THE
INTERRUPTED DIALECTIC

PARALLAX Re-visions of Culture and Society
Stephen G. Nichols, Gerald Prince, and Wendy Steiner
Series Editors

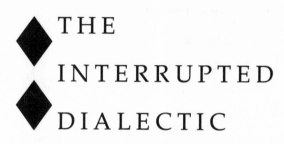

THE INTERRUPTED DIALECTIC

Philosophy, Psychoanalysis, and Their Tragic Other

Suzanne Gearhart

THE JOHNS HOPKINS UNIVERSITY PRESS
BALTIMORE AND LONDON

© 1992 The Johns Hopkins University Press
All rights reserved
Printed in the United States of America

The Johns Hopkins University Press
701 West 40th Street
Baltimore, Maryland 21211-2190
The Johns Hopkins Press Ltd., London

The paper used in this book meets the minimum requirements of the American National Standard for Information Sciences—Permanence of Paper for Printed Library Materials, ANSI Z39.48-1984.

LIBRARY OF CONGRESS CATALOGING-IN-PUBLICATION DATA

Gearhart, Suzanne, 1947–
  The interrupted dialectic : philosophy, psychoanalysis, and their tragic other / Suzanne Gearhart.
      p.   cm.—(Parallax)
  Includes bibliographical references and index.
  ISBN 0-8018-4359-6 (hc : alk. paper)
    1. Literature—Philosophy.   2. Psychoanalysis and literature.   3. Tragedy.
  4. Tragedy—History and criticism.   I. Title.   II. Series: Parallax (Baltimore, Md.)
  PN49.G44   1992
  801—dc20   91-44187

For *Thomas, Matthew,* and *David*

◆ Contents

THE
INTERRUPTED DIALECTIC

Introduction: The Birth of

Philosophy and Psychoanalysis

The principal thesis of this book is that both speculative (Hegelian) philosophy and (Freudian) psychoanalysis are modeled after and elaborated to an important extent in terms of a particular view of tragedy, that is, that the interpretation each gives to tragedy plays a central role in their self-constitution and theoretical self-justification. In fact, it could even be argued that much of the critical force of each is derived from the strength of their interpretations of individual tragic works and the manner in which they develop and generalize the insights that they claim are already to be found in tragic literature. If this is so, then it follows that those currents of contemporary theory that are either explicitly or implicitly indebted to either dialectical philosophy or psychoanalysis—indebted either positively or negatively— also are rooted in and limited by a particular relation to the tragic.

In the chapters that follow, I analyze the implications for modern (speculative) philosophy and for psychoanalysis of their profound interest in tragedy and the theoretical effects of their interpretations of tragedy. Through critical readings of works of philosophy, psychoanalysis, and literature, my aim is to clarify what draws Hegel, Freud, and others to tragedy as well as the significance of their ability to find in it a confirmation of many of their most important theoretical insights. If, in *The Birth of Tragedy*, Nietzsche traced the life of tragedy from its birth in Dionysian festivals to its death in Socratic philosophy, *The Interrupted Dialectic* focuses rather on the birth of speculative philosophy and psychoanalysis in tragedy and the consequences of this birthplace for each.

Questions concerning the fundamental relation between tragedy and what we would now call modern theory, at least in its psychoanalytic form, are certainly not new. For example, this relation is the basis of Jean Starobinski's essay "Hamlet and Oedipus" (in his *La Relation critique* [Paris: Gallimard, 1970]), in which he examines the role played by Freud's interpretation of these two exemplary tragic works in relation to psychoanalysis. Starobinski's conclusion is that *Oedipus*, in particular, not only serves as an especially noteworthy case study for psychoanalysis but also must be considered a matrix or model for psychoanalytic theory itself. As various chapters of this book argue, this thesis is of crucial importance for understanding not just the nature and critical force of psychoanalysis, as Starobinski argues, but also, and in my mind equally important, its limitations.

The problem Starobinski addresses in his essay on *Hamlet* and *Oedipus* extends beyond Freud and psychoanalysis, where the fundamental debt to at least these two exemplary tragedies is explicitly acknowledged. It includes not only Hegel but also a much broader philosophical and critical tradition, which has also viewed tragedy as an exemplary—if not the exemplary—form of literature and art generally, and in some sense situated and even constituted itself in terms of what it postulated as the essence of this exemplarity. In the chapters that follow, I argue that if psychoanalysis and various forms of philosophy and criticism find their theoretical insights confirmed in tragedy, it is because they are already being "thought" by tragedy, but not necessarily in the same terms that they project onto it. That is to say, tragedy prefigures philosophy and psychoanalysis in their major lines, confirming certain of their insights but also providing the grounds for questioning others.

Because of its self-consciously dialectical nature, the philosophy of Hegel plays a crucial role in dramatizing the process through which philosophy interprets tragedy. From the perspective of Hegelian philosophy, tragedy cannot be a mere object for philosophical interpretation. Philosophical interpretation must find itself in tragedy. In other words, philosophy must be seen as a negation and at the same time a retention and sublation of tragedy; and philosophy itself can claim to be higher than tragedy only because it incorporates tragedy into itself, because its own truth has a tragic dimension. The dialectic of tragedy and philosophy is a process out of which philosophy itself emerges as absolute, because of the way it is able to recognize itself in tragedy and merge with it without losing its own identity. Hegel's interpretation of tragedy, however, offers only the most explicit version of a dialectic that can be found in implicit form in the work of other interpreters of tragedy—including Lessing, Nietzsche, Freud, and Eric Auerbach, to name only those philosophers and critics I treat at some length in this work.

As my title indicates, what is especially significant for me about the dialectic of philosophy and psychoanalysis with tragedy is that it is an interrupted dialectic. It is interrupted not just by accident or from without—as dialectical reasoning itself readily admits as part of the process of the negation and incorporation of the exterior within the interior—but rather, of necessity and from within. The problem is not that in tragedy, philosophy and psychoanalysis confront a form of alterity so radical they cannot incorporate it into themselves and become its *Aufhebung*. Rather, it is that tragedy lends itself all too well to philosophical or psychoanalytical interpretation, and, as a result, the question becomes whether philosophy itself or tragedy better exemplifies philosophy, whether psychoanalysis itself or tragedy better exemplifies psychoanalysis. The mirror tragedy offers to philosophy and psychoanalysis is one in which they can indeed recognize themselves, but always at the risk of losing themselves, becoming totally disoriented and unable to tell which is other and which is self. In other words, the identification between philosophy or psychoanalysis and tragedy is radically problematical because it undermines as much as it confirms the identity of philosophy and psychoanalysis.

I argue that it is never completely clear whether tragedy is an (inferior) form of philosophy or psychoanalysis, or if philosophy and psychoanalysis are simply forms or derivatives of tragedy and thus expressions of *its* "truth." In this sense, the idea that the dialectic leads to a reconciliation of tragedy and theory which is commanded by theory must itself be put into question. The dialectic appears to be constantly in danger of being broken off before reconciliation is achieved, interrupted by a conflict between two rival forms of either psychoanalysis, philosophy, or tragedy. The interrupted dialectic is one in which philosophy and psychoanalysis are joined in conflict with tragedy, and the conflict is irreconcilable precisely because it stems from what in each case each has in common with the (its) other.

The dialectic of philosophy (or psychoanalysis) and tragedy can be understood as merely one version among others of a dialectic that unites—and also divides—philosophy (or psychoanalysis) and art as a whole. But this dialectic is of particular critical significance to modern theory as a whole because of the central role played by the process of identification in tragic poetics and texts. The term *identification* as such is, of course, not found in the work of Aristotle, Lessing, Kant, Hegel, Nietzsche, or that of the French dramatists I discuss in this book. I argue, however, that if the term itself is not present, a contradictory *process* of identification, as it will be belatedly defined and elaborated by Freud, is at work. My argument is that this process of identification is as central to the interpretations of tragedy given by all of the above thinkers and writers—and thus to the constitution of speculative philosophy and important currents of contemporary theory—as the concept is to Freud's theory of the psyche. Thus, I argue, it is legitimate to read their work in terms of the issues raised by the complex role Freud attributes to identification, especially in the complicated history through which the subject is constituted.

For some of the figures I deal with, the process of identification implicit in their discussion of tragedy is positive, in the sense that by "putting oneself in the place of the other," as Freud puts it, the subject confirms or "authentifies" itself. For others, it is a negative moment of a dialectic through which the subject must pass, a moment in which the subject is menaced with or experiences destruction and loss as it moves outside itself, but one that ultimately allows it to (re)confirm itself on a higher level, with the successful overcoming of negativity and otherness. In most cases, in fact, the process is both positive and negative at the same time. But, as I argue, what is ultimately at stake in the work of each of these figures, including Freud, is the question of whether the process of identification is secondary, in the sense that it can only confirm or negate a pre-given subject, or primary, that is, prior to any (sense of) self and in that sense constitutive of, rather than derived from, the subject. For modern speculative philosophy, with its emphasis on the subject as the starting and end point of reason, knowledge, ethics, and aesthetics, the task of theorizing tragic identification is thus crucial for its own self-constitution.

Lessing's *Hamburg Dramaturgy* provides a particularly significant indication of the link between Aristotle's concept of catharsis, Lessing's own interpretation of Aristotle, which I treat as emblematic of all modern interpretations of catharsis, and Freud's concept of identification. In his extensive commentary on the *Poetics*, Lessing stresses that the Aristotelian term *fear* imparts a self-reflexive quality to the pity or compassion with which Aristotle associates it. As contrasted with terror, which Lessing asserts is what we might feel for a misfortune affecting another, Aristotle's notion of fear, he argues, arises from a sense of "the similarity of our position with that of the sufferer. It is the fear that the calamities impending over the sufferers might also befall ourselves."[1] Fear causes us to refer the compassion we feel for the tragic character back to ourselves (179), thus putting ourselves in the position of the tragic character, and it is this self-reflexive process that constitutes the core of Aristotelian catharsis, according to Lessing.

As I have already suggested, even if Lessing does not use the term *identification* itself, a process closely related to what Freud will later explicitly call identification is implicit in his discussion of catharsis. In *The Interpretation of Dreams*, when Freud formally introduces the term *identification*, his definition clearly echoes Lessing's commentary of Aristotle. In a spirit similar to that in which Lessing distinguishes terror from fear, Freud distinguishes simple imitation, based on a conscious reproduction of the behavior and feelings of another, from an assimilation that would be based on a much deeper, unconsciously created or perceived resemblance. Using the dream of one of his young patients as an example, Freud argues that as a result of just such an unconscious assimilation, she had "put herself in [the] place" of another, "or, as we might say, . . . she had 'identified' herself" with another.[2]

The poetics of tragedy, whether of Aristotle or of later theoreticians and writers, and psychoanalysis are not the only two fields in which identification holds a prominent place, however. Though the term itself is not used by either Kant or Hegel any more than it is by Lessing, I argue that the concept and process of identification play as important a role in their philosophies as in his commentary on Aristotle.

In the case of Kant, a primary process of identification is the implicit ground of aesthetic judgment in particular, because the "demand for universality," which is an inherent feature of all aesthetic judgments according to Kant, presupposes that in making such judgments the subject will be able to free itself from "the limitations that contingently affect [its] own estimate" and to put itself "in the position of everyone else."[3] In the case of Hegel too, identification emerges as a process central to—if not identical with—the dialectic itself. Hegelian philosophy is based on a series of identifications through which the subject forms ties with the object and, even more, comes to be confounded with the object, thus putting itself in the place of the other, only to find and reaffirm itself once again, at the higher level of self-consciousness achieved at the end of the dialectical process. The central role played by what I call a process of identification in Hegelian and Kantian philosophy as well as in tragedy is thus an important part of what links them to each other and to psychoanalysis. It is also the locus of many of the principal and most fundamental conflicts between them.

I thus read Freud's predecessors from a perspective that is indebted to his work. But this does not mean that Freud is necessarily of more assistance than they are in revealing the deeply problematic nature of identification. As I also argue, a critical investigation of the interpretation of tragedy offers the occasion for an exploration of the ambiguous character of identification long before Freud uses the term explicitly. In the terms of Aristotle's *Poetics*, that ambiguous character can be seen in the strange fusion that tragic identification effects between pity and fear. It is with respect to tragedy, in particular, that something negative or painful emerges as central to identification, or at least to certain forms of it, something that corresponds to the negative character of tragedy itself—in the simplest terms, to the suffering of the tragic character or characters.

To put this point in more modern language, one could say that it is in relation to tragedy that an ambivalence is revealed as central not only to the emotions of the spectator of tragedy, but also perhaps to all cases of identification. As I argue in my readings of Kant, Freud, Racine, and Diderot, in particular, this ambivalence, this mixture of the diametrically opposed feelings of pleasure and pain, has the effect of radically problematizing the pleasure associated with art in general and thus greatly complicates the philosophical task of producing a unified theory of art. Equally important, the identity of the subject is seriously disrupted by the conflict between pleasure and pain, by the ambivalent character of (tragic) identification. Tragedy, in other words, confronts philosophy and psychoanalysis with the possibility that the process of identification is at bottom radically disruptive of identity. Thus it is also disruptive of any dialectic that tries to make identification an instrument with which to confirm the identity of art, of an individual subject, or of philosophy and psychoanalysis themselves.

Philosophy and psychoanalysis are linked not only by the dialectic and the corresponding theory of identification that in each case underlies their interest in tragedy, however. They are also linked inasmuch as a theory of the difference between the sexes dominates the interpretation each gives of tragedy. For both Hegel and Freud, the conflict at the basis of the tragedy which each takes to be exemplary of tragedy as a whole is a more or less direct consequence of the differences between the sexes. As a result, the dialectic must overcome not only tragedy, but also the sexual difference that, for both psychoanalysis and speculative philosophy, is fundamental to tragedy. Psychoanalysis and speculative philosophy thus confront the problem of sexual difference in much the same dialectical manner in which they confront tragedy.

In the case of the difference between the sexes, the dialectic is also interrupted, however, and, once again, not by something radically other—in this case, by a form of (feminine) sexuality that could be absolutely opposed to the dominant (masculine) form of sexuality. As I argue in my readings of Hegel's interpretation of *Antigone*, Freud's interpretations of *Hamlet*, and also through readings of Corneille's *Horace*, Racine's *Iphigénie*, Prévost's *Manon Lescaut*, and Beaumarchais's *Le Mariage de Figaro*, it is interrupted instead by what could be called a "femininity" (or a "masculinity") common to both sexes. The difference between the sexes proves to be irreconcilable in much the same manner as the difference between theory and tragedy—not so much because of what distinguishes the two terms but more because of what the opposed terms have in common, which is defined by or contained in neither term alone.

The interest of philosophy in the problem of tragedy is not exclusive to a specific period in the history of Western philosophy but is evident in many phases of its history. Nonetheless, I have chosen to analyze the dialectic of philosophy and tragedy in the terms of a modern version of it because of the way modern speculative philosophy, as exemplified by Hegel, makes that dialectic explicit. It is precisely because of the dialectical—or, in other words, self-conscious—nature of the confrontation between philosophy and tragedy in the work of Hegel that the interruption of the Hegelian version of this dialectic is particularly significant. In contrast to the philosophy of Plato, in which the tragic and epic poets are banished from the city ruled by philosophy, or even to the philosophy of Aristotle, in which tragic poetics appears as one branch among others of philosophy, Hegelian philosophy embraces tragedy and openly acknowledges its own tragic roots. That tragedy should nonetheless in some sense resist Hegel's interpretation, that the dialectic should nonetheless stall, can mean only that philosophy itself is interrupted by tragedy: philosophy itself is divided from itself by its relation to the tragic other with which it so readily identifies.

This view of philosophy places it in a different light from the one in which it presents itself, and in this sense it is a critical view, one that undercuts certain of the claims made by philosophy on its own behalf. But though critical, this perspective is not simply negative, because it also makes it possible to grasp the dynamic or even dramatic character of philosophy and, in this sense, to see its lack of absolute autonomy, universality, and objectivity as precisely what in many cases is the source of its critical force.

The reasons I have chosen to treat the problem of tragedy to such an important extent in terms of the work of French dramatists and writers of the seventeenth and eighteenth centuries are closely related to those that prompt me to focus on Hegelian philosophy. Despite their diversity, the works of each of the literary figures I analyze can be interpreted in the light of an attempt to create a modern form of tragedy or to surpass tragedy by instituting a modern genre that would not be simply tragic, a form or genre that, like Hegelian philosophy, would go beyond the ancient tragic models that each implicitly or explicitly designates for itself. Like Hegelian philosophy, these modern tragedies seek to negate, retain, and raise ancient tragedy to a higher, that is, truly modern level. It is because of the philosophical nature of their ambition that the judgment that philosophy and criticism make of these works is especially revealing.

Because its own aim of surpassing ancient tragedy is exemplified in the works of the neoclassical French literary texts I treat in this book, it would seem natural for speculative philosophy to embrace them as an expression of its own truth. In fact, however, the reverse is more often true. For reasons that vary somewhat in each case, Hegelian philosophy refuses to recognize itself in the work of the modern French tragedians. Hegel's own refusal echoes that of Lessing and A. W. Schlegel, among others, and it is in turn echoed in works such as Nietzsche's *Birth of Tragedy*, Benjamin's *Origin of German Tragic Drama*, or Erich Auerbach's *Mimesis*.

Hegel's lack of sympathy for the French, however, cannot be explained in terms of a vulgar nationalism—that is, a lack of appreciation for anything that is not German or that does not conform to what is, not just for Hegel but for German philosophy and criticism as a whole, the work of the supreme modern tragic dramatist, Shakespeare. As I argue in my reading of the passages from Hegel's *Aesthetics* in which he criticizes Corneille and Racine, Hegel's relation to the

French should instead be understood as another instance of conflict based on identification: what opposes Hegel to the French is the modern ambition they share. The modern, self-conscious version of the dialectic of philosophy and tragedy is thus perhaps disrupted less by ancient tragedy, which it considers to be the supreme form of *art*, than by modern tragedy, which it holds to be the *Aufhebung* (failed in some cases and successful in others) of ancient tragedy, an *Aufhebung* that doubles or mimes the one that speculative philosophy itself proposes.

What is interrupted by modern (French) tragedy is not just the formal dialectical relationship between philosophy and tragedy, however, but also the theory of sexuality that grows out of the Hegelian and Freudian interpretation of tragic conflict. In each of the literary works I examine, sexuality is defined in and through conflict between the masculine and the feminine. But the conflict is in each case irreconcilable not because the feminine is absolutely other than the masculine, but because of what they share. For different reasons, Corneille's Camille, Racine's Eriphile, Prévost's Manon Lescaut, and the heroines of Beaumarchais's *Le Mariage de Figaro* all exemplify the critical force of an alterity that is not simply other, that is, the contrary of the same, but rather an alterity that affects and displaces the same and the identical from within.

In chapter 1, I discuss the work of three modern thinkers, each of whom uses an interpretation of tragedy to criticize traditional philosophy and aesthetics: Nietzsche, Benjamin, and Freud. I argue that the force of the critical strategy of each stems from the way he is able to identify in tragedy elements that can be opposed to traditional philosophy and aesthetics in order to overturn both. But I also argue that the limitations of their critical strategies are evident in that each privileges one form or model of tragedy—whether the Dionysian in the case of Nietzsche, the Oedipal in the case of Freud, or the baroque *Trauerspiel* in the case of Benjamin—over all others and thus seeks to give tragedy *an* identity. By doing this, each in effect constructs a tragedy that is the absolute other of philosophy and thus also proposes a new dialectic of tragedy and philosophy—a tragico-centric dialectic in which tragedy itself is endowed with the absolute character to which philosophy previously laid claim.

Chapter 2 analyzes the uneasy relations between philosophy and tragedy through a reading of Hegel that focuses on his interpretation of the philosophy of Kant and also of what for him is the exemplary tragedy, Sophocles' *Antigone*. From Hegel's perspective, Kant's work embodies a radical conflict between the transcendental and the real, the universal and the particular, the ethical and the practical, and finally between the aesthetic and the rational. Hegel thus turns to *Antigone* because, according to his interpretation of the play, it portrays a similar conflict manifest in the life of the "ethical community." This community is at the heart of Hegel's interpretation of tragedy because it serves as the context for the unfolding of the tragic drama but also because it provides a sense of how and in what terms such conflict can be resolved.

In this manner, *Antigone* emerges as the embodiment of Hegelian philosophy and more specifically of its ability to reconcile conflict, whether of an ethical, aesthetic, or rational-philosophical nature. But as I also argue, Hegel's interpretation of *Antigone* reveals a conflict at the heart of the Hegelian dialectic itself, between, on the one hand, the need to absolutize conflict in order that its reconciliation be pure and total and, on the other, a need to limit conflict by subordinating one term of the conflict to the other, in order to assure that the conflict not become permanent and irresolvable. In terms of his interpretation of *Antigone*, Hegel is caught between a need to stress the equally ethical nature of Antigone and Creon, and hence the radical nature of the contradiction that their conflict introduces into the ethical community, and the need to subordinate the figure of Antigone by qualifying *her* relationship to the ethical as intuitive and natural.

Hegel's interpretation of *Antigone* is designed to overcome a conflict that, in the terms of Kant's philosophy, appears to be inherent in ethics, art, and reason itself. But it is also intended to overcome the ambivalence of the Kantian version of identification, that is, the deeply problematic nature of the process through which the Kantian subject puts itself in the place of the other. Through a discussion of Kant's *Critique of Pure Reason* and his *Critique of Judgement*, I argue that, in his tragic version of identification, the subject can never be sure it knows the other (or the self), and in this sense identification appears to be based not on a common *identity*, but on something held in common prior to any sense of self. The Kantian dialectic of identification, insofar as one could say there is such a thing, is interrupted by the lack of identity of either party in it, and thus no third term can emerge from this dialectic that could be the synthesis—and the completion—of the other two.

In chapter 3, I analyze the way Hegel confronts tragedy once again, this time in its modern form. Through a discussion of his contrasting interpretations of the tragedies of Shakespeare and Corneille, I argue that Hegel's attitude toward modern tragedy is of necessity ambivalent. This ambivalence is evident in Hegel's condemnation in Corneille's tragedies of what he praises in those of Shakespeare—and, in particular, in *Hamlet*. The project of Corneille's plays, I argue, is as dialectical as the one Hegel attributes to the plays of Shakespeare, as can be seen in the mediating function that Corneille, like Hegel, attributes to the modern tragic hero. And yet, like the Hegelian dialectic of modern tragedy, Corneille's dialectic of the hero, as exemplified in his *Horace*, is also interrupted when Horace is challenged by his sister, Camille. Her challenge reveals an irreconcilable conflict between the "law of the man" and the "law of the woman," one based not on a simple opposition but rather, once again, on what the two figures share. Given the fidelity with which Corneille's own project for modern tragedy prefigures Hegel's project for modern philosophy, the failure of *Horace* to reconcile these two figures, a failure that is both formal and conceptual, serves as an indication of the radically problematic nature not only of modern tragedy but of modern philosophy as well.

Chapter 4 discusses both the importance of Freud's concept of tragedy for his theory of psychoanalysis and also the problematic nature of this concept, which stems from the conflicting implications of his interpretations of the two tragic works that are the most constant literary references of psychoanalysis: *Oedipus* and *Hamlet*. I argue that, from the perspective of psychoanalysis, as from the perspective of speculative philosophy, it is the modern tragedy—in Freud's case, *Hamlet*—which gives rise to the greater uneasiness and poses the greater theoretical challenge. That challenge is to theorize what in traditional terms is the problem of tragic guilt or what in Freud's own terms it would be more proper to call the (specifically modern) problem of repression—its origin and nature. What makes this challenge so serious emerges as Freud's examination of the problem of repression unfolds in the series of essays beginning with "Psychopathic Characters on the Stage" and culminating in *Civilization and Its Discontents*. Freud cannot find an origin for repression without acknowledging the primacy of a certain displeasure that his own economic theory of the psyche, centered on his interpretation of *Oedipus*, never effectively accounts for, even when he abandons pleasure as the unifying principle of that economy. The result is that *Hamlet*, despite Freud's attempts to interpret it as another *Oedipus*, comes to appear as exemplary of a (modern) version of the psyche which diverges significantly from the Oedipal version because its principle is not pleasure or even stability but rather displeasure or uneasiness.

The primary nature of displeasure, which is being indicated in Freud's reading of *Hamlet* and also in the texts that relate to that reading, is, I argue, even more apparent in Racine's *Iphigénie*. I thus confront Freud's analysis of the origins of repression with an interpretation of this play and of the character of Eriphile in particular, in order to show the implications of the primary nature of (tragic) displeasure in relation both to Racine's universe and to psychoanalysis. Eriphile is considered in this interpretation not only as a female Hamlet but, more important, as a character whose complex femininity holds the key to the problem of the origin of displeasure. In Racine's play it is precisely Eriphile's feminine sense of guilt that serves as the model for tragic guilt itself. *Iphigénie* thus indicates that, just as displeasure cannot be reduced to a form or forerunner of pleasure, so the feminine cannot be seen simply as a form or figure of the Oedipal and the masculine—any more than tragedy itself can be seen as the mere prefiguration of a psychoanalysis based on a single, Oedipal form of tragedy.

Chapter 5 discusses the dialectic through which Erich Auerbach's narrative of the history of Western literature finds its literary culmination in nineteenth-century realism and its literary-critical culmination in historicism. Like the dialectics of speculative philosophy and of psychoanalysis, this dialectic too is interrupted when it confronts a work that I argue should be understood as a modern French tragedy—Prévost's *Manon Lescaut*. Auerbach's condemnation of this novel contravenes a central thesis of realism—that all literature represents reality, even if the literature of each period does this in varying manners and according to differing literary conventions. Nonetheless, that condemnation is absolutely necessary when one looks beneath the random character that Auerbach attributes not only to the real but to his own history of realism to find the ethico-aesthetic values informing his narrative and driving it toward its culmination in nineteenth-century realism and historicism.

While Auerbach explicitly incorporates certain aspects of tragedy—what he calls tragic seriousness—into his concept of realism, in his interpretation of *Manon Lescaut* another aspect of tragedy emerges as the antithesis of the real. Auerbach's theory of literary realism rests on a refusal or a failure to entertain the possibility of there being a profound link between the sexual and the tragic. His discussion of *Manon Lescaut* is thus less an interpretation of the novel than a justification of the reasons why he chooses to exclude it from realism (and thus from history). He does so because, by associating the sexual and the tragic, *Manon Lescaut* degrades the tragic, according to Auerbach, emptying it of what he considers to be its seriousness. In contrast to Auerbach, I argue that *Manon Lescaut* shows (or confirms) not only that sexual conflict is fundamental to tragedy, but also that sexuality—even or perhaps especially the sexuality of Manon, because it has ethical significance or tragic seriousness—cannot be simply eliminated from the real or its (historicist) history. It is precisely because of this ethical or tragic significance that the sexuality of Manon, like *Manon Lescaut* itself, can be said to interrupt the dialectic of realism from within.

As I have indicated, the problem of identification is virtually as central to this book as the problem of tragedy itself, given its fundamental and contradictory role in the theory of tragedy. In chapter 6, which focuses on Hegel's reading of Diderot's *Le Neveu de Rameau* in the *Phenomenology of Spirit*, I argue that the special privilege Hegel accords to Diderot's text, the special fascination it holds for him, lies in the way it personifies or exemplifies a particularly radical, all-encompassing form of identification in the figure of Rameau's nephew. The specular basis of Hegel's interest in Diderot's text is clear: as a figure who has already occupied all positions that are apparently opposed to his own, the Nephew is also a figure for the dialectic itself, in its identification with—and ultimately its transcendence of—all forms of alterity.

Hegel's interest in this text relates not only to his concern with modern French history and culture, but also to his interpretation of tragedy and more particularly of catharsis. In a manner that recalls Lessing, Hegel sees Aristotelian catharsis not just as feeling or emotion but as a manner of understanding involving a process that confounds or identifies self and other. His interpretation of *Le Neveu* is thus indicative of the link that exists from his standpoint between this modern text, on the one hand, and ancient as well as modern tragedy, on the other. The central place and character that the *Phenomenology of Spirit* assigns to Rameau's nephew corresponds to speculative philosophy's own "absolutization" of the tragic—and philosophical—process of identification. At the same time, speculative philosophy itself, insofar as it is both a practice and self-conscious theory of identification, emerges from Hegel's reading of Diderot's text as the heir and the culmination of the tragic, and the *Aufhebung* as the philosophical—that is, the absolute and purely rational—version of catharsis.

Hegel's reading of *Le Neveu*, however, ignores those elements of the text which place the perspective of the Nephew in an ironic light and deny him the central position in the text which Hegel claims for him. Correspondingly, it ignores the way the question of passion or feeling intrudes itself into a process of identification which in the terms of Diderot's text can be said to originate neither solely in reason nor in feeling. There is indeed a dialectic of identification in *Le Neveu*, but it is an open or unfinished dialectic in which reason may well make use of passion for its own ends, but, just as likely, passion may make use of reason for its ends. This uncertainty indicates that reason and passion, like art and philosophy, are not completely different, simple opposites, even if they are not completely identical either. It points to a fundamental ambiguity concerning the ends of identification, which Diderot's text, in spite of the force of Hegel's interpretation, does not resolve.

In chapter 7, I turn once again to a philosophical interpretation of a text by Diderot, in this case, Philippe Lacoue-Labarthe's reading of the *Paradoxe sur le comédien*. Lacoue-Labarthe's approach to Diderot's text is informed by a critical strategy in which art and identification play a key role, because for him they represent what he calls the matrix of philosophy.[4] That is, they represent something other than traditional philosophy, especially speculative philosophy, without it being possible to merely oppose them to—and thus turn them into another version or another confirmation of—speculative philosophy. For Lacoue-Labarthe, Diderot's text exemplifies the critical force of art and identification in relation to speculative philosophy, but it also betrays an attempt to submit them to a concept of the subject in which their paradoxes would find a resolution and their disruptive force would be contained.

This interpretation of Diderot, I argue, rests on an implicit privileging of a generalized form of identification, exemplified in a purer form by the work of Hölderlin, in contrast to another limited form of identification, exemplified by speculative philosophy and, in the end, by Diderot's text on acting. Through this distinction, Lacoue-Labarthe indirectly gives an essence to art, based on its affinity with the generalized form of identification, and thus, despite his insistence on the speculative nature of art, in the last instance simply opposes it to philosophy, particularly speculative philosophy. In this sense, Lacoue-Labarthe's reading of Diderot can be said to represent an attempt to resolve an irreconcilable contradiction between philosophy and art—irreconcilable because it stems from what they have in common—and in the process to betray his own interpretation of the nature of their conflict.

In chapter 8, I first address the problem of identification through a reading of texts by Freud which offer a psychoanalytic perspective on social theory and then compare Freud's theory of the social to Beaumarchais's depiction and dramatization of identification in *Le Mariage de Figaro*. My particular purpose in this chapter is to explore the political and social implications of a problematical concept of identification such as emerges from a critical confrontation of theory and drama.

I focus especially on the way Freud's theory of identification both is limited by and points beyond his views concerning the Oedipal basis of societies. My decision to confront Freud with Beaumarchais's *Figaro* lies in part in the way this play, in which tragic elements are central and clearly discernible, confirms many of the social principles Freud draws from *Oedipus*. But it also stems from the way *Figaro* situates the Oedipal in terms of a concept of identification which is the basis of the comic character of the play. As exemplified in the figure of Chérubin, the process of identification, without being pre-Oedipal, nonetheless makes the significance of Oedipus fundamentally ambiguous. Like Freud's Oedipal model of society, it too points beyond the self as the basis for society, but unlike the Oedipal model its result is not to identify the social with any single male or paternal figure. It points to the femininity of all paternal figures, the masculinity of all maternal figures, and therefore, to the radically ambiguous—but for that very reason radically social—nature of the subject of identification.

My discussion of the tragic involves the investigation of highly technical and abstract theoretical questions as well as readings of literary texts; it touches on philosophy, psychoanalysis, and social theory as well as literature and literary criticism. Even within the field of literature, it is not focused exclusively on the interpretation of works that belong narrowly to the tragic genre as such. This book does not, however, owe what might be called its multidisciplinary character to any faith in the intrinsic desirability of interdisciplinary approaches to critical problems. Its perspective, which continually moves between theory and literature, emerged rather as a necessary correlative of its complex and paradoxical tragic subject. As Gerard Genette (disapprovingly) remarks in his *Introduction à l'Architexte* (Paris: Seuil, 1979), as part of his commentary of Aristotle's *Poetics*, "there thus . . . exist elements of the tragic outside of tragedy" (24). Unlike Genette, I think this is one of the most critically important aspects both of tragedy and of theories and interpretations of it: that tragedy does not have a natural place as the object of any specific discipline. It is neither simply a literary genre or theme, nor an outlook, nor a dramatic spectacle involving spectators, actors, and a script.

A similar ambiguity is characteristic of attempts to deal with identification, as is evident in the debates over its importance in relation to tragic poetics. The question of whether identification is an aesthetic or purely psychological or social process is virtually as old as the *Poetics*, and if it has been debated so long and so inconclusively, it can only be that identification, like tragedy, is all of these things at the same time and never a process characteristic of or determined by one of them alone.

The Interrupted Dialectic thus follows the thread connecting speculative philosophy and psychoanalysis to tragedy and at the same time separating them from each other. Its chief critical purpose is to indicate the limitations of these specific theoretical apparatuses and those theories and critical strategies or positions derived from them or, in the logic of the dialectic, diametrically opposed to them. I emphasize the way in which the tragic, as the privileged other of philosophy and psychoanalysis, interrupts and thus opens up their particular dialectics from within. My purpose in doing so is not to argue that critical thinking should have nothing more to do with speculative philosophy or psychoanalysis, that we have come (or should come) to the end of them, even in the way, for example, that Hegel proclaimed "the end of art." On the contrary, this book proposes that new critical life can be found in both dialectical philosophy and psychoanalysis by opening them up to a tragic other different from the one they explicitly model themselves after and claim to have mastered. And this is so only because this other tragic other is from its birth profoundly philosophical and psychoanalytical, although not in a way that either philosophy or psychoanalysis determines.

CHAPTER 1

The Identities of Tragedy:
Nietzsche, Benjamin, Freud

The idea that art, or certain interpretations of art, can provide critical perspectives on philosophy, social theory, and various historical empiricisms is by now familiar, even if it continues to be contested by many. A large and important current of contemporary criticism and theory is concerned with investigating basic philosophical assumptions from the standpoint of problems that have long been the focus of literary criticism and the philosophy of art. A list of these problems would include, for example, the role of figure and metaphor not just in poetic language but in language in general; the role of imagination in thought; and the status of fictional objects in the world. There are numerous signs that those who see art as possessing a critical potential are increasingly interested in analyzing that potential in relation to political and social institutions. This current is powerful enough that even the work of many whose relationship to it is polemical shows unmistakable signs of having been influenced by it.[1] Furthermore, those works that make use of perspectives provided by art or literature to question the assumptions of traditional philosophy, and in a growing number of cases history and social theory as well, hardly constitute a group or a "school." Their diversity and even opposition to one another are an additional sign of the potential critical power and significance of the problem of art, an indication of a promising critical agenda that continues to emerge as aesthetic concerns cease to be confined exclusively to aesthetics in its traditional sense.

For the contemporary thinkers and writers in whose work art is viewed as offering a perspective from which various empiricisms and also traditional philosophy can be viewed critically, Nietzsche, either implicitly or explicitly, is a crucial figure. His work as a whole provides a model of the way in which the question of art can play a role in undermining philosophy, or at least a philosophy characterized by its confidence in thought and science and their ability to "penetrate the deepest abysses of being."[2] Through his interpretation of art and more specifically, of tragedy, Nietzsche's work throws into relief those elements in art that can be regarded as the most problematic from the standpoint of his principal target in *The Birth of Tragedy*: the philosophical-aesthetic tradition he claims originates in "Socratic optimism."

Tragedy is at the center of Nietzsche's conception of art, and the critical force of art is synonymous with what he argues is the dynamic core of tragedy. If "the problem of science cannot be recognized in the context of science" (18), Nietzsche implies that it *can* be recognized in the context of something radically alien to science: a Dionysian tragic art, from the perspective of which the cornerstones of (Socratic) philosophy—the self, logic, knowledge, and morality—appear no longer as firm foundations, but rather as a constantly shifting and subsiding substratum. "We may recognize in Socrates the opponent of Dionysus" (86), and in the terms of *The Birth of Tragedy* this means that we may recognize in (Dionysian) tragedy the opponent of and the most efficacious weapon in the struggle against (Socratic/Platonic) philosophy.

Nietzsche's critique of traditional philosophy also entails a critique and rejection of a traditional form of tragedy and, more specifically, of a traditional form of tragic identification. His interpretation of identification emerges in his discussion of the tragedies of Euripides, whom he considers to be the poetic alter ego of Socrates. Though he does not explicitly employ the term *identification*, Nietzsche's comments on Euripides provide a sense of his own interpretation of the process associated by Aristotle with tragic catharsis and later with what Freud explicitly terms identification. Nietzsche is contemptuous of the realism of Euripides because its aim is, in his words, to bring "the *spectator* onto the stage" in all his "civic mediocrity" (77). What I would call Euripidean identification puts the spectator in the place of the other, but the place of the other is in reality the place of the self— the mediocre, moralistic, civic self. Instead of elevating the spectator to the level of art, Euripidean identification drags art down to the level of the self. Nietzsche appears to include the Aristotelian notion of catharsis in his critique of Euripidean identification when he says that those for whom the feelings of pity and terror are "the effect of tragedy . . . have had no experience of tragedy as a supreme *art*" (132). These feelings, he argues, ought to be treated as "medical or moral phenomena," and the triumph of an aesthetic in which they figure prominently is one more sign that authentic, Dionysian tragedy is dead.

At first glance, the process that Nietzsche opposes to Euripidean identification might appear to have nothing in common with it. Instead of a confirmation of self, the Dionysian form of tragedy involves a loss of self. For example, Nietzsche argues that in the Dionysian festivals in which tragedy originated, there was "no opposition between public and chorus" (62), with the result that audience, hero, and chorus all merged into a single, "great sublime chorus" (62). Instead of putting the spectator in the place of the other, Dionysian tragedy dissolves the distinction between self and other and thereby seemingly destroys the possibility of identification. Moreover, what makes the Dionysian festivals and even, at least implicitly, the tragedies of Aeschylus and Sophocles different from the tragedies of Euripides, in Nietzsche's view, is that in them the experience of tragedy is disorienting and even painful (65), and its result is the surrender (64) of individuality.

Despite all this, Dionysian tragedy still involves a form or variant of Euripidean identification, because while the individual subject is radically negated by the tragic experience, another subject can be seen to emerge from its destruction. Nietzsche's term for that other subject is the lyric "I" of the Dionysian poet, and true subjectivity belongs to him rather than the Euripidean subject: "The images of the *lyrist* are nothing but *his very self:* . . . of course, this self is not the same as that of the waking, empirically real man, but the only truly existent and eternal self resting at the basis of things, through whose images the lyric genius sees this very basis" (50). Behind and beneath the Euripidean ego lies an "eternal self," a self that is implicitly the focus of another, deeper process of identification in which subjectivity is produced and confirmed — not the subjectivity of the mediocre citizen, but a lyric subjectivity that belongs to no particular individual. In terms of the Dionysian festival, the lyric subject is revealed only when the ego is surrendered. It takes the form of a "great sublime chorus of dancing and singing satyrs or of those who permit themselves to be represented by such satyrs" (62). If there is now "no opposition between public and chorus," there *is* still a process of identification similar in a crucial respect to the one Nietzsche associates with Euripidean tragedy, inasmuch as the process of fusion of the audience, chorus, and tragic hero produces and confirms a (higher form of the) subject.

Nietzsche's use of an interpretation of tragedy as the framework within which to criticize traditional philosophy and even traditional art is of course not unique. Walter Benjamin's *Origin of German Tragic Drama*[3] represents another instance in which an interpretation of tragedy—though significantly different from that of Nietzsche—has similarly critical implications. While at first glance this work might appear to be only a narrow, scholarly monograph on a previously neglected period in the history of German drama, in reality it elaborates the theory of a specifically modern version of tragedy through which Benjamin in effect breaks with—or at any rate reinterprets—traditional concepts of art and philosophy. Freud's psychoanalytic theory offers another major instance in which many of the presuppositions of traditional philosophy and theory are put into question through an interpretation of tragedy. Like Nietzsche, Freud too finds a logic or reason in tragedy in relation to which the reason of traditional philosophy and theory appears limited and superficial. Freud's psychoanalytic theory is also like Nietzsche's interpretation of tragedy in giving a central place to identification, labeled as such by Freud, in its description of the tragic unconscious. In the context of Freud's work, as in the context of Nietzsche's, the form of identification associated with tragedy is complex and highly problematical, and for that reason, I would argue, it has the greatest critical potential for undermining the various concepts of the subject and the traditions that support them.

The Birth of Tragedy offers a model in terms of which the critical nature of the projects of Benjamin and Freud can be understood. But it also exemplifies a tendency that can be found in varying degrees in their work as well—the tendency to equate a single version or interpretation of tragedy with an essence of tragedy, which becomes in turn essence pure and simple. It is because of this tendency to assign an absolute value to art and in particular to tragedy that Nietzsche's work has come to exemplify not only the critical force of art but also the danger of aestheticism—as it does already for Nietzsche himself when, in his "Attempt at Self-Criticism," he writes of the "artists' metaphysics in the background" of *The Birth of Tragedy* (18).

The idea forming the basis of this artists' metaphysics—that "existence and the world seem justified only as an aesthetic phenomenon" (141)—undoubtedly seems highly questionable to us, as it did already to him, not just for ethical or political reasons but for philosophical reasons as well; that is, because such an idea is ultimately every bit as metaphysical as the Socratic optimism it opposes and strives to over-turn. Nietzsche's description of tragedy reveals a heterogeneous entity, divided among conflicting tendencies—the Dionysian, the Apollinian, and the Socratic-Euripidean—and the metaphysical character of his interpretation of tragedy is evident in his decision to separate out the Dionysian element and privilege it as the absolute form or version of tragedy. Nietzsche overturns absolute reason only to replace it with something that in the end seems to resemble it very closely—an absolute (form of) tragedy, which comprehends all other forms of tragic art (and philosophy) within itself.

The tendency to privilege one form or version of tragedy at the expense of others can also be discerned in the work of Benjamin and Freud as well as Nietzsche. It should be stressed that in no case is it totally uniform or consistent in its effects, and in no case does it wholly negate the critical implications of their interpretation of tragedy. Reading these figures together makes it possible not only to assess the effects produced by such a tendency but also to question the interpretation of tragedy of each in terms of the interpretation of tragedy of the others. It thus provides a picture of the complex, indeterminate nature of tragedy, and in the case of Nietzsche and Freud, of identification as well. It confirms that tragedy is not an essence, that there is no single version or form of it that subsumes all other forms or interpretations, but rather that the term *tragedy* designates a problem, a point of both intersection and divergence among major philosophical, aesthetic, and social theories.

The dogmatic tendency to assign an essence to tragedy has numerous effects in *The Birth of Tragedy*. One of the most important is to oppose art to philosophy, to see them as radically different and contrary entities, each with its own sphere or stage. This is the consequence of Nietzsche's decision, at least at the most polemical moments of *The Birth of Tragedy*, to identify tragedy with what he calls the Dionysian. He writes that with the appearance of Socrates, Dionysus is "scared from the tragic stage" (82), and as a result tragedy itself dies, the victim of a suicide that is the "consequence of an irreconcilable conflict" between tragedy and philosophy (76). Similarly, when he argues that, in his plays, Euripides "conscientiously reproduces even the botched outlines of nature" and thus provides the citizen of Athens with a mirror in which he can recognize himself in all his "civic mediocrity" (77), Nietzsche indicates that Euripides has

be seen as an attempt to carry out major aspects of Nietzsche's critical agenda with respect to art, while at the same time overcoming or at least avoiding many of the pitfalls of Nietzsche's aestheticism.

Benjamin's differences with Nietzsche emerge almost immediately in his choice of subject and in his manner of defining it. For Benjamin, German baroque drama, or the *Trauerspiel*, is distinguished from classical (and presumably from neoclassical drama as well) because of its preeminently historical themes and character, and he holds the distinction to be much more than the indication of a relatively superficial transformation in the tragic genre. Instead, the historical nature of the *Trauerspiel* signifies a profound reformulation of the notion of the tragic and the emergence of a specifically modern form of tragedy or art, one that points beyond the various models of art–including the Romantic model–still indebted in one form or another to classicism and hence to ancient tragic models. The effect of Benjamin's argument, when contrasted with that of Nietzsche, is to open up the question of the essence of tragedy by indicating the existence of another, modern version, one radically different from classical tragedy but with an equally legitimate claim to represent tragedy as a whole.

Inasmuch as baroque drama comes to stand for modern art itself in the course of Benjamin's discussion, *The Origin of German Tragic Drama* can be considered a defense and illustration of the importance of modernity for our understanding of art as a whole. Moreover, Benjamin's discussion of what for him is this quintessentially modern art points beyond *The Birth of Tragedy* precisely because the notion of the *Trauerspiel* points beyond beauty, and for Benjamin this means it points beyond art itself. This aspect of the *Trauerspiel* is also evident in Benjamin's discussion of what distinguishes the baroque from classicism, that is, both ancient and neoclassical tragedy. He argues that whereas classicism "was not permitted to behold the lack of freedom, the imperfection, the collapse of the physical, beautiful, nature" (*Origin of German Tragic Drama*, 176), baroque drama, thanks to its historical nature, presents us with a historical process that "does not assume the form of the process of an eternal life so much as that of irresistible decay" (178). The allegorical mode of baroque drama corresponds to its deeply historical and modern character. Like history and modernity, allegory also points beyond nature and hence beyond beauty, because it is characterized by ambiguity, multiplicity, and an uneconomical extravagance of meaning and is thus no longer bound by the law of beauty, which is a law of economy and simplicity (177). Unlike Nietzsche, who defends the importance of the most ancient forms of Greek tragedy because for him they best exemplify art itself, Benjamin focuses on this modern form of tragedy because of its unaesthetic or extra-aesthetic quality.

The Origin of German Tragic Drama remains a Nietzschean work, however, despite its attempt to rethink the relations among art, history, and philosophy, and despite its attempt to rethink art in terms of modernity itself. For even though Benjamin emphasizes the negative forces at work within history and the discontinuous nature of history which results from those forces, history—and hence modern art—is no less metaphysical for him than Dionysian tragedy is for Nietzsche. Just as Nietzsche presents the Dionysian version of tragedy as the fullest embodiment of the nature or essence of tragedy, so in the end the *Trauerspiel* comes to signify not so much the existence of another possible version or interpretation of art as the true nature of art, a nature that for Benjamin is now intrinsically historical and dialectical but remains a nature nonetheless in the sense that it is universal: "The object of philosophical criticism is to show that the function of artistic form is as follows: to make historical content, such as provides the basis of every important work of art, into a philosophical truth" (182).

In the final analysis, Benjamin's conception of modern art as exemplified in the *Trauerspiel* does not point beyond (classical) art (or beyond truth). Or at any rate, in pointing beyond them it points back to them, back to a historical conception of them which, according to Benjamin, it is and always has been the object of philosophical criticism to reveal. Philosophical criticism is the specific form of criticism that complements the true nature of (modern) art. According to Benjamin, it strips off the ephemeral beauty of the work of art but in the process reawakens a deeper beauty that is "more than empty dreaming" (182). This reawakening of beauty is a reawakening of art itself, of an art whose essence now lies in its historical rather than beautiful nature. Benjamin's theory of German baroque drama thus represents an important antidote to Nietzsche's metaphysics of art and tragedy. But it also exemplifies a metaphysical tendency of its own, because Benjamin's conceptions of allegory, history, and modernity constitute a new form of beauty that is "more than empty dreaming" and thus a new essence of art.

The metaphysical nature of Benjamin's conceptions of history, modernity, and allegory is not the only problematic aspect of his interpretation of the *Trauerspiel*, however. Another lies in the ethical-theoretical decision defining the limits of the corpus that forms the basis of his discussion of baroque drama. Like Hegel and a number of Hegel's immediate predecessors and contemporaries, Benjamin is concerned in *The Origin of German Tragic Drama* with defining a German aesthetic, albeit one not exemplified uniquely by German authors. Benjamin's approach to this project is somewhat different from most of those who came before him. In their case, the aim is not to establish modern art as the sovereign opposite of classicism, as is the case with Benjamin. They seek, first of all, to distinguish between an authentic classical art—that of the Greeks—and an unauthentic classical art—of the Latins (that is, principally of Rome and modern France). Second, their goal is to create a modern equivalent of the first classicism which would reveal what they hold to be the inferior nature of the second. Benjamin's study of the *Trauerspiel* breaks with the nostalgia of his predecessors in the sense that, in treating baroque drama as the exemplary form of art, he is displacing both French neoclassical art and ancient art from their preeminent positions.

But where French neoclassicism is concerned, the parallel between Benjamin and many of his predecessors holds, nonetheless. In the case of Shakespeare and Calderón, for example, Benjamin reveals that he is willing to go beyond the confines of German literature and German history in order to define his object, German baroque drama, inasmuch as *Hamlet* is cited as a great example of the genre (136) and Calderón is considered a master of the drama of fate, that is, of baroque drama (133).[9] But Benjamin's concept of the *Trauerspiel*— and his corresponding concept of modern art—is not similarly extended to include any French dramatist. He never discusses or analyzes the work of Racine, Corneille, or any other French dramatist of the baroque period in *The Origin of German Tragic Drama*, and this omission is entirely consistent with his attempt to refocus the question of art and define modern art in terms of a field that is *explicitly* nonclassical but *implicitly* non-French.

Of course, there is always a risk of unfairness in speaking of a given work in terms of what it does not do rather than in terms of what it actually does. Certainly if *The Origin of German Tragic Drama* were the narrowly focused scholarly work it at certain moments appears to be, it would be meaningless to raise the issue posed by the limitation Benjamin imposes on his corpus. The exclusion of French neoclassicism, however, does take on significance, a transcendental significance, so to speak, inasmuch as *The Origin of German Tragic Drama* is much more than a scholarly monograph: it is, rather, a philosophical-critical investigation into the nature of art itself. Because of the way it equates (modern) art and the German, and because of the corresponding tension it implies as a result between the non-German (that is, between the French neoclassical) and the German (that is, baroque drama), Benjamin's work should be seen as prolonging a tradition that includes Lessing, Hegel, and Nietzsche (to mention only those figures I shall treat in my own discussion of the problem) rather than breaking with it.

Nietzsche's work, once again, both exemplifies this same type of limitation and offers a critical perspective on it. It is true that he is not directly concerned, as is Benjamin, with a German literary corpus – Greek drama and the Greek Dionysian festivals define the tragic in *The Birth of Tragedy*. But because, for Nietzsche, the tragic is irretrievably lost, the problem of gaining insight into its nature is virtually insurmountable. And according to Nietzsche, we would have no insight into it at all were it not for a handful of German thinkers and artists who, if they have not fully penetrated "into the core of the Hellenic nature," have at least shown us a path leading to it.[10] In this sense, Nietzsche's object in *The Birth of Tragedy* is not just the Greeks but, rather, the Greeks as they have been revealed to us by these figures who exemplify the German spirit.

The privilege Nietzsche gives to the German is even more explicit in the notes and drafts that are contemporaneous with *The Birth of Tragedy*, where he not only writes of an affinity between but even assimilates the Greek and the tragic with the German: "We have the feeling that the birth of the [new] tragic age simply means a return to itself of the German spirit" (Sallis, *Crossings*, 136). In another passage, Nietzsche depicts Germany as a "backward-stepping Greece: we have reached the period of the Persian wars" (136, n. 28). At the same time, he assimilates French culture with the antitragic elements in Greece's history. A notebook entry from 1869 states that "Euripidean tragedy is, just like French tragedy, framed according to an abstract concept" (119, n. 7).

Freud's statement in *Civilization and Its Discontents* linking German nationalism and anti-Semitism is certainly relevant to passages such as these.[11] If the nationalist spirit of *The Birth of Tragedy* and its anti-Romanism are perhaps less striking than in the above lines from Nietzsche's notes, the anti-Semitism Freud holds to be an inevitable correlate of extreme forms of German nationalism is in evidence. In section 9 of *The Birth of Tragedy*, Nietzsche contrasts the Aryan and the Semitic in terms of the manner in which each "community of peoples" supposedly conceives of the origin of evil (70). In the case of the Aryan community, we see "their gift for the profoundly tragic" in the myth of Prometheus. Nietzsche holds Prometheus to be the Aryan myth par excellence because it confers dignity on sacrilege. This myth, he continues "contrasts strangely with the Semitic myth of the fall in which curiosity, mendacious deception, susceptibility to seduction, lust—in short a series of pre-eminently feminine affects was considered the origin of evil" (71). That the distinction Nietzsche makes here between the Aryan and the Semitic is not neutral is evident not only inasmuch as the tragic and the Aryan are being equated but also inasmuch as the Prometheus myth, unlike the Semitic myth of original sin, does not constitute an attempt to "interpret away" the "misfortune in the nature of things" (71).

Just as in the "Attempt at Self-Criticism" Nietzsche distances himself from the aestheticism of *The Birth of Tragedy*, so in the same text he distances himself, albeit in a more elliptical and hence ambiguous manner, from the related and analogous privilege given to the German, as when he asserts in the opening lines that *The Birth of Tragedy* was written in *spite* of the Franco-Prussian War (17). A later passage from *Ecce Homo* leaves no ambiguity as to Nietzsche's diametrically opposed, though perhaps equally disturbing attitude toward both the French and the German: "I believe only in French culture and consider everything else in Europe today that calls itself 'culture' a misunderstanding—not to speak of German culture."[12] Like Benjamin in *The Origin of German Tragic Drama*, Nietzsche discusses neither French neoclassical tragedy nor French criticism as it relates to the tragic in *The Birth of Tragedy*. But in each case, an underlying tension between "the French" and "the German" colors the discussion and serves as one of its crucial and ultimately unexamined presuppositions. As long as the question of the tragic can be posed in terms of a single, national corpus of literary works, or at any rate, a corpus that is homogeneous in terms that are derived from a national perspective on art, then the theoretical identity of tragedy can be better assured and its diversity, complexity, and heterogeneity overlooked.

At the risk of stating the obvious, it is important to stress that the tendency to define art in terms of a national identity is hardly unique to German critics and philosophers of art. Many of them frequently stress the importance of eliminating national biases from criticism, and they often criticize the French, especially but not only Corneille and Voltaire, on just these grounds. One has only to read one or two of Voltaire's most celebrated prefaces to his own tragedies to feel that, at least in certain instances, these critics and philosophers had ample justification for their view.[13] The real issue, then, is not whether the French or the German (or any other national) perspective on art is "more national," assuming for a minute that the issue is one of degree and that there can be a modern art and theory of art that is not national. The tendency to separate out the German and the French is problematic not just because it inevitably results in the elevation of the one at the expense of the other, but, more importantly, because it tends to obscure the common ground between the opposed terms used to delineate the problem of art by a Nietzsche, a Benjamin, or a Hegel. In Benjamin's terms, for example, it obscures the parallels and the affinities between (French) (neo)classicism and the (German) baroque. In Nietzsche's terms it obscures the affinities between the Euripidean and the Dionysian, between an authentic and an unauthentic art, between the tragic and the philosophical. And, as we shall see, in Hegel's terms, it obscures the way speculative philosophy is prefigured in modern (French) tragedy.

In focusing for the most part on French writers in relation to German theorists and critics, my aim is not to reopen the Racine versus Shakespeare debate (as interpreted by A. W. Schlegel, Hegel, and others), although I hope to have shown the arbitrary nature of the criteria in whose terms that debate was (and in many cases is still) framed. It has been, rather, to indicate some of the ways in which the national dimension of the theory of art is intertwined with its philosophical and theoretical dimensions, and how at times it even becomes the dominant indicator of its metaphysical character. Because of the national dimension of the problem of art, I have used texts of French literature to provide a critical perspective on literary-philosophical theories that in some way exemplify a tendency to suppose that a natural affinity exists between art and "the German."[14] But this is not to deny the existence of a French version of the phenomenon I have sought to analyze—quite the contrary. The texts of Corneille, Racine, Prévost, Beaumarchais, and Diderot certainly in no way escape from the problem posed by the contamination of nationalism and art, either by virtue of their literary nature or by virtue of being French.

The national dimension of the theory of modern tragedy is just one example of the way it touches extra-aesthetic areas and takes on a political and social meaning. In this respect too, Nietzsche's *Birth of Tragedy* is instructive, inasmuch as it conveys a sense of the social dimension of the problem of tragedy—it is a critique of received social as well as aesthetic ideas. The contrast Nietzsche draws between a Dionysian and a Socratic (or Euripidean) version of art is paralleled by another contrast between a Dionysian version of the subject and a Socratic version, and it is through this second contrast that Nietzsche conveys the political and social implications of his critique of philosophy.

For Nietzsche, soberness is a cornerstone of Socratic optimism, and the value Socratic philosophy attaches to sobriety and consciousness represents a reaction against the "drunken" or unconscious poets whom Nietzsche considers to be the authentic representatives of the Dionysian character of art. Nietzsche's critique of Socrates thus reacts in turn to the celebration of sobriety with a celebration of "the 'I' of the lyrist [which] sounds from the depth of his being; [and whose] 'subjectivity,' in the sense of modern aestheticians is a fiction" (*Birth of Tragedy*, 49). When contrasted with the "I" of the lyrist, the self defined by Socratic philosophy appears superficial in every aspect— aesthetic and theoretical, but also ethical and political. *The Birth of Tragedy* thus conveys a sense of the urgency of the question of art: the idea that the inertia of the tradition Nietzsche is criticizing, on the one hand, and the critical potential of art, on the other, are of concern from a social as well as a theoretical or aesthetic standpoint. From Nietzsche's perspective, Socratic optimism is not just a narrowly philosophical position but also a kind of ethico-theoretical infrastructure subtending culture, politics, and education and thus shaping the modern, posttragic individual.

But in the most crucial respects, the political and social dimension of Nietzsche's critique of Socratic optimism has the same metaphysical character as his critique of its theoretical or philosophical dimension. Nietzsche's dialectic of art relates to politics and society as well as theory—it negates, retains and raises politics to the level of absolute art, that is, an art that comprehends not only philosophy but also politics "within" it. And just as Nietzsche identifies tragedy with what for him is its Dionysian core, so he identifies the essence of the political with the Dionysian festival, as is evident in his description of the prototragedies out of which the tragedies of Sophocles and Aeschylus evolved: "We must always keep in mind that the public at an Attic tragedy found itself in the chorus of the *orchestra*, and there was at bottom no opposition between public and chorus: everything is merely a great sublime chorus of dancing and singing satyrs or of those who permit themselves to be represented by such satyrs" (62). Located between the *skene* and the *theatron*, the *orchestra* is the place where all activity is subsumed as artistic activity, and "everything is merely a great sublime chorus" in which the citizen and the actor can no longer be distinguished. Its position at the heart of the larger tragic theater represents the central place of music in relation both to tragedy and to society as a whole. The *orchestra* is the space in which the Dionysian subject finds its true place; one in which the lyric "I" presents itself and finds itself immediately at one with the other spectators/actors who make up the sublime chorus.

The critical implications of this description of the Dionysian festivals in relation to the Socratic-Euripidean polis are clear. In the city as it is projected by the philosophy of Socrates, the mediocrity of each individual citizen-subject must of necessity correspond to the superficiality of the bond uniting him to the other citizens. Implicitly, what separates each citizen of the Socratic polis individually and the citizenry collectively from the Dionysian tragic also separates them from one another by imprisoning each in a fictive individuality.

It is in Nietzsche's description of the Dionysian festival that identification, or at least a particular version of identification, emerges as what immediately links the lyric subjects of the Dionysian chorus together—and hence as the social bond of the Dionysian collective. Unlike Aristotelian catharsis, Dionysian identification, as we have already seen, is not supposed to bring art down to the level of the civic mediocrity of the spectators. Instead, it supposedly raises the (Dionysian) spectators to the level of art by raising each of them above and beyond his individuality. In this Dionysian form, identification is a social process that immediately links together the Dionysian subjects of Nietzsche's "aesthetocracy." In his description of the Dionysian chorus, what could be called Nietzsche's aestheticizing of the political takes the form of an ultimate, total, and frenzied process of identification in which all boundaries between individuals and between the aesthetic (the tragic) and the political are overcome.

There are many points in terms of which Freud's interpretation of tragedy can be contrasted to that of Nietzsche, but one of the most important is its synthesis of the aesthetic and the political. Freud's psychoanalytic theory points beyond Nietzsche's aestheticized politics, even as it gives a central place to both the tragic and the process of identification, which Freud states is "known to psychoanalysis as the earliest expression of an emotional tie with another person."[15] What emerges in Freud's discussion of the relation between the individual and society is the model of a paradoxical process of identification (and a correspondingly complex sense of tragedy), one whose nature is problematic not only in relation to the superficial phenomenon of consciousness but also from the standpoint of the unconscious as well. The implication of this Freudian model of identification as compared to the (implicit) Nietzschean one is that identification is never immediate or simply positive, even in relation to the unconscious or "lyric" subject. Unlike the Dionysian "I," the core of the unconscious Freudian subject is fundamentally heterogeneous, and its relationship to itself and therefore others is fundamentally complex.

Like *The Birth of Tragedy*, Freud's theory of the psyche reinterprets tragedy and in the process reveals the relative superficiality of traditional concepts of reason, logic, and science. Tragedy, in the form of the unconscious, is not just one object among others for reason; it is the foundation upon which reason—or the rational and the conscious—are erected. Though every aspect of Freud's analysis of the unconscious is related to his interpretation of tragedy, two processes in particular—identification and the related process through which the superego is constituted—indicate what is most problematic and at the same time most critical in Freud's interpretation of the tragic.

These two processes deserve to be called tragic for two principal reasons. First, Freud's analysis of them is linked consistently with his interpretation of Sophocles' *Oedipus Rex* and Shakespeare's *Hamlet*, two plays that, as Jean Starobinski has argued, serve not only as examples for psychoanalysis but also as matrixes out of which psychoanalytic theory itself can be said to emerge.[16] Second, the problems posed to psychoanalytic theory by identification, by the emergence of the superego, and by the processes related to them are directly linked to what, borrowing from Freud, could be called the irreducibly masochistic dimension of identification. As I argue in chapter 4, the economy within whose framework Freud initially interprets dreams is not able to account for this dimension of identification, and his revisions of his theory can be seen as an attempt to elaborate a framework within which the tragic—that is, the uneconomical or "originally" masochistic—character of identification can be theorized.

Of course, the significance of Freud's work in relation to the theoretical and political dimensions of identification and tragedy is not without ambiguity. Freud can be seen as misrecognizing many of the most important implications of his interpretations of *Oedipus Rex* and *Hamlet* and as resolving by arbitrary means the various difficulties posed by the problem of identification for psychoanalytic theory. Several aspects of Freud's work reflect such misrecognition and reveal an attempt to integrate the tragic elements of the psyche (principally the superego, but also the process of identification, insofar as it serves as a proto-superego) into an economic description by reducing and simplifying what he elsewhere indicates is their complex and even contradictory nature. I argue in chapter 4 that Freud's account of the "anatomical differences between the sexes" is one of the most spectacular in a series of attempts to contain the uneconomical tragic processes within a logic of economy. And as I show in chapter 8, another attempt is evident in Freud's insistence on understanding the process of identification from the perspective of the murder of the father of the primal horde and thus on (re)affirming the theoretical supremacy of *Oedipus* and of the economic principles that, he holds, it exemplifies.

Through his discussion of the themes associated with the preeminently modern figure of Hamlet (the themes of repression, melancholia, primary narcissism, primary masochism, the emergence of the superego, and, above all, identification), Freud nonetheless breaks decisively with the Nietzsche of *The Birth of Tragedy*. First, Freud's exploration of these themes leads him at least implicitly to problematize tragedy itself as a model for the unconscious. *Oedipus Rex* alone can no longer guide him as he explores the territory these problems open up. *Hamlet* now emerges as the figure of another model of tragedy, one that is linked to but at the same time cannot be wholly assimilated with Oedipus. Freud never totally renounces his view that his interpretation of *Oedipus Rex* is the cornerstone of psychoanalysis. However, the increased importance taken on by the themes associated with *Hamlet* in his work undercuts the position of *Oedipus Rex* within the psychoanalytic theory and signals the necessity of abandoning the project of comprehending the interpretation of art and theory within a conceptual framework derived from a single model of tragedy.

Second, Freud's exploration of the themes that emerge in connection with the figure of Hamlet leads to the construction of what could be called a model of a modern psyche in which the tragic (or the unconscious) is not simply visited from without by the censoring agency but is instead involved in the censoring process as well. In the light of this modern model of the psyche, it is no longer possible to oppose an unconscious subject to a conscious one, as Nietzsche seeks to do when he contrasts Dionysus and Socrates, and as Freud himself tends to do when he initially interprets the Oedipus myth in *The Interpretation of Dreams*. Because of the uneconomical nature of the tragic processes (repression, censorship, primary masochism, identification), the Freudian subject is even more radically split than the subject in whom we can purportedly distinguish an unconscious and a conscious self. The split can no longer be localized, it no longer divides the inside from the outside, the conscious from the unconscious, the libidinal from the death drive, or the self from the other. Nor can the split in the Freudian subject be located between a core or central element and a peripheral or superficial one; instead, it is within and between each element, agency, or process. In this sense, Freud's interpretation of the unconscious is incompatible with Nietzsche's interpretation of the subject in terms of a pure Dionysian element or core.

From the perspective of the more complex sense of the relation between the unconscious and the censoring agency that typifies the "modern" psyche in the work of Freud, Nietzsche's lyric "I" appears as an absolute, and therefore metaphysical, subject. This absolute subject has displaced the subject of reason but retains its essential qualities of integrity and sovereignty and, in place of the self-reflexive knowledge of absolute reason, possesses a self-reflexive experience of the Dionysian essence of tragedy—of its own essence—in the form of the tragic celebration. The Freudian subject and the Nietzschean lyric "I" are alike in that neither ever knows itself. But they are unlike inasmuch as the Freudian subject also never grasps itself self-reflexively through the manifestations of the unconscious, whether they take the form of acts, dreams, or works of (Dionysian) art. From the perspective of this radically divided, Freudian subject, it is possible to reverse Freud's famous dictum by saying that there is "no royal road to the unconscious" precisely because the unconscious is everywhere.

The contrast between the complex nature of the Freudian subject and the still relatively simple, homogeneous character of the Dionysian "I" corresponds to a similar contrast between Freud's treatment of the theme of identification and the sense of identification implicit in Nietzsche's description of the Dionysian festival. At bottom, what is at issue for psychoanalysis in the discussion of identification is the question of how primary a phenomenon it is, and the answer given to this question also indicates how primary the social is in relation to the subject.

Though Freud frequently appears to draw back from the implications of certain of his affirmations in relation to identification, those implications emerge clearly nonetheless. When he entertains the possibility of a primary masochism in his essay "The Economic Problem of Masochism," he also in effect recognizes that it presupposes or implies an equally primary process of identification. For primary masochism is a form of aggression that the "not-yet-a-subject," not even an unconscious subject, directs against itself, thus putting itself in the place of the other by simultaneously defining the subject as other and same. As a result, identification must of necessity share in the primary—and complex—nature of this form of masochism. The tragic or masochistic character of identification is thus the aspect of it that points to its primary nature—and therefore, to the fundamental character of the split it creates in the subject through the very process by which the subject begins to be constituted.

As exemplified in the "great sublime chorus," in which the spectators, chorus, and hero of Dionysian tragedy become one, Nietzschean identification confirms that the Dionysian subject itself is outside and prior to identification and thus the ultimate source of all other psychological and social phenomena. The Freudian sense of the tragic character of identification, on the other hand, implies both a subject that, because it is already an other for itself, is fundamentally open and a correspondingly open and problematic sense of the social.

Freud's theory of the unconscious is thus also a theory, if not of society, then of the inherent, fundamental, constitutive sociality of the subject, a sociality that is indicated by the primary—and ambiguous—nature of identification. Just as identification is the social bond in Nietzsche's interpretation of tragedy, so for Freud it is also the social bond, implicitly so in his psychological essays and explicitly in the context of his essays on society. But from the perspective of the more complex sense of identification that emerges in Freud's discussion of primary masochism, the bond linking the unconscious subject to other unconscious subjects in Nietzsche's description of the Dionysian chorus appears relatively superficial and simplistic. For it both precludes the idea that the other plays a role in relation to even the unconscious subject and also ignores the manner in which (unconscious) identification splits as well as unifies.

Despite all that Freud and Nietzsche share, Freud's theory thus also offers a critical perspective on the social dimension and implications of *The Birth of Tragedy*. What opposes Freudian psychoanalysis to Nietzsche's interpretation of tragedy in this respect is not that the former offers an alternative theory of the subject, defined in terms that are purportedly better grounded in logic, reason, or experience. It is, rather, that many aspects of Freudian psychoanalysis can be seen as constituting a process of questioning of the subject, a constantly renewed effort to situate it in terms of deeper processes, which then become the objects of attempts to situate them in turn. It is perhaps above all through this process that Freud conveys a sense of the modernity of the psyche—that is, a sense that no subject is ever pregiven but can only be a protosubject, a "subject" of identification.

It is also through the constant revision of psychoanalytic theory that the identity of the tragic model guiding Freud in his elaboration of his theory of the unconscious is constantly put into question. Just as the unconscious, according to Freud, is characterized by a fusion of antithetical drives, so the idea of tragedy that emerges from his work is one in which two—in many respects antithetical—models of the unconscious, Oedipus and Hamlet, are fused without the tension between them being completely erased. Like Benjamin's *Origins of German Tragic Drama*, Freud's work indicates the critical potential of a specifically modern form and concept of tragedy. Unlike the *Trauerspiel*, however, modern tragedy as exemplified by Shakespeare's *Hamlet* never completely displaces ancient tragedy as exemplified by *Oedipus Rex*. Like the Freudian subject, tragedy in Freud's work has no clear identity. Instead, it is defined by a conflict between contending models of tragedy, and the critical effects of Freudian theory in relation to philosophy, aesthetics, and social theory are directly related to the way it keeps the question of tragedy open.

It could be argued that, no matter how carefully and critically construed, no work whose subject is the tragic or even the modern tragic can avoid falling victim to what could be called tragico-centrism: that is, the tendency to create a metaphysical concept of tragedy that mirrors the metaphysical conceptions of art, philosophy, the subject, and society that it criticizes. Such a work inevitably focuses on tragedy at the expense of an equal consideration of the other arts (and on art at the expense of philosophy, history, and science) and on a single tradition in the history of art (a tradition that comprehends Greek tragedy, [French] neoclassicism, and [German] idealism and Romanticism). As a result, it necessarily runs the risk of endowing tragedy with a specificity and exemplarity and in this manner of giving it an absolute identity.

The risk of such tragico-centrism is an integral part of the critical projects of Nietzsche, Benjamin, and Freud, inasmuch as each seeks to highlight elements of the tragic that have critical potential and thus continuing relevance for the contemporary age. There is no denying that, both despite and because of their projects, each shares much with the traditional philosophies, aesthetics, and social theories they all criticize. But their work, taken both individually and collectively, also indicates the heterogeneous character of the philosophical, literary, critical, national, and social perspectives defining the larger system that serves as the context in which the problem of tragedy emerges. In their different approaches, the irresolvable conflicts and irreconcilable identifications between philosophy and art, between the subject and society, and between national entities as well, emerge as the fundamental components of what in this context could be called the age of modern theory, which is also an age of modern tragedy. This is why it can be said that tragedy is in the last analysis less an object than a problem, less an entity that can be studied from differing theoretical perspectives—be they psychoanalytical, literary-critical, philosophical, or social—than a space in which these different perspectives meet and clash.

CHAPTER 2

Philosophical Identification,

 Tragedy, and the Sublime:

Hegel, Kant, and *Antigone*

Kant's Categorical Imperative is thus the heir of the Oedipus complex.

—Freud

This idea of art as immanent critique is perhaps best symbolized by the agon *of Greek tragedy.*

—Adorno

Aesthetics should leave the controversy between Kant and Hegel behind without trying to smooth it over.

—Adorno

Philosophy against Itself: Hegel versus Kant

What is tragedy? Even the literary historian who prides herself on the empirical nature of her research, even the connoisseur of dramatic literature cannot escape this question, and yet no individual tragedy, nor even the largest imaginable collection of works that could reasonably be called tragedies, can provide an answer to it. Put simply, tragedy itself is not given in the tragic work; this does not mean, however, that tragedy is a purely abstract, formal idea. Its nature cannot be determined without reference to tragic works of literature—there is no *tragedy* without them. But neither can it be determined solely with reference to these works.

The result, according to the logic of Hegel's *Aesthetics*, is that tragedy—that is, the concept of tragedy and hence tragedy itself—belongs to philosophy. From Hegel's perspective, the philosopher alone can fully respond to the question, What is tragedy? for the same reason that only the philosopher can fully respond to the question, What is art?

Thus the work of art, . . . in which thought expresses itself, belongs to the sphere of conceptual thinking, and the spirit, by subjecting it to philosophic treatment, is thereby merely satisfying the need of the spirit's inmost nature. . . . Art, far removed, as we shall see more definitely later, from being the highest form of spirit, acquires its real ratification only in philosophy.[1]

In this passage, Hegel does not yet answer the question What is art? but he does take what in his terms is the indispensable first step toward an answer. Once it has been established that philosophy alone can provide us with the deepest insight into the nature of art, then all that is needed is patience. If we are willing to wait for "an encyclopedic development of the whole of philosophy and its particular disciplines" (25), then we will at last be given the whole, complete answer to the question of art.

Even though it is tempting to do so, it would be a mistake to criticize Hegel too severely for the privilege he gives philosophy in this passage and in the *Aesthetics* in general. For where else can we turn for the concept and theory of art if not to philosophy? To say that the artist, the work of art itself, or the critic can establish what art is as well as or better than the philosopher is not a satisfactory argument. If we do not already possess the definition of art, how can we be sure the artist or critic is something other than a philosopher, and the work of art itself, which Hegel calls an expression of thought (13), is something other than philosophical? Hegel's view of the relation between art and philosophy cannot be refuted simply or globally, because it is impossible to argue that art is the same as or other than philosophy without making a (philosophical) presupposition concerning the nature of each.

Heidegger argues in the epilogue to his "Origin of the Work of Art" that Hegel's *Aesthetics* is "the most comprehensive reflection on the nature of art that the West possesses—comprehensive because it stems from metaphysics."[2] He thus pinpoints the source of the significance and influence of this work, not only for avowedly Hegelian aestheticians and theorists, but for Hegel's critics as well. The *Aesthetics* is notable not only for the scope and variety of the works of art and the periods in the history of art that it encompasses. What distinguishes it perhaps even more is the force and clarity with which Hegel constantly reiterates the necessity for philosophy to be the absolute starting point of aesthetics and the correspondingly systematic nature of the link that binds (his) philosophy of art to (his) philosophy as a whole. Hegel's work reveals why even a particularly radical opponent of systematic, dialectical philosophy such as Nietzsche will not be able to drive a wedge between philosophy and tragedy without himself reconfirming the link between them, albeit in different terms, through what could be called a metaphysics of tragedy. This is why for many critical philosophers today, even those whose affinity with Nietzsche is very great, the philosophy of Hegel has come to stand for a given state of things, the context in which and against which critical thinking takes place. Even after Nietzsche, Hegel's work retains its cogency and metaphysical force—or inertia.

But if there is no way simply to sever the link between philosophy and tragedy, this does not mean that the first step Hegel takes in the direction of the true concept of art and hence of tragedy establishes a clear direction. Despite appearances, Hegel's thesis concerning the philosophical nature of art is not straightforward but, rather, full of ironic significance in relation to both art and philosophy. For, once it has been determined that art is not the other of philosophy, but rather that its essence is to be found in philosophy, then any disagreement concerning the true concept of art concerns philosophy directly and in *its* very essence. That the philosophical character of art is irrefutable only heightens the irony—it only ensnares philosophy all the more inexorably in a logic it only partially masters.

The logic in question, the one that underlies the relationship between art and philosophy in Hegel's *Aesthetics*, is what I call a logic of identification, understood as a process through which philosophy finds itself in its other: art. Hegelian philosophy is speculative not only in the sense that it involves prolonged analysis of a systematic nature or that it is based on a form of reason that transcends simple experience. Also and perhaps most important, Hegelian philosophy is speculative in the sense that it is based on a *specular* relation between subject and object, in which object and subject are no longer opposed but seen as if each were a mirror reflection of the other. Through this process of mirroring, the Hegelian subject repeatedly puts itself in the place of the other in a series of identifications that structure not only the *Phenomenology of Spirit* but Hegelian philosophy as a whole. According to the logic of this specular process of identification, philosophy can always see art as an image of itself. It can find its own reason and its own concept in art, and this is why philosophy can claim that art "acquire[s] its real ratification only in philosophy."

But the philosophical nature of art also, at least implicitly, poses a difficulty for philosophy. If it is true that the image and concept of philosophy can be found in art, then a question arises as to whether art or philosophy is more truly and profoundly philosophical. Instead of confirming that art is a subdiscipline within a larger philosophical system, identification links art and philosophy together in a rivalry whose basis is the claim implicitly shared by each to be the embodiment of the concept of absolute reason. Another version of the impasse to which its identification with art leads philosophy is apparent in the distinctions that speculative philosophy is forced to make between the "essential," philosophical elements of art and those of lesser philosophical status or importance. Such distinctions are always problematic, and as a result they point to the uneasy character of the identification between philosophy and art. They indicate the possibility that the philosophical and the "a-philosophical" elements of art cannot ultimately be separated and that, as a consequence, philosophy cannot extricate itself from its identification with art but is itself contaminated precisely by what it considers to be the less properly philosophical elements in art. Hegel's attempt to make identification the basis of a dialectic that begins and ends in philosophy thus places philosophy itself at risk of losing itself and becoming another version of art.

Hegel's philosophy as a whole is designed to obviate the risks inherent in the uneasy identification between philosophy and art, but they remain particularly evident nonetheless in two closely related areas. One is in relation to Kantian aesthetics. Hegel presents his philosophy generally as the reconciliation of the Kantian antinomies, and his stance in relation to Kantian aesthetics and in particular to Kant's concept of the sublime is strictly analogous to his position in relation to Kantian philosophy as a whole. This not only means, however, that his critique of Kant's aesthetics is subordinate to broader philosophical concerns. It also means that from Hegel's perspective, to overcome the Kantian sublime is to overcome Kantian philosophy itself.

In Kant's version of aesthetics, the sublime is equal to and in certain respects more significant than the beautiful for the aesthetic as a whole. In Hegel's system of "the three forms of art," however, the sublime occupies an inferior position, inasmuch as its fate is to be transcended by classical art. In Hegel's interpretation of art, classical art and in particular classical tragedy overcome what he holds to be the purely negative character of the relationship between imagination and reason, between nature and the Idea in Kant's "Analytic of the Sublime." Classical art "clears up [the] double defect [of the sublime]; it is the free and adequate embodiment of the Idea in the shape peculiarly appropriate to the Idea itself in its essential nature" (*Aesthetics*, 77), and in this manner, classical art stands for Hegelian philosophy itself in relation to Kantian philosophy. However, the process through which classical art overcomes the opposition and negativity of the sublime involves not simply a rejection and a leaving behind but, rather, an identification in which the negative elements of the sublime are incorporated into its own substance. The reconciliation of nature and Idea achieved by classical art and in particular classical tragedy is one that, at least in principle, can be effected only at great cost and only as a result of the tragic conflict between nature and Idea having reached a maximum of intensity.

The relationship between Hegel's conception of classical tragedy and the Kantian sublime, however, like the relationship between Hegelian philosophy and art as a whole, can be reversed. The following analysis of Kant's philosophy highlights those aspects of Kant's *Critique of Pure Reason*, his *Critique of Judgement*, and, in particular, his "Analytic of the Sublime" which can be seen as implicitly, before the fact, drawing Hegelian philosophy into an irresolvable conflict concerning the nature of art and tragedy—and hence, concerning its own nature as philosophy. Kant's critique of aesthetic judgment provides the grounds for arguing that the aesthetic is as much an interruption of the dialectic of nature and Idea as a means of reconciling them in philosophy—and that therefore the tragic (and ultimately philosophy itself) is as much sublime as classical.

The reading of Kant which I propose will provide the background against which Hegel's interpretation of tragedy and, more particularly, his reading of Sophocles' *Antigone* are analyzed in the second half of this chapter. As we shall see, *Antigone* is in Hegel's view the supreme example of tragedy and art in general precisely because of what he considers to be its effective reconciliation of the oppositions structuring the Kantian sublime. Despite the overwhelmingly positive, philosophical significance Hegel attaches to this play, however, what Jacques Derrida, for example, calls Hegel's fascination with the figure of Antigone[3] cannot be understood wholly in terms of a simple confirmation of the philosophical dialectic. *Antigone* should also be seen as a figure of the sublime—that is, of a conflict that philosophy cannot overcome in and through art because it touches the relation not only of nature to reason but also of reason to itself.

I shall show that identification emerges as a central issue in the conflicting perspectives on art and tragedy offered by Kant's concept of the sublime and Hegel's concept of classical art, despite the absence of the term from the work of both. In Kant's case, I shall argue that a primary process of identification can be uncovered in the *Critique of Judgement* and in the *Critique of Pure Reason* as the very basis not only of aesthetic judgment but of reason itself. When this primary form of identification is contrasted with the one implicit in Hegel's interpretation of tragedy, both Hegel's interpretation and the intimately related project of grasping philosophy itself through an identification with art appear deeply problematic. In the "Analytic of the Sublime," in particular, the process of what I would call aesthetic identification, which makes possible judgments relative to the sublime, can be shown ultimately to limit and divide reason and philosophy against themselves rather than affirm them. From the perspective of the second "Analytic," Hegel's project appears compromised not because art and philosophy are totally opposite but, rather, because what separates them appears to be as much within philosophy (and within art) as between philosophy and art.

"Pure Reason" and the Aesthetic: The Problematic Character of Kantian Identification

Unlike Hegel's, Kant's major philosophical works contain no references to tragedy. Nonetheless, in *The Birth of Tragedy*, Nietzsche gives an important place to Kant, arguing that he "introduced an infinitely profounder and more serious view of ethical problems and of art,"[4] even going so far as to say that Kantian philosophy is "Dionysian wisdom comprised in concepts" (112). A. W. Schlegel, in his *Course of Lectures on Dramatic Art and Literature*,[5] also affirms the existence of a profound affinity between Kantian philosophy and tragedy. He argues that the reason tragedy does not shun even the harshest subject is "that a spiritual and invisible power can only be measured by the opposition which it encounters from some external force capable of being appreciated by the senses." This fundamental aspect of tragedy can best be understood, he goes on, by referring to the section on the sublime in Kant's *Critique of Judgement*, "to the complete perfection of which nothing is wanting but a more definite idea of the tragedy of the ancients, with which he does not seem to have been very well acquainted" (*Dramatic Art and Literature*, 69).

To some, these assertions of the importance of Kant's philosophy in relation to art and tragedy might sound paradoxical, especially when one considers the place his work has been assigned by many historians of philosophy thanks to its rationalism. And yet Nietzsche's view concerning the affinity between Kantian philosophy and the question of art is based on two aspects of Kant's philosophy. First, it can be seen in the way Kant elevates the problem of aesthetic judgment from a secondary to a primary concern and in the critical implications of his critique of aesthetic judgment in relation to knowledge and reason themselves. Second, the idea that there is a special affinity between Kant's philosophy and tragedy is also borne out by considering the specific nature of aesthetic judgment as it emerges in the *Critique of Judgement*.

What gives the critique of aesthetic judgment its central position in Kant's philosophy as a whole is that a form of identification, which is central to both philosophy and the aesthetic, emerges with particular clarity in the Third Critique, and the specific character of this Kantian version of identification also provides the link between his philosophy and the problem of tragedy. A. W. Schlegel's view that Kant's "Analytic of the Sublime" is the part of his work with the greatest relevance to tragedy is especially pertinent in this regard because the Kantian interpretation of identification is highlighted in precisely this section of the "Critique of Aesthetic Judgment." As we shall see, the Kantian sublime is based on a highly problematic form of identification, one that, like Aristotelian catharsis, is both pleasurable and painful, reassuring and disorienting at the same time.

I argue that Kant's "Analytic of the Sublime" both gives the process of identification a fundamental role in relation to reason and aesthetic judgment and, at the same time, highlights what is most problematic in identification. However, this is not to imply that the problematic of identification cannot be found in other sections of the Third Critique or in the other Critiques. On the contrary, the "Analytic of the Beautiful" and even the *Critique of Pure Reason* prepare the way for the "Analytic of the Sublime" in their double and conflictual approach to this problem. In the case of the "Analytic of the Beautiful," an implicit concept of identification provides the foundation for the discussion of aesthetic judgment from the very start. As Jean-Luc Nancy has argued:

> "To think for oneself and at the same time in the place of others": beginning with German aesthetics of the eighteenth century, and with Baumgarten in particular, this formula— which mixes the same and the other, which thinks or which requires the simultaneity of the same and the other in the same— characterizes judgments of taste and the capacity proper to the artist. Kant will transform it from an empirical thesis into a transcendental determination with [his notion of] the "demand for universality" of judgments of taste in the Third Critique.[6]

Nancy's commentary clearly echoes the language of the Third Critique itself, in which Kant argues that disinterested judgments—that is, judgments to which, in the language of the Third Critique, one can demand universal assent—presuppose the possibility of "putting ourselves in the position of everyone else."[7]

This same possibility of putting oneself in the place of everyone else, or, in Nancy's terms, of mixing the same and the other, is just what, for Freud, defines the process of identification when he first introduces the term in *The Interpretation of Dreams*. In the course of an interpretation of the dream of one of his patients, Freud asserts that her dream acquires new meaning if one supposes that it concerns not the dreamer herself but her friend, and that the dreamer has therefore "put herself in her friend's place, or, as we might say, . . . she has 'identified' with her friend."[8] In Kant's "Analytic of the Beautiful," it is just such a process of identification that is being indicated as the basis of aesthetic judgment, but now in terms not of a specific other but, rather, of an undetermined plurality of others.

As a consequence of its disinterested character, Kant argues, aesthetic judgment implies the existence of a common sense, by which he means not the common (or vulgar) understanding but, rather, a public sense (151), that is, a capacity for feeling delight in the beautiful which unites all of humanity. It is because of the importance of Kant's notions of universality and common sense that Hannah Arendt and Jean-François Lyotard, for example, despite the significant differences between their respective approaches to the political and the aesthetic, both see Kant's *Critique of Judgement* as providing the basis for a Kantian politics. For each of them, this politics would entail a form of association with others based on something other than convergent interests, on the one hand, or a totalitarian concept of the body politic, on the other.[9] Their view of Kant's philosophy contrasts significantly with that of Hegel, from whose perspective a Kantian politics is by definition impossible, given what he sees as the constitutive inability of Kantian practical reason to actualize itself. Jean Hyppolite formulates this Hegelian critique in modern terms when he writes about Kant:

> Without doubt, the "I think" is the summit of Kantian architecture, but this Cogito is a cogito in general, it is the common essence of individual consciousness, and the issue of *transcendental intersubjectivity* is not really raised. . . . This *intersubjectivity* has been considered . . . in our own time as an original "phenomenon" of our experience, and Heidegger has described it with the name of "Mitsein." This being-with would be constitutive of human reality and would belong to it on the same grounds as its being-in-the-world.[10]

The implication of Arendt's and Lyotard's reading of Kant, however, is that this Hegelian reading does not take seriously enough the role that the other plays in making aesthetic judgment possible—or, in other words, the fundamental nature of identification in relation to aesthetic judgment. To borrow Hyppolite's terms, though not his conclusions, it is in terms of aesthetic judgment that the transcendental character of intersubjectivity is affirmed by Kant.

The specific nature of the form of identification that unites humanity in aesthetic judgment is indicated in Kant's insistence that "the assertion is not that everyone *will* fall in with our judgment, but rather that every one *ought* to agree with it" (*Critique of Judgement*, 84). The (transcendental) other whose agreement I seek (82— *Man wirbt um jedes andern Beistimmung*) when I pronounce a judgment of taste is another (human) subject like myself. This is why it is *possible* that he or she will agree with me. However, that other is truly other, in the sense that I cannot know whether or not he or she *will in fact* agree with my judgment. If the judgment of the other were always in principle in agreement with mine, then the other would be another (version of) myself. Judgment would be rational, but there would be no relationship to the other as other. If, however, the judgment of the other were simply different from mine, if he or she were swayed by other, purely personal tastes, then the otherness of the other would indeed be affirmed, but not in relation to reason. The relationship to others would be merely empirical and in this sense subject to the vicissitudes of accident and personal history. The relation to the other is transcendental in Kant's terms, that is, it affects reason itself, precisely because the other is neither simply same nor other.

What is already being indicated in this discussion of the universality of taste in the "Analytic of the Beautiful" is the problematic character of the process of identification which is the condition of aesthetic judgment. Aesthetic judgments relative to the beautiful are based on an identification with others: this is what is meant by their universality. But the problematic character of identification is being indicated in the ambiguous status of the other—neither simply an other nor simply identical to myself. In aesthetic judgment, I cannot choose which aspect of the other my demand is addressed to. Aesthetic judgment mixes the same and the other in the sense that it is addressed to both a stranger and myself, both to myself as stranger and to a stranger as myself.

A putting oneself in the place of the other accounts for the universality not only of taste, as it is understood by Kant, but also for the universal or categorical character of moral law. In this sense, identification is as fundamental to Kantian ethics as to Kantian aesthetics. Of course, Kant's *Critique of Practical Reason*, like his critique of aesthetic judgment, stresses the subjective character of moral law. But what has been said above concerning the transcendental character of the relation to others applies to the Second as well as to the Third Critique. In the *Critique of Practical Reason* as well as in the *Critique of Judgement*, the place in which I put myself—or in which conscience puts me—when I put myself in the place of the other is the place of the freedom of the other, and thus of what is other both in relation to myself and in relation to the other. Nietzsche's remark that Kant's philosophy made possible a "more serious view of ethical problems and of art" can be interpreted in terms of the transcendental (or in Freud's terms, the primary) character of this identification with others. Unlike Euripidean identification, which according to Nietzsche's argument drags art, ethics, and the other down to the level of the mediocre self, Kantian identification raises the subject to the level of this "transcendental alterity."

The "Analytic of the Beautiful" is not the only place in Kant's philosophy where the "Analytic of the Sublime" is being anticipated in terms of the problematic sense it conveys with respect to identification, however. In the *Critique of Pure Reason*, identification also plays a primary role and has an analogously ambiguous significance. Moreover, it is significant that identification should play this role. Not only does the *Critique of Pure Reason* thus offer an additional confirmation of the importance of identification in the philosophy of Kant, but it also indicates that the process of identification is constitutive with respect not only to aesthetic judgment but also to reason itself, even in its theoretical form. It is certainly true that Kant, because he had already recast his notion of identification in transcendental rather than empirical terms in the *Critique of Pure Reason*, was able in the *Critique of Judgement* to bring a bold new solution to many of the dilemmas that the question of taste had posed for his predecessors. But the reverse is true as well. Because the logic of identification, even as it is described in the *Critique of Pure Reason*, is already an aesthetic logic, because it is already a logic of primary identification with others, the First Critique (and ultimately Kant's philosophy as a whole) appears not only as a theory equal, at least in certain respects, to the task of understanding the aesthetic. It also appears as a theory in which the aesthetic, or at least a certain aesthetic conception of identification, founds reason, and in which, as a result, reason itself is confronted with the question of art from the (its) beginning.

In the simplest terms, identification is primary in relation to reason because, in the language of the *Critique of Pure Reason*, the rational subject as such is not and cannot be an object of knowledge. From the perspective of the First Critique, the inaccessibility of the rational subject to its own knowledge is implicit in the distinction between what Kant calls the empirical unity of self-consciousness and the transcendental unity of self-consciousness. Since all knowledge relates concepts to intuitions, and since there is no intuition where there is no object to effect the sensation or intuition, there can be no knowledge of the rational subject, inasmuch as, in Kant's terms, it does not coincide, at least not fully, with an empirical entity.

The radical implications of this distinction become fully explicit in chapter 24 ("Of the Application of the Categories to the Objects of the Senses in General") of the Second Section (whose subject is the "Transcendental Deduction of the Pure Concepts of the Understanding") of the *Critique of Pure Reason*. There Kant finally addresses himself directly to

> the paradox [*das Paradox*], which must have struck everybody in our exposition of the form of the internal sense; namely, how that sense represents to the consciousness even ourselves, not as we are by ourselves, but as we appear to ourselves, because we perceive ourselves only as we are *affected* internally. This seems to be contradictory, because we should thus be in a passive relation to ourselves.[11]

The paradox could not be clearer. In his essay *Kant's Critical Philosophy*, Gilles Deleuze expresses it by borrowing a well-known poetic formula from Rimbaud: "Je est un autre" – "I is an other."[12] Rimbaud violates the rules of grammar in order to render the radical character of the alienation of the self from itself, and the radical character of this alienation – in this case the split within the Kantian subject – is what Deleuze is also underscoring. Thanks to the active nature Kant attributes to the understanding and the passive nature he attributes to sensibility, the self is an other for itself. At the same time, the other is the self, but a "strange" self from which the self is alienated. The "I think" is an actor who is both absent and present in the self that occupies the empirical stage – absent because it cannot find itself in the empirical self, but present in the sense that it cannot be found anywhere else, that is to say, in the sense that it is nothing apart from this empirical self that "it in effect *produces* . . . by *affecting* the internal sense" (91).

That the notion of paradox imposes itself on Kant at this point in his analysis is itself indicative of the violence his description of the subject does to even the most supple forms of logic. No single synthesis and no simple dialectic can wholly comprehend within itself the contradictory and primary process of identification Kant is in fact describing here. On the contrary, according to the (paradoxical) logic of this primary process of identification, passivity and activity mutually reinforce each other in their contradiction. The activity of the understanding is what produces the unity of the subject, but the rift between understanding and sensibility can only be accentuated by that same activity. The more the subject is "I," the less "I" it is.

These passages from "Of the Application of the Categories to the Objects of the Senses in General" are, of course, to be found not in the first edition of the *Critique of Pure Reason* but, rather, in the second. This is a highly important distinction from the standpoint of Heidegger, who argues, in *Kant and the Problem of Metaphysics*, that Kant betrayed the most radical implications of the *Critique of Pure Reason* when he rewrote it for the second edition.[13] From Heidegger's perspective, the passages quoted above, because of the stress they lay on the active nature of the understanding, on its unique ability to produce unity, would clearly exemplify the general tendency of the second edition to promote the understanding at the expense of the transcendental imagination in particular and at the expense of sensibility or intuition as well.

Despite the undeniable importance of Heidegger's reading, it is nonetheless possible to question his view that, in rewriting the First Critique, Kant decides in favor of the pure understanding (175) and thus betrays the most radical and critical implications of his philosophy.[14] In making this argument, Heidegger does not give sufficient weight to the highly problematic character of the theoretical subject as it emerges in the second version of the *Critique of Pure Reason*. The effect of Kant's revisions, as exemplified in the passage quoted above, is in my mind more complex than Heidegger acknowledges. On the one hand, it is quite true that they appear to downplay the unifying role of the transcendental imagination and thus subordinate the whole subject to a triumphant understanding. On the other hand, it is *also* true that, by accentuating the passivity of sensibility and the activity of the understanding, Kant in effect radically splits the subject. The effect of this split is not merely to benefit the understanding but, from another standpoint, to subject it to a radical limitation, inasmuch as this split makes the subject inaccessible to the understanding itself.

In this sense it could be argued that the second version of the *Critique of Pure Reason* is much more effective than the first in combating—to borrow the terms of Nietzsche's *Birth of Tragedy*—the theoretical optimism of the Socratic tradition. To Socrates' famous dictum "Know thyself," it opposes another imperative: Recognize the limits of (self)-knowledge.

> Of [the real] subject [in which knowledge inheres], however, we have not and cannot have the slightest knowledge, because consciousness is that which alone changes representations into thoughts, and in which, therefore, as the transcendental subject, all our perceptions must be found. Besides the logical meaning of the I, we have no knowledge of the subject in itself, which

forms the substratum and foundation of it and of all our thoughts.
(*Critique of Pure Reason*, 253)

Kant's philosophy never ceases indicating and approaching the "subject in itself," which in its terms forms the foundation of all thought; however, Kant maintains that the same subject is completely inaccessible to our knowledge. Self-reflexivity is an imperative, perhaps *the* imperative of his philosophy, but it is a self-reflexivity without a self. The Kantian subject is an "as-if" self, a theatrical subject split between reflection and sensibility—that is to say, split between the unknowable nothing that is the "I think" and the pathetic subject with which, from a certain standpoint, the "I think" has no necessary connection. The Kantian "I think" yields no proof or certainty that "I am." In this sense, Kantian philosophy is *not* subjective. That is to say, it is not based on self-knowledge or on any perspective on the subject to which the subject itself would have privileged access.

The character Kant ascribes to the subject relates directly to the central role played by identification in both the *Critique of Pure Reason* and the *Critique of Judgement*. The radical nature of the split in the self lies in the fact that the Kantian self exists for itself *in exactly the same terms in which it exists for others*—my relation to myself is as passive or as active as that of others to me. A transcendental alterity, which comes to the fore as the central principle of the *Critique of Judgement*, is already clearly being indicated in the passivity of the internal sense in relation to the understanding. The place of the subject *is* the place of others, for whom it is appearance—or abyss—just as it is for itself. The split in the subject, which is the result of the inaccessibility of the subject to its own faculty of understanding, makes it impossible to ground the subject in self-knowledge. In doing so, it implicitly creates the possibility of another "ground" for the subject: a "transcendental" identification with others.

In terms of the fundamental but problematic nature of the role played by identification, the *Critique of Pure Reason* and the "Analytic of the Beautiful" prepare the way for and permit a fuller appreciation of the implications of the "Analytic of the Sublime," in which identification is once again central. Nonetheless, the problematic character of Kantian identification can be said to emerge with special force and clarity in this Second Analytic. In the case of judgments relative to the sublime, the ambivalent nature of identification is linked, once again, to an identification of the subject with itself, understood as what is other and unfathomable for it—that is, with what Kant calls the supersensible or the Idea. This identification is accompanied by or manifest in a "rapidly alternating repulsion and attraction." Kant explains these conflicting feelings by asserting that, on the one hand, the mind is repelled by the supersensible, because, for the *imagination*, which is only at ease in relation to the intuitable phenomena of nature, the supersensible is "like an abyss in which it fears to lose itself" (*Critique of Judgement*, 107). On the other hand, the mind is attracted to the supersensible because *reason* identifies with the supersensible: for it, the feeling associated with the sublime is a confirmation of its own supersensible nature (107).

The result of this identification of the subject and a supersensible realm in which it recognizes its own self is a "vibration" (107) or even a "violence" (108). This violence concerns the imagination first of all, because the imagination in particular is frustrated by the impossibility of representing the supersensible and thus of reconciling it to the realm of nature and intuition. Hence, from the standpoint of the imagination, it can already be said that what is experienced by the subject in the case of the sublime is something radically different from itself. However, the imagination is not alone in being touched by the violence of the sublime. As Kant puts it, that same violence not only affects the imagination but is "final *for the whole vocation* [*Bestimmung*] of the mind" (108, translation modified). If reason, unlike the imagination, can identify with the supersensible, still that identification is not merely reassuring. Like the imagination, for which the supersensible is other, reason, for which the supersensible is an image of itself, experiences a feeling of violence as if before an abyss. The split whose existence is being indicated in the violence of the sublime is not only between nature and the Idea, or between imagination and reason, but also within the Idea or reason itself. The process of primary identification is thus both positive and negative for reason as well as for the imagination—that is, reason is its own abyss.

It should be stressed once again that this conclusion applies not only to reason in the form in which it is brought into play in aesthetic judgment. Just as the split in the subject of knowledge already indicates the possibility of a transcendental alterity, so Kant's analysis of the violence associated with the sublime is already being indicated in the First Critique, in a passage in which Kant describes the malaise experienced by human reason when it confronts the notion of freedom: "The unconditioned necessity, which we require as the last support of all things, is the true abyss of human reason. Eternity itself, however terrible and sublime it may have been depicted by Haller, is far from producing the same giddy impression" (409). Like the supersensible in the case of the sublime, the notion of an unconditioned necessity occasions a feeling of malaise in us greater than that produced by eternity, not despite but rather because we find it in ourselves as subjects.[15]

The Third Critique is thus made necessary by the First, not exactly because, as Hegel would have it, art is a particular, that is, unconscious form of knowledge (*Aesthetics*, 59). Rather, it is because the idea of a primary form of identification is the foundation of Kant's critique of aesthetic judgment and is also presupposed in his affirmations concerning the paradoxical character of the knowing and even of the rational subject. Reason cannot think itself without thinking in the place of the other. That is also why reason cannot think itself without identifying with the aesthetic—without being confronted by the fact that the primary form of identification exemplified in aesthetic judgment is analogous to the problematic process through which reason itself is constituted. The idea that the question of the aesthetic could be just a subquestion within a larger encyclopedic system of science or philosophy seems inadequate to describe the more complex relationship that emerges in Kant's work. What comes to the fore instead, to borrow some of the terms, if not the overriding logic, of Hegel's interpretation of tragedy, is the idea that both knowledge and aesthetic judgment have equal *theoretical* justification.

The Third Critique, however, is necessitated by the First in another sense: because the "Analytic of the Beautiful" and, even more, the "Analytic of the Sublime" spell out the ambivalence that is the necessary correlate of a fundamental or primary process of identification. It is because identification is primary that self-knowledge is radically limited, and this means that identification is of necessity not merely pleasurable or reassuring. In the sublime version of identification, delight is mixed with violence, attraction is mixed with repulsion, much as, one is tempted to say, in Aristotelian catharsis, pity is mixed with fear. In the final analysis, Nietzsche's assertion concerning the affinity between Kantian philosophy and tragedy is sustained most unequivocally by the nature of Kantian identification. When Kant's philosophy as a whole and his *Critique of Judgement* in particular are read in terms of the problematic of identification, they appear in a different light from the one in which Heidegger and others have placed them. Jubjectivity is not confirmed but rather, to an equally important extent, surrendered (*Birth of Tragedy*, 64); contradiction and pain (55) play as great a role as reconciliation and delight; and a faith that knowledge "can penetrate the deepest abysses of being" (95) gives ground to a sense of the way knowledge is limited by the very process of identification that constitutes the rational subject.

The Divided Subject of Tragedy: Hegel against Hegel

The work of Hegel, unlike that of Kant, contains many explicit references to tragedy and, in particular, to Sophocles' *Antigone*, which he considers the most important and exemplary tragedy of all.[16] Significantly, Hegel's reading of *Antigone* is directly linked to his interpretation of the philosophy of Kant. From his earliest theological writings to the final pages of the *Aesthetics*, Hegel can be seen to be working to bridge the abyss opened by Kant's description of the subject and thus implicitly to qualify and delimit the process of identification whose primary nature is indicated in Kant's text. The passages in Hegel's work that most directly relate to this project are also frequently those where *Antigone* is evoked.

But though the philosophy of Kant and Sophocles' *Antigone* are closely linked in Hegel's texts, the link from Hegel's own perspective is negative. In his introduction to the *Aesthetics*, Hegel makes it clear that art in general plays a key role in effecting the conciliation of the various oppositions, which in his view structure Kant's philosophy. Examples are the opposition "between subjective thinking and objective things, between the abstract universality and the sensuous individuality of the will," and between "the practical side of the spirit" as opposed to "the theoretical" (Hegel, *Aesthetics*, 56). If art as a whole effects conciliation and thus represents the sublation of Kantian philosophy, drama implicitly accomplishes these two aims more fully and perfectly than any other form of poetry or art, inasmuch as Hegel holds it to represent the highest form of both: "Because drama has been developed into the most perfect totality of content and form, it must be regarded as the highest stage of poetry and of art generally" (1158).

What drama is to art and poetry as a whole, tragedy itself is to drama. In fact, for the young Hegel, the mediating function of the tragic is so distinct and powerful that he qualifies it as "the expression of the absolute position."[17] Finally, what tragedy is to drama, *Antigone* is to the tragic genre itself, as Hegel indicates when he calls Sophocles' play "the most magnificent and satisfying work of this kind" (*Aesthetics*, 1218). While art as a whole is assigned the task of reconciling the terms that are opposed in Kant's philosophy, the preeminent positions of tragedy within the sphere of art and of *Antigone* within the tragic genre indicate that this Greek tragedy performs that task better than any other work of art.

The mediating role that Hegel attributes to *Antigone* is thus in part a function of its nature as the supreme work of art, but it is also, equally important, a function of the conflict it depicts and the manner in which in Hegel's view the play resolves that conflict. The excellence of *Antigone* should be understood not only in terms of Hegel's concept of drama but also in terms of his view of classical art and its ability to overcome the sublime phase of art. Classical art, as has already been suggested, is metasublime because it mediates between the two terms whose opposition is for Hegel the substance of the sublime: nature and Idea. The sublime is "a *mere search* for portrayal [rather] than a capacity for true presentation" of the Idea (76). In classical art, on the other hand, the Idea achieves adequate, concrete presentation, and as a result Hegel holds classical art to be "concretely spiritual" (78). The human form is the central figure in classical art, according to Hegel, because it is "the existence and natural shape of the spirit" (78).

Antigone embodies the mediating function of art not only because of its position as the supreme work of art, but also because of its depiction of the conflict between reason and nature and the manner in which that conflict is overcome. There are in effect three actors in *Antigone* as read by Hegel: the two antagonists, Antigone and Creon, and the chorus, which is the tragic embodiment of what Hegel calls the ethical community of which Antigone and Creon are a part. The significance of Hegel's concept of the ethical community lies precisely in that it encompasses both nature and reason in its ethical life, that it harmonizes their claims and thus permits their conflict to be overcome. According to Hegel, the ethical community is firmly rooted in nature insofar as "nature, not the accident of circumstances or choice,"[18] assigns each sex to its appropriate sphere in the life of the community—the family or the state—and also implicitly constitutes the distinct spheres themselves in their differences and essential harmony. But the community is also rational, insofar as it also encompasses an ethical life that is rooted not in natural feeling or even natural particularity but, rather, in consciousness (274). It is the woman whose ethical life is rooted in nature, that is, in the natural particularity of the family. In contrast, the life of the man is rooted in reason, that is, the self-conscious activity of the state. From Hegel's perspective, the conflict between Antigone and Creon is thus one between the family and the state, woman and man—and it is also a properly sublime conflict between nature and reason.

Hegel attempts to bear out his thesis concerning the mediating function of art and drama in his reading of *Antigone*, in which he constructs a dialectical interpretation of tragedy that is intended to heal the split in the subject opened up by Kant's thought and to restore philosophy to its position as both the starting point and the end point of aesthetics and ethics.

Of course, the central role that devolves to tragedy both in Hegel's *Aesthetics* and in his earlier work relates not only to his view of the mediating function of tragedy, but also to the depth and intensity with which it brings out division and conflict. Peter Szondi argues that this distinctive quality of Hegel's interpretation of tragedy is evident even at the earliest stages of his work: "In contradistinction to Schelling, Hegel directs his attention not only to the identity [of individual morality and the universal], but also to the perpetual conflict of the powers grasped in their identity and to the movement inherent in their unity" ("Notion of the Tragic," 49). The young Hegel's notion of tragedy as the expression of the absolute position would be misleading if we conceived of the absolute position itself in terms of an indifference—in which the oppositions analyzed by Schelling always culminate. Instead, as expressed in tragedy, the absolute is already being thought in dynamic terms as conflict and movement, which pit the tragic characters against each other and against their own fate. In the *Phenomenology*, as Szondi once again notes, Hegel was to reproach Schelling in veiled terms for his haste in advancing to the stage of harmony. Hegel's interpretation of tragedy requires that we tarry (*Phenomenology*, 19) with the division and conflict introduced by the tragic into the ethical/aesthetic sphere and not pass over them too quickly or superficially.

Hegel's own interpretation of *Antigone*, in other words, comprises both a Kantian and a Hegelian moment, both a sublime and a classical dimension. Conflict or opposition must reach a maximum of intensity and gravity in order that their resolution be total and pure. Harmony cannot succeed conflict too quickly because harmony becomes actual only insofar as we recognize conflict and disruption as essential to it. This means, however, that only absolute, irreconcilable conflict can produce absolute harmony. But how? Hegelian philosophy, in other words, can be only Hegelian and not Schellingian, insofar as it is Kantian. In this way, the dialectic appears not only as a powerful machine for converting all forms of alterity into versions of its (same) self, but also as a gigantic double bind, which causes the dialectic to work constantly against itself, to be in constant danger of losing itself, of being interrupted before it has recovered itself.

The logic of the dialectic in relation to its tragic phase is thus radically contradictory over and above the usual meaning of contradiction, understood as the "work of the negative" or, in other words, as a process that leads to Absolute Knowledge. As a result, the progress of the dialectic toward its resolution in philosophy can be assured only through an active intervention designed to rescue philosophy from its potential interruption by tragedy. Hegel's interpretation of *Antigone* has a correspondingly dual focus. One side of his analysis reflects a need to affirm the depth and intensity of the tragic conflict, in order that the reconciliation proposed by tragedy be total and absolute. Another side of it, however, reflects a need to limit the depth and intensity of the same conflict, in order to ensure that the dialectic not be interrupted and that its progress toward its culmination in philosophy, while threatened, not ultimately be impeded.

Hegel thus evokes and then rejects the possibility that what separates Antigone and Creon might be constitutive with respect to the community of which they are members, and it is in terms of this community that he portrays their conflict as ultimately superficial and resolvable. In order to do this, he appeals to the figure of Antigone herself and to a theory of the predominantly natural character of the woman, and it is in terms of this theory that he harmonizes the conflicting claims of Antigone and Creon. The dominant tendency of Hegel's interpretation of *Antigone* is thus a sublation of the conflict between the principals, which enables Hegel to use the play, or at any rate his interpretation of it, to sublate the philosophy of Kant. But because of the relatively arbitrary nature of Hegel's decision to subordinate the element of conflict in Sophocles' tragedy to the element of reconciliation, his interpretation of *Antigone* also, and against its dominant argument, indicates the possibility of another equally plausible interpretation of the play—one in terms of which *Antigone* would appear as an exemplary tragedy thanks to its sublime rather than classical nature.

The dominant tendency in Hegel's analysis of *Antigone* is evident above all in what he writes about the chorus. Like Nietzsche's *Birth of Tragedy*, Hegel's interpretation of Greek tragedy also has as a central feature a discussion of the origins and significance of the Greek chorus. The chorus, Hegel argues, "belongs essentially to the dramatic action itself and is so necessary to it that the decay of tragedy is especially manifested in the deterioration of the choruses which no longer remain an integral part of the whole but sink down into being an unnecessary ornament" (*Aesthetics*, 1212). However different the terms in which they conceive of the chorus, for Hegel as for Nietzsche, tragedy dies when the chorus ceases to be its central feature.

In Hegel's terms, the central position of the chorus in tragedy stems from the fact that only when the spectator considers the outcome of tragedy from its perspective is he or she afforded a sense of satisfaction. Though the destruction of the principals might appear unjust when one considers the ethical nature of their characters, it nonetheless gives rise to what Hegel calls a sense of eternal justice, inasmuch as the community itself is thereby preserved: "In Greek tragedy it is eternal justice which, as the absolute power of fate, saves and maintains the harmony of the substance of the ethical order against the particular powers which were becoming independent and therefore colliding, and because of the inner rationality of its sway we are satisfied when we see individuals coming to ruin" (1230). Whatever the moral worthiness of his or her actions, the individual *as individual* can only be a disruptive element when he or she asserts himself or herself from within the ethical community, and his or her tragic flaw, his or her guilt, and the spectator's own sense of satisfaction at the tragic outcome are ultimately understandable always in relation to it. Hegel's interpretation of the role of the chorus in Greek tragedy corresponds clearly to his critique of Kantian subjectivity, which, he claims, is cut off from the ethical community and constitutes a moment that is abstract and formal in relation to the life of the community. The chorus, in other words, is like "a temple surrounding the image of the gods." In another image, Hegel writes of the chorus as "the scene of the spirit" (1211). It encompasses the subject, providing a context for it that is both its other and its own substance, and in this sense it prefigures philosophy in its harmony and in its reconciliation of self and other.

What is striking in the passages from the *Aesthetics* dealing with the chorus is not only the consistency with which Hegel highlights its mediating function but also the ethical terms in which he discusses it and *Antigone* as a whole. The chorus is described as the embodiment of an ethical order; the play as a whole provides above all a sense of eternal justice; and the conflict between Antigone and Creon is said to exemplify a clash between two ethical powers. To say that the play has an ethical dimension from Hegel's perspective does not go far enough in suggesting the role played by Hegel's conception of the ethical in his interpretation. It would be more accurate to say that, in his interpretation of *Antigone*, Hegel appears to be doing what one critic has accused him of doing in the section of the *Phenomenology* in which he interprets Diderot's *Le Neveu de Rameau*: totally ignoring the boundaries separating the ethical and the aesthetic.[19]

From Hegel's perspective, however, it is perfectly legitimate to speak of *Antigone* in ethical terms, and there is no risk that in doing so the properly aesthetic dimension of this Greek tragedy will be ignored or reduced. Why this should be the case is indicated in a passage from the *Aesthetics* in which Hegel describes the fusion of the ethical and the aesthetic in Greek life. He tells us that the Greeks not only *produced* supremely beautiful works of art, but that they *were themselves* supreme works of art. It is not just "the heroic figures in epic and drama" who must be considered from the standpoint of their plasticity and beauty, according to Hegel:

> After all, in the beautiful days of Greece men of action, like poets and thinkers, had this same plastic and universal yet individual character both inwardly and outwardly. . . . The Periclean age was especially rich in such characters: Pericles himself, Phidias, Plato, Sophocles above all, Thucydides too, Xenophon, Socrates — each of them of his own sort, unimpaired by another's; all of them are out-and-out artists by nature, ideal artists shaping themselves, individuals of a single cast, works of art standing there like immortal and deathless images of the gods, in which there is nothing temporal and doomed. (*Aesthetics*, 719–20)

With this passage, Hegel's implicit view that, in discussing the ethical significance of *Antigone,* he is also considering it as an aesthetic object is explained, for the essence of the Greek ethical community *is* aesthetic. In a manner that anticipates Nietzsche's assertions concerning the fusion of spectators and actors, of life and art in the "great sublime chorus" of the Dionysian festival (*Birth of Tragedy,* 62), Hegel's view of the Greeks implies that *Antigone* is not just an (artistic) representation or expression of the ethical life of the Greeks. Greek life and art, the ethical community and *Antigone,* are one and the same, a single entity that should be considered the Greek's supreme aesthetic-ethical work.

Hegel's conception of the Greeks thus accounts for, if it does not authorize, the way in which the different versions of his reading of *Antigone* collapse the ethical and the aesthetic. It also reveals the theory of identification that is implicit each time Hegel reads Sophocles' play. That the ethical community and *Antigone* are one and the same is perhaps the clearest indication of the unambiguous, essentially positive form of identification that prevails at all levels of Hegel's interpretation of art, ethics, and, ultimately, knowledge. The Greek is of necessity at home in Greek art insofar as his own substance and Greek art are one, and thus it can be seen that the ultimate nature of aesthetic experience lies in an authentication (*Phenomenology,* 278) of the Greek rather than a confrontation that is potentially violent or repellent, to borrow from Kant. The process of identification that implicitly links the Greek to Greek art can also be understood in ethical terms, as the process linking the individuals in the ethical community to one another and to the community as a whole; and it is, moreover, in terms of the wholeness of this community that Hegel criticizes the Kantian subject as being cut off from the other in which it must find itself or with which it must identify positively. Finally, an essentially positive version of identification is also implicit in Hegel's description of the relationship between the ethical powers, whose common *ethical* nature is for Hegel the guarantee of their fundamental harmony and ultimate identity.

These points emerge more clearly in the fuller discussion of the ethical community that appears in the *Phenomenology* and the *Philosophy of Right.* Though in these other works the interpretations given of *Antigone* are entirely consistent with that given in the *Aesthetics,* both in their details and in the way they too implicitly condense the ethical and the aesthetic, they also provide a fuller, more complex picture of the ethical community. In these additional descriptions of *Antigone*, we see more clearly the dynamic nature of the life of the community and of tragedy underscored by Szondi. Far from being undifferentiated or homogeneous, the life of the ethical community, according to Hegel, is full of contrasts between human and divine laws, among the institutions to which they give rise, and above all, between the Greek woman and the Greek man, whose separate and at times overlapping spheres of activity define the chorus/ethical community as a whole. In *Antigone*, Hegel tells us in *The Philosophy of Right*, we see family piety as "principally the law of woman," and he goes on to characterize this law in Sophocles' own terms as "'an everlasting law, and no man knows at what time it was first put forth.'"[20] According to this more developed description of the ethical community, then, the basis of the harmony of the community, or the reconciliation that it spontaneously effects between the rational-ethical and the natural, lies in the sexual—that is, in the difference between the sexes and the manner in which that difference is incorporated into Greek life.

Despite the contrasts between the human and the divine, the state and the family, and the man and the woman, or rather, thanks to them, Hegel nonetheless insists in the *Phenomenology* that the ethical realm is "in its enduring existence an immaculate world, a world unsullied by any internal dissension. Similarly, its process is a tranquil transition of one of its powers into the other, in such a way that each preserves and brings forth the other. We do indeed see it divide itself into two essences and their reality; but their antithesis is rather the authentification of one through the other" (278). The ethical is for Hegel a community in the strongest possible sense: a whole in which each part—be it ethical power or individual—is "at home in this whole" (277). This harmony reflects the fact that at bottom, the two sexes authenticate each other and the antithesis between them is superficial (267).

The critical thrust of this description of the ethical community in relation to the philosophy of Kant is clear. Like Heidegger much later, Hegel implicitly faults Kant for having subjected the ethical sphere to a triumphant faculty of reason at the expense of intuition—or nature. His aim is thus to connect reason and nature once again. That is why for Hegel the law of the ethical community is not and cannot be an abstract categorical imperative. It is, rather, rooted in nature, understood as custom and particularity, in the differences between the divine and human law, in other words, in the specificity of the relations between the state and the family, among family members, and above all, between members of the opposite sex. The sexual enters into the law, which is to an important extent its expression, and gives it its concrete character.

The oneness of the chorus and hence its ethical and aesthetic importance is thus rooted in Hegel's interpretation of the natural and more specifically the sexual. As Jacques Derrida indicates in *Glas*, in the light in which it is placed by Hegel's reading, *Antigone* appears not only as the common root of the Greek tradition to which it originally belonged, and of German idealism, but also of modern psychoanalysis as well. With Hegel's reading of *Antigone*, the question of sexuality—or at any rate, of sexual difference—becomes central to Hegelian philosophy. The sexual emerges as the underpinning of reason in both its ethical and aesthetic forms.

The other element of tragedy, which Hegel contrasts with the chorus, is "the individual 'pathos' which drives the dramatis personae, acting with an ethical justification, into opposition with others and thereby brings them into conflict" (*Aesthetics*, 1209). The individual and the conflict that results when he or she emerges from against the background provided by the ethical community are the "properly dramatic" elements of tragedy (1171). The chorus provides a stage, but the action—the play proper—belongs to the individual characters. Though he appears to contradict his earlier claims about the importance of the chorus, Hegel nonetheless asserts in commenting on the role of the individual characters that neither the chorus (as poetic form) nor the monologue is central to tragedy. Instead, *dialogue* is the one "completely dramatic form" (1172). Implicitly this is the case because monologue can show us the individual, but not in conflict, and the chorus can show us only the ethical community. Dialogue alone can show the individual in conflict—can show, in other words, that the essence of the individual is the conflict that he or she introduces into the ethical world.[21]

This interpretation of the relationship between the formal elements of tragedy is consistent with Hegel's treatment of the relationship between the individual and tragic conflict in the *Phenomenology* as well. The self and conflict are so intimately connected that one looks in vain for a means of distinguishing them. Even the idea that the self

is the cause of conflict is too weak; that is, it gives a misleading picture of how they are related from Hegel's perspective. The individual
and conflict are neither causally connected nor structurally equivalent. They are simply identical:

> The way in which the antithesis is constituted in this ethical
> realm is such that self-consciousness has not yet received its due
> as a particular individuality. There it has the value, on the one
> hand, merely of the universal will, and on the other, of consan-
> guinity. *This* particular individual counts only as a shadowy
> unreality. And yet, no deed has been committed; but the deed
> is the *actual self*. It disturbs the peaceful organization and move-
> ment of the ethical world. What there appears as order and har-
> mony of its two essences, each of which authenticates and
> completes the other, becomes through the deed a transition of
> opposites in which each proves itself to be the non-reality, rather
> than the authentification, of itself and the other. (*Phenomenology*,
> 279)

The deed introduces conflict into the ethical order, but the deed—and
the conflict—is already given in and by the individual self, insofar as
the deed is nothing more than what Hegel calls the *actual self*. The
deed and the actual self emerge abruptly and simultaneously in the
midst of the ethical community, whose harmonious character is dramatically altered by this emergence.

It should be noted that for Hegel, the disruption of the ethical totality by the self is not simply negative. However beautiful the community, the actualization of the self, the transcendence of the ethical
community, and tragic conflict itself are all necessary: "Spirit is the
ethical life of a nation in so far as it is the *immediate truth*—the individual that is a world. It must advance to the consciousness of what it is
immediately, must leave behind it the beauty of ethical life, and by
passing through a series of shapes attain to a knowledge of itself"
(265). In the sense that Hegel affirms the destruction of the ethical
world by the individual, he is also affirming the conflict introduced
into that world by the individual. This is still another way of understanding what Szondi calls the dynamic nature of Hegel's interpretation of tragedy, or, in other words, the productive nature of
negativity, which, according to Hegel, is introduced into the ethical
community by the self. By simultaneously affirming the individual
and the dissolution of the ethical world, Hegel is doing what must be

done if the reconciliation of tragic conflict is to produce an ultimate harmony: he is affirming conflict itself, its absolute nature and necessity.

But if Hegel is not crudely nostalgic for the ethical community, if he also affirms conflict and/as the individual, he also defends his view of their relationship—the idea that they are identical. Of course, this also means he is defending the idea that the ethical community itself is unsullied by any dissension, that conflict befalls the ethical community rather than being an essential part of its structure as community. In Hegel's analysis, in other words, the individual subject is made the bearer of conflict, and thus, just as the individual is both a part of and other than the ethical community, so conflict is in the ethical community, but only in the sense that it is contained by it, not in the sense that it is a constitutive element of the community as well. In this sense, Hegel's affirmation of the importance of tragic conflict simultaneously implies a limitation of it.

In his interpretation of *Antigone*, Hegel himself seems at one point to entertain the possibility of a conflict that would be much more deeply rooted in the ethical substance when he writes: "There is immanent in both Antigone and Creon something that in their own way they attack, so that they are gripped and shattered by something intrinsic to their own actual being" (*Aesthetics*, 1217–18). The immanence in Antigone and Creon of the very thing they are attacking indicates the possibility that their conflict is absolute, because no ultimate reconciliation would seem to be possible if a given conflict stems from the element or elements the antagonists have in common. In this sense, the ethicity common to Antigone and Creon would not necessarily guarantee the ultimate harmony of the ethical powers they represent but, on the contrary, could also be interpreted as an indication that the ethical substance itself is divided by conflict.

But while Hegel's comments on the characters of Antigone and Creon evoke the possibility of fundamental and thus absolute ethical conflict, he dismisses this same possibility in the *Phenomenology*, in a passage that clearly anticipates his critique in the *Aesthetics* of the tragedies of Corneille and Racine. Hegel writes that in the case of tragic conflict between competing ethical powers, we are not faced "with the sorry spectacle of a collision between passion and duty, nor with the comic spectacle of a collision between duty and duty. . . . The collision of duties is comic because it expresses a contradiction: viz. the contradiction of an Absolute that is opposed to itself" (*Phenomenol-*

ogy, 279). Tragedy, he argues here, would not be tragedy if it presented us with an opposition between duty and duty, that is, an opposition intrinsic to the ethical itself. But it would be more accurate to say that tragedy would not be classical, it would not accomplish the work of the philosophical dialectic, and it would not exemplify better than any other form of art the philosophical vocation of art itself, if it depicted a collision that involved not only the individual characters but the ethical community itself.

The possibility that tragic conflict concerns not just the individual in his or her relation to the ethical community but also—or even rather—the ethical community itself is evident in Hegel's analysis of the relation between man and woman as it emerges as the central conflict in *Antigone*. As we have seen, in the ethical community conceived of as an immaculate world, the difference between the two ethical powers, a difference that at bottom corresponds to the difference between the sexes, is only a contrast, and the two opposed terms constantly merge, each finding authentication in the other. Hegel nonetheless finds it necessary to distinguish between the two terms, in order to effect a marriage between the particularity and richness of natural life, on the one hand, and, on the other, ethical life as constituted by a purely formal, rational imperative from the standpoint of which all particularity is irrelevant.

The wedding of the self-conscious and the natural, in which the latter is brought forth into daylight (274), is possible thanks to the special and even paradoxical character Hegel ascribes to the family, which is one of two ethical powers or institutions encompassed by the larger community, the other being the state. Hegel calls the family the *"natural ethical community"* (268), and the reasons for this designation are clear. For the family (and ultimately the ethical community) to fulfill its function as conceptual mediator, it must be both natural and ethical—it must be firmly rooted in the differences and relations given by nature and also clearly transcend them. The family can play this role within the ethical community thanks to its own mixed but harmonious nature, for the family is the unity—or marriage—of "universal Self-conscious Spirit" with its "element," "unconscious Spirit"— that is, of man with woman (278).

This marriage between nature and spirit, between woman and man, however, does not in itself suffice to heal the rift between the natural and the rational. It merely displaces it, so that it becomes a rift within the family rather than one between an abstract moral imperative and actual existence. It is not enough that one set of family members – the women – should exemplify nature and another set – the men – should exemplify reason as the ethical principle; for if this is true, then the family cannot fulfill its mediating function but is itself divided. In attempting to mediate between the ethical/rational and the natural, Hegel is thus caught in a double bind. While the logic of his argument dictates that the family be comprised of natural and ethical elements, it also necessitates that he demonstrate the ethical and therefore implicitly rational character of women and of the divine law that ultimately regulates their relationship to the family. The *unconscious* force that women represent must be *primarily* natural and also *primarily* ethical if the family itself is to be ethical. Both arguments are a logical consequence of Hegel's position; both are needed if there is to be a reconciliation of the natural and the rational. However, the validity and necessity of both make such a reconciliation impossible; for if the family as a whole represents the ethical principle, then the opposition within the family between the natural and the ethical divides the ethical from itself – it becomes an opposition within the ethical itself understood as the Absolute.

The relationship between brother and sister most clearly reveals the ethical character of the family, and the sister herself possesses "the highest *intuitive* awareness of what is ethical" (274). The absolute position Hegel assigns to *Antigone* in relation to both ethics and art relates directly to this point, inasmuch as the character of Antigone herself represents this intuitive ethical sense and thus signifies/effects the reconciliation of nature and reason toward which (classical) ethics and (classical) art both tend. Antigone represents such awareness because, while her femininity ties her strongly to nature, her relationship to her brother is the most nonnatural of all family relationships – in Hegel's words, it is "pure and unmixed with any natural desire" (275). Derrida comments on this passage that "in truth sexual difference is still needed, a sexual difference that is sexual as such and nonetheless without desire" (*Glas*, 169). But Derrida goes on to ask: "Is it impossible? Is it in contradiction with the whole system? Are we any longer in the natural sphere of the *Sittlichkeit* (the family) once sexual difference is superseded?" (169).[22] Indeed, nowhere does the dialectic seem further removed from the *natural* ethical community and closer to a Kantian community based on the disinterested nature of desire or will than with the pure relation between Antigone and her brother.

Antigone thus exemplifies the non-natural or purely ethical dimension of the natural ethical substance with particular force and clarity, but, as Derrida notes, this same ethical quality is frequently discussed without Antigone being expressly named. In this manner Hegel indicates that her ethical character is not specific to her alone but is, rather, the essence of woman-in-general: "In the ethical household, it is not a question of *this* particular husband, *this* particular child, but simply of husband and children generally; the relationships of the woman are based, not on feeling, but on the universal" (*Phenomenology*, 274). Against his dominant argument, Hegel is thus obliged to argue that as ethical being, the woman's relation to nature, that is, to feeling and desire, is negative—every bit as negative as that of the man in his role as citizen, which takes him out of the family and into the self-conscious activity of the state.

Whereas initially it appeared that the ethical finds a natural expression in the life of the family, the picture changes as Hegel advances in his analysis. The great majority of the activities associated with family life as a whole are only, it turns out, expressions of natural desires and feelings, which are accidental in relation to this ethicity. In the ultimate analysis only one concrete act realizes the ethical character of the family, and that is the performance by Antigone of rites whose purpose is to protect her dead brother from being devoured by wild animals and corrupted by natural processes. Antigone's deed is not merely prompted by feeling for another member of her family: in the context of family life it is *the* foremost ethical duty, and in performing it, she gives expression to the ethical nature of the family as a whole: "Blood-relationship supplements, then, the abstract natural process [of death] by adding to it the movement of consciousness, interrupting the work of Nature and rescuing the blood-relation from destruction" (271). The ultimate expression of the ethicity of the woman and of the family is this interruption of "the work of Nature." Though implicitly it is only thanks to it that the woman and the family can be said to be ethical as well as natural, this passage reveals that the ethical character of the family consists precisely in a negation of nature. The natural ethical community, which at first glance seemed to represent a marriage of the ethical and the natural, now appears as an oxymoron. Though a major purpose of Hegel's interpretation of *Antigone* is to root the ethical in natural life, its result is to reveal the profoundly non-natural character of the family, the ethical, and Antigone, the woman, as well.

Despite the distinctions Hegel lays down between the woman and the man, his discussion of *Antigone* reveals that the various elements of the family are all equally ethical and thus equally rational. The feminine form or embodiment of the ethical cannot be any less ethical, any more natural than the masculine, because the ethical resides in the *negation* of nature and is not a question of degree of proximity to nature. From this perspective, the conflict between Antigone and Creon appears to be rooted not in the difference between (her) nature and (his) reason but rather in their shared ethicity and rationality, and in this sense it cannot be resolved in terms of the underlying harmony or unity of the ethical substance.

Of course, Hegel himself seems to say as much when he writes that in the ethical community "the two sexes overcome their [merely] natural being and appear in their ethical significance, as diverse beings who share between them the two distinctions belonging to the ethical substance" (275). That Hegel is unwilling to assume the ultimate implications of this shared ethicity is evident, however, when he characterizes the ethical character of Antigone as intuitive and the ethical life of the family as "strictly speaking, negative" (275)—that is, when he seeks to establish a difference within Antigone (and thus within the family) that would allow her (and it) to mediate nonetheless between the natural and the ethical. But the revelation of the non-natural character of the ethicity of Antigone, as exemplified in her performance of the religious rites for her dead brother, undercuts the distinction between an intuitive (or natural) and a self-conscious (that is, rational) ethicity. It shows that the conflict in *Antigone* is sublime in the sense that it pits not only nature against reason but also, more importantly, reason against itself.

The conflict in *Antigone* is absolute for the same reason it is sublime: because the ethical community is touched by this conflict and hence itself already tragic even prior to the outbreak of the properly dramatic clash between individuals. Despite Hegel's dominant argument, what emerges in his interpretation of *Antigone* is not just the philosophical version of the dialectic of tragedy, but rather also, alongside it, another dialectic, which interrupts the dynamic process both of the ethical community and of speculative philosophy. The action in this other version of the dialectic of tragedy is no longer encompassed by the environment of an immaculate ethical community, and the "mere *difference* of [its] constituents" can no longer be seen as having been "*perverted* [my emphasis] into *opposition* and collision" (Hegel, *Aesthetics*, 1196)—because in it opposition and collision have been revealed instead to be the very substance of the community and an irreducible dimension of the sexual.

Kant's sublime aesthetics and ethics are thus as present in *Antigone* as Hegel's version of aesthetics and ethics. This means that *Antigone* represents not only a means by which to posit, negate, retain, and raise aesthetics and ethics to a higher level, but also a necessary risk of regression toward a phase of the dialectic in which the theoretical is continually disrupted by the aesthetic and ethical. When the problematic aspects of Hegel's interpretation of *Antigone* are stressed, it becomes apparent that aesthetic and ethical questions belong to philosophy as Hegel argues, but in a manner different from the one he suggests. Not only can they be resolved in and as philosophy, as Hegel holds, but also, philosophy is divided from itself by the aesthetic and the ethical—that is, divided between a Kantian and a Hegelian version of itself (and of tragedy), between a dialectic that effects reconciliation of opposing ethical and aesthetic claims and a dialectic that (re)engenders their conflict. The claim of philosophy to be an inescapable starting point in defining the nature of tragedy is confirmed, but philosophy no longer appears as the only starting point, and the philosophical interpretation of tragedy no longer appears as the only necessary or the ultimate interpretation.

The fundamental nature of identification is confirmed in a similarly ambiguous manner by Hegel's reading of *Antigone*. Identification links the two sexes together, but it also pits them against each other, dividing them *because* their conflict is between equally ethical powers. The other is the same as well as other, and this contradictory logic does not immediately or necessarily result in harmony and reconciliation. It is no longer self-evident that the Hegelian version of identification, in which the contrasting parties or terms involved in the process of identification are authenticated by it, is the more fundamental version. The unity it grows out of and perpetuates now appears as superficial, or at any rate, only one aspect of a more complex relationship and process.

Equally important, the aesthetic, or, in Hegel's terms, art and in particular *Antigone* no longer appear as the immediate expression of an ethical/aesthetic community and of a sexual harmony based on the sublation of the differing natures of the sexes. Instead, tragedy emerges as the *philosophical* figure for forms of the sexual, the ethical, and the aesthetic that lie outside or beyond philosophy.

The Interrupted Dialectic of Modern Tragedy: Hegel, Corneille, and the Feminine Challenge to *Aufhebung*

It is Corneille who has done the greatest harm and exercised the most pernicious influence on these tragedians. Racine only seduced by his example, Corneille by his examples and doctrines together.
—Lessing

In a dream I saw myself in Goethe's study. . . . The side of the writing desk abutted on the wall opposite the window. Sitting and writing at one side was the poet, in extreme old age. I was standing at one side when he broke off to give me a small vase, an urn from antiquity, as a present. I turned it between my hands. An immense heat filled the room.
—Walter Benjamin

Art, Philosophy, and Modern Tragedy

As we have seen, tragedy (and *Antigone* in particular) plays an ambiguous role in Hegel's version of aesthetics, ethics, and philosophy. On the one hand, it represents a means by which to posit, negate, retain, and raise art to a higher level. On the other, it also represents a necessary risk of regression toward a phase of the dialectic in which the aesthetic can be seen continually to disrupt the theoretical. This disruption, it should be recalled, occurs not because *Antigone* lies beyond the reach of philosophy or because the philosophical interpretation that Hegel gives of it has no plausibility. Rather, it occurs because the aesthetic is neither wholly different from nor identical to philosophy and because *Antigone* lends itself equally well to two opposing interpretations, one emphasizing resolution of conflict in terms of its dialectical nature, the other underlining the ultimate irresolvability of its radically conflictual character.

As we have also seen, tragedy is not just one genre among others for Hegel; it is the genre of genres, and *Antigone*, the exemplary tragedy, is in essence *the* exemplary work of art. And though, as I have argued, tragedy fails him when he attempts to use it as the instrument with which to reconcile philosophy and art, the logic that confers such a special status on tragedy is so strong that Hegel turns again to tragedy in a renewed attempt to resolve the conflict between art and philosophy in the terms of philosophy. Only this time, he turns not to ancient but to modern tragedy, not to *Antigone* but to *Hamlet*.

In the terms of Hegel's system of fine art, the dialectical role played by modern tragedy relates directly to the particular role played by modern art as a whole in mediating between art and philosophy. Modern art or, as Hegel calls it, romantic art, can mediate between art itself and philosophy because its own nature is a fusion of art and philosophy. If we want to understand and see such a fusion in concrete terms, all we have to do is look at modern, especially German art: "In our day, in the case of almost all peoples, criticism, the cultivation of reflection, and in our German case, freedom of thought have mastered the artists too."[1]

But though the fusion of art and philosophy is argued to be a simple matter when we look at modern German culture, when considered from a conceptual perspective, it is, on the contrary, highly complex and difficult. In bringing art and philosophy together, modern art is obliged to be a "self-transcendence of art but within its own sphere and in the form of art itself" (80). Modern art, it seems, can reconcile art and philosophy only at a very great cost to itself, since it must transcend art itself in order to do this. But what is equally difficult is that it must accomplish this self-transcendence while remaining in its own sphere. With Hegel's concept of modern art, the tension between art and philosophy appears to be at a maximum. But given the logic of the dialectic, the attainment of such a maximum can be taken as the sign that a fundamental reconciliation has occurred in and through the concept of modern art.

Hegel's concept of modern tragedy is assigned a function similar to that of modern art as a whole in reconciling art and philosophy, and because of the particular nature that Hegel ascribes to modern tragedy, it also serves to elaborate the terms in which such reconciliation can take place. The dialectical role of modern tragedy is evident in Hegel's treatment of what for him is the fundamental element distinguishing ancient dramatic poetry from the modern: character. In a significant departure from Aristotle's *Poetics*, Hegel's philosophy of tragedy makes character the principal element of drama as a whole and modern drama in particular. According to Hegel, dramatic poetry "must, in the first place, like epic, bring before us a happening, a deed, an action; but its first step must be, above all, to strip externals away and put in their place as the ground and cause of everything the self-conscious and active individual" (1160). As in Aristotle's *Poetics*, drama is still defined by Hegel as the imitation ("bringing before us") of an action. But action itself has ceased to be more important than character, as Aristotle held it to be.[2] Instead, character, the individual character, has become the ground of everything.

Character plays the central role in Hegel's analysis of modern tragedy because of its inherently philosophical or dialectical nature. In other words, the work of the dialectic in negating, retaining, and raising the preceding stage of art to a higher level will be carried out by this crucial element of dramatic poetry. Character, however, can only do this if it becomes modern, that is, if the modern playwright delineates it with greater intensity and attaches greater aesthetic (and ethical) importance to it than the ancient playwrights did. In the case of ancient tragedy, as we have seen, character does the work of the dialectic by introducing conflict into the previously harmonious ethical substance. But the individual in this case is a still abstract version of individuality, defined only by an identification with one of the ethical powers and not by his or her "subjective inner life" (Hegel, *Aesthetics*, 1223). Hegel compares the heroes of ancient drama to works of sculpture in order to indicate not only their great beauty and grandeur but also their abstraction as compared to the heroes of modern drama (1195). Implicitly, the individual in ancient tragedy plays such a different role than the individual in modern drama because of this relative abstraction.

By introducing conflict into the ethical substance (the ancient conception of) character does a part of the work of the dialectic. But only in the case of modern drama does character perform the whole of the work of the dialectic by achieving reconciliation. This means that only in modern drama is character revealed to us in its fully developed, concrete form. In modern drama, "there comes before our contemplation . . . the victory of [the characters'] own subjective personality which nevertheless persists self-assured" (1199). Conflict, which is only precipitated by the individual character in ancient tragedy, is overcome by the modern tragic hero, not just at the level of the action of specific plays but at the level of modern tragedy as a whole.

In a passage that condenses the modern sense of character into a single image and also shows us its dialectical power, Hegel writes: "The intensity and depth of subjectivity come all the more to light, the more endlessly and tremendously is it divided against itself, and the more lacerating are the contradictions in which it still has to remain firm in itself" (178). The individual character in all its intensity and depth can be revealed only if it is divided against itself and beset by contradictions, but it is revealed in this situation precisely because it remains firm in the face of it. The notion of firmness, which plays the central role in Hegel's discussion of character, is brought forward here in terms that explain why it is a philosophical or dialectical and not just a psychological concept. The individual character, the central element of modern drama, negates, retains, and raises to a higher level conflict and contradiction, and thereby elevates the subject from a still relatively undeveloped to a much more concrete, more fully mediated form. In this sense, modern drama not only differs from ancient drama but, even more, becomes what every historical stage in Hegel's system is in relation to the preceding stage: its *Aufhebung*. In other words, character, conceived in terms of or as the private individual with his or her inner feelings, is already in itself the theoretical or philosophical sublation of the ancient.

Hegel's striking and lapidary thesis concerning art—"Art, considered in its highest vocation, is and remains for us a thing of the past" (11)—should be interpreted in terms of the dialectical force he ascribes to modern art and in particular to modern tragedy. As Heidegger is quick to point out in the epilogue to "The Origin of the Work of Art," in positing his thesis concerning the pastness of art, Hegel "never meant to deny [the] possibility" of the coming into existence of "new art works and new art movements."[3] One can go further, however, and say that not only does Hegel have no intention of denying the possibility of a modern or, one could even claim, a post-modern art. He is not even denying the importance of such an art. On the contrary, with his thesis concerning the pastness of art he indicates the value he attaches to ancient art as art itself but also, indirectly, the equally great—if not greater—value he attaches to modern art because of its more properly philosophical and dialectical rather than purely aesthetic character.

In the last analysis, art "in its highest vocation is . . . for us a thing of the past," because the vocation of modern art and modern tragedy is not art but philosophy, not the correspondence of form and idea but the transcendence of form by idea. The vocation of modern art is no longer the highest vocation to which *art* can aspire, but, for just that reason, modern art should be considered to have an even higher vocation, insofar as it paves the way for the sublation of art by philosophy. In the self-assurance with which the hero of modern tragedy persists in the face of even the most lacerating contradictions, we can already see modern philosophy itself beginning to emerge. The notion of modern tragedy is thus ineluctable in the terms of the dialectic of art, because of the way it both retains ancient, tragic art and also begins to raise art to the level of philosophy.

As has already been suggested, the concept of modern art is effective in bridging the gap between art and philosophy because it also exemplifies the tension between them thanks to its highly paradoxical nature as a "self-transcendence of art but within its own sphere." But at moments, the dual nature of modern art and, in particular, of modern tragedy seems on the verge of becoming outright contradiction or even paradox and hence of failing to perform its dialectical function. One such moment is when Hegel attempts to situate tragedy in relation to the historical-conceptual framework of the *Aesthetics*. In the passage in which he formulates the relation of the *generic* difference between tragedy and comedy with the *historical* difference between the ancient and the modern, he indicates that tragedy is essentially ancient:

> The same principle which gave us the basis for the division of dramatic art into tragedy and comedy provides us with the essential turning-points in the history of their development. For the lines of this development can only consist in setting out and elaborating the chief features implicit in the nature of dramatic action, where in tragedy the whole treatment and execution presents what is *substantial* and fundamental in the characters and their aims and conflicts, while in comedy the central thing is the character's *inner* life and his *private* personality. (Hegel, *Aesthetics*, 1205)

The division between tragedy and comedy corresponds with the historical turning point dividing the ancient from the modern, the substantial from the properly individual. This means that, strictly speaking, there is no such thing as ancient comedy and, by the same token, no such thing as modern tragedy, or, at the very least, that modern tragedy is an inferior, essentially "comic" version of tragedy. The logic of this historical-generic framework is thus consistent with the more inclusive logic of modern art as a whole: as we might expect, tragedy, like art, is a thing of the past.

But Hegel defines the historical and conceptual framework of the *Aesthetics* in just the opposite manner when he makes character the "ground and cause of everything" not just in modern drama, but in drama as a whole. If character is indeed the central feature in tragedy, then ancient tragedy appears to be at best a defective version of tragedy bordering on the untragic: "At its plastic height in Greece, tragedy remains one-sided by making the validity of the substance and necessity of ethical life its essential basis and by leaving undeveloped the individuality of the dramatis personae and the depths of their personal life" (1222). Modern tragedy thus reveals itself to be the most authentic form of tragedy because it "adopts into its own sphere from the start the principle of subjectivity" (1223).

The idea that modern rather than ancient tragedy better exemplifies tragedy as a whole is also implicit in Hegel's decision to place his discussion of tragedy under the heading of the Romantic rather than the classical arts. The reasons why tragedy should be discussed in this concluding section of the *Aesthetics* and, even more, in the concluding pages of this section itself are clear, though they are at odds with the equally compelling reasons that caused him to equate tragedy with the ancient. If tragedy is to be the highest form of art, and modern tragedy in particular is to be the form of tragedy that prepares the way for the transcendence of art by philosophy, then it is fitting that tragedy as a whole be designated the highest and last stage in the dialectical unfolding of the concept and history of art narrated in the *Aesthetics*. But such a designation implies that tragedy as a whole is modern and that ancient tragedy is therefore a lesser form of (modern) tragedy.

The contradictory manner in which Hegel situates modern tragedy both in historical and conceptual terms of course relates directly to the complex nature of the reconciliation that modern tragedy is supposed to effect between art and philosophy—and also between the ancient and the modern. But now, instead of appearing just difficult, that reconciliation appears radically problematic, if not impossible. Modern tragedy and ancient tragedy each have an equal but incompatible claim to represent tragedy as a whole, with the result that tragedy can be argued to belong as much to the age of philosophy as to the age of art. This seemingly irresolvable clash, in which each appears to be the potential sublation of the other, threatens to contaminate both tragedy and philosophy. In other words, it threatens to make tragedy and art as a whole irreducibly modern and hence philosophical—to make both things of the present. But it also threatens to reduce modern tragedy to a form of ancient tragedy and, in the process, to undermine the integrity of philosophy itself, making it what it has pronounced tragedy to be: a thing of the past.

In the light of Hegel's difficulty in deciding to what age tragedy belongs, the radically contradictory nature of the notion of modern tragedy begins to emerge. It no longer appears as the most sensitive but nonetheless most successful link between art and philosophy but appears, rather, as a highly unstable border zone in which the two meet, conflict, and are contaminated by each other.

The "Quarrel" between the Moderns: Corneille and Shakespeare in Hegel's *Aesthetics*

The passages from the *Aesthetics* focusing on individual works of modern tragedy reinforce what emerges in Hegel's more general discussion of the distinctions between the genres of dramatic literature and the historical periods—a sense of the impossibility of establishing with any rigor the boundaries delimiting the ancient and the modern, art and philosophy. In broadest terms, the general impression given by these passages is that Hegel is engaged in a struggle with his immediate predecessors and contemporaries to determine at what point the ancient and the modern begin and end and, equally important, how to situate the age of (the) philosophy (of tragedy) in relation to these two ages in the history of art. The Oedipal dimension of this struggle is fairly obvious. It is clearly one to determine who is the legitimate modern heir of the Greeks, and as a result, what is unresolved and ambiguous in it is Hegel's relationship both to ancient tragedy and also to those other modern figures whose work, like that of Hegel, is born as tragedy dies its seemingly interminable death. For very different reasons, Shakespeare and Corneille are two of the most important of these modern figures. When read against the background of Hegel's problematic concept of modern tragedy, the contrast Hegel implicitly draws between their works appears as an attempt to neutralize the destabilizing effects that the contradictory notion of modern tragedy would otherwise have on the philosophy of art as a whole.

Though Hegel criticizes the French on several grounds, the specific criticism he makes of Corneille is that his heroes (like those of Racine) do not display the firmness of character Hegel requires in the best examples of dramatic poetry. If a character is not "*one* in himself," Hegel argues, "the different aspects of his diverse characteristics fall apart." The result is not only that the hero becomes "senseless and meaningless" (240), but also that he becomes incapable of playing the dialectical role assigned to him in the *Aesthetics*.

> In Corneille's *Cid*, the collision of love and honor plays a brilliant part. Such a "pathos"[4] in different characters can of course lead to conflicts; but when it is introduced as an inner opposition in one and the same character, this provides an opportunity for splendid rhetoric and affecting monologues, but the diremption of one and the same heart, which is tossed hither and thither out of the abstraction of honor into that of love, and *vice versa*, is inherently contrary to solid decisiveness and unity of character. (241)

The reference to Rodrigue's monologue in act 1, scene 5, is clear. Given the central importance Hegel attaches to character, the inner opposition that Rodrigue demonstrates in this scene—an inner opposition that Hegel interprets as the infallible sign of a lack of firmness and self-assurance—is not just one flaw among others. From the standpoint of the *Aesthetics*, it is *the* fatal flaw from which no drama can be rescued, not even by "splendid rhetoric and affecting monologues."

Because, in the case of *Le Cid*, conflict afflicts not just the tragic universe but the hero himself, the play as a whole fails to perform the dialectical role assigned to it by the philosophy of art. But this negative version of the tragic hero corresponds to another, negative version of the dialectic, which, according to Hegel, is exemplified in French neoclassical tragedy as a whole. In the French plays, he writes, "a sort of dialectical machinery" is inserted "into the individual's own character" (1229). This construal of character, Hegel argues, is "what is worst of all," and it produces, not a true but rather "a sort of perverse and sophistical dialectic" (1229).

The full force of Hegel's negative assessment of Corneille becomes apparent only when one contrasts it with his judgment of Shakespeare, the modern dramatist he holds to be supreme. Though there are a number of points on which Shakespeare is compared favorably to other dramatists, when one considers the central importance Hegel attaches to character, it comes as no surprise that Shakespeare's supremacy is most apparent in precisely this respect.

> In the portrayal of concretely human individuals and characters it is especially the English who are distinguished masters and above them all Shakespeare stands at an almost unapproachable height. (1227)

> Such a purely self-dependent individual rests on himself and in this firmness either realizes himself or perishes. . . . Shakespeare's characters especially are of this kind; in them it is precisely this taut firmness and one-sidedness that is supremely admirable. (577)

Because of his masterful depiction of character, the plays of Shakespeare are held by Hegel to be not just excellent examples of modern tragedy but the standard by which all modern dramatic poetry should be judged.

Shakespeare is supreme in his depiction of character, but *Hamlet* occupies the position in relation to Shakespeare's other plays that those plays, taken as a group, occupy in relation to modern drama as a whole. The prince of Denmark is not just one hero among others for Hegel; he is clearly *the* modern tragic hero. When Hegel wants to illustrate his thesis concerning the difference between the ancient and the modern tragic hero, he need only refer to Shakespeare's *Hamlet* in order to feel he has fully justified his point: "In order to exhibit in more detail the difference in this respect [that is, with respect to character] between Greek and modern tragedy, I will direct attention only to Shakespeare's *Hamlet*" (1225–26). The failure of the French to equal Shakespeare in their depiction of character is thus far-reaching in its implications, for it makes of him, not the French, the true heir of

Sophocles and Aeschylus, even if he must reinvent the notion and concept of character in order to show himself worthy of them.

Hegel's argument is structured in such a way that Hamlet ought, therefore, to be a model of the firmness, decisiveness, and unity that Hegel argues are characteristic of the modern tragic hero in general. In certain passages in the *Aesthetics*, Hegel does indeed argue that this is the case, despite some indications to the contrary. "Hamlet," he writes, in an apparent response to Goethe, "indeed is indecisive in himself, yet he was not doubtful about *what* he was to do, but only *how*" (244). In another long passage in which he discusses Hamlet's firmness, or lack of it, Hegel first asserts that "Hamlet's nature is weak in practice; his beautiful heart is indrawn," but then he goes on to argue in the concluding lines of the same passage: "Hamlet hesitates because he does not blindly believe in the ghost. . . . Hamlet doubts, and, by arrangements of his own, will get certainty for himself, before he embarks on action" (231). Though these passages do not immediately confirm Hegel's claims that Shakespeare's heroes are distinguished by a "taut firmness and one-sidedness," they still are not wholly in contradiction with it. They still can be seen as consistent with a view that Hamlet remains at bottom firm and decisive, even if he is superficially and initially vacillating and torn by contradiction.

At other moments, however, the idea that Hamlet's firmness of character leads him to triumph over an initial doubt or uncertainty is simply contradicted. Hamlet appears no longer as an example of firmness, but rather as one of "character as inner but undeveloped totality" (580):

> But such a deep tranquil heart, which keeps its energy of soul pent up like the spark in the flint, which does not give itself outward form, and which does not develop its existence and reflection on it . . . remains exposed to the grim contradiction of having no skill, no bridge to reconcile its heart with reality and so to ward off external circumstances, to be supported against them, and to be its own support. . . . So, e.g., Hamlet. (583)

Hegel's description of Shakespeare's hero has a familiar ring for more than one reason. Like other of his references to Hamlet, it recalls Goethe's interpretation of Shakespeare's play and its hero. It also very clearly evokes his own description in the *Phenomenology* of "the beautiful soul," who, like Goethe's Hamlet, is a figure of anything but firmness and decisiveness:

> The "beautiful soul," lacking an *actual* existence, entangled in the contradiction between its pure self and the necessity of that self to externalize itself and change itself into an actual existence, and dwelling in the *immediacy* of this firmly held antithesis, . . . being conscious of this contradiction in its unreconciled immediacy, is disordered to the point of madness, wastes itself in yearning and pines away in consumption.[5]

This picture of Hamlet no longer leaves any room for an eventual reassertion of his unity of character, of his firmness in the face even of the most "lacerating" contradictions. When presented as an example of "inner but undeveloped totality," Hamlet's disorder appears no less serious than the "diremption" of Rodrigue; and the contradiction between the "pure self" and "the necessity of that self to externalize itself" appears no less inimical to decisiveness and firmness of character than the contradiction between love and honor.

On the face of it, Hegel's vacillation in relation to Hamlet is very difficult to understand. His whole system would seem to make it imperative that Hamlet be a model of firmness, because only in that case can modern tragedy perform its dialectical function of negating and retaining ancient tragedy and also serve as the intermediate link between (ancient) art and (modern) philosophy. Moreover, Hegel himself does at times find a way of arguing that in the most fundamental terms Hamlet is indeed firm and decisive. The question is, Why does Hegel not consistently hold this to be the case; Why does he at times interpret Hamlet's character in the opposite manner—as totally "exposed to grim contradiction" without any bridge to reconcile it?

The answer can only be that at some level Hegel also "wants" Hamlet to be like Rodrigue, an inferior version of the modern hero, unable to perform his dialectical work. In other words, he wants to negate what he started out affirming—the philosophical character of modern art—because there is something threatening as well as desirable about it. All modern tragedy—whether that of Corneille, Racine, Shakespeare, or others who figure in the *Aesthetics*—is potentially the ally and even in a sense the instrument of philosophy in its reflection of and on the ancient. But all modern tragedy is also potentially the rival of philosophy, inasmuch as the task it performs is vital to philosophy itself. What is threatening about modern tragedy is that through its depiction of character it may already have completed the work of philosophy, it may already in itself represent the ultimate "transcendence of form by idea" and the "end of art" that philosophy claims it alone can represent. Modern tragedy must do its job of linking philosophy to art, but it must not do it too well. It must be like philosophy, but not too much like philosophy. In the light of his contradictory interpretations of *Hamlet*, Hegel's criticisms of *Le Cid* appear to be a projection of the negative element in his relation to Shakespeare. They appear, in other words, to have less to do with Corneille's play and more to do with Hegel's own uneasy relation to Shakespeare and to modern tragedy in general.

One could argue according to the logic, though not the letter, of Hegel's *Aesthetics* that the modern tragic hero can take two forms. One is an explicitly negative form in which he is no more than the expression of a "perverse and sophistical dialectic" (*Aesthetics*, 1229), and in which as a result he produces no authentic reconciliation, as Hegel holds is the case in the plays of Corneille. The other is an apparently positive form in which we see a "victory [of his] own subjective personality which nevertheless persists self-assured" (1191). In fact, however, both of these results are undesirable. In the first case, art becomes less than art or an inferior—that is, not genuinely dialectical—version of art. In the second case, art becomes more than art—a philosophy-as-art in which the subjectivity of the hero does the work of the dialectic and thereby threatens to complete the work of philosophy before the age of philosophy has begun.

"Corneille" is the name Hegel gives to the first case; "Shakespeare" is the name he gives to the second. But in a deeper sense, Shakespeare *is* Corneille, that is to say, Shakespeare also exemplifies a negative concept of modern tragedy, or at any rate, the negativity inherent in the concept of modern tragedy. His *Hamlet* raises the possibility that the reconciliation between art and philosophy takes place in the terms of tragedy rather than philosophy and thus serves to undermine the distinction(s) between tragedy and philosophy, the ancient and the modern, through which Hegel seeks to assure the eventual transcendence and triumph, if not of Hamlet-Rodrigue, then of philosophy itself. Given the contradictory nature of Hegel's interpretation of the character of Hamlet, that character comes to represent as much the return of the ancient and the tragic as it does the victory of the modern and the philosophical, because in it the modern and the philosophical can only triumph as tragedy.

Corneille and the Modern Tragic Hero:
Horace Confronted by Camille

Despite the almost uniformly critical nature of Hegel's remarks on the French theater in general and Corneille in particular, Corneille's critical texts and plays contain important parallels with the theory of tragedy that Hegel elaborates in the *Aesthetics*. Though they diverge on a number of specific points, Corneille and Hegel nonetheless share something on the order of a common and uneasy theoretical condition in which they are placed because of their interest in tragedy in general and modern tragedy in particular, and this common condition ultimately accounts for the deeper parallels in their work. Corneille's problem, like Hegel's, is to develop a concept of modern tragedy that can both account for its specific character and permit it to be seen as another version of (ancient) tragedy. The solution to this problem, in Corneille's case as in that of Hegel, is found in a dialectical concept of modern tragedy and of the modern tragic hero. In the terms of both his critical writings and his plays, Corneille's concept of modern tragedy can be said to negate, retain, and raise ancient tragedy to a higher level, and thus to reconcile the ancient and the modern in terms of a movement that progresses in the direction of the modern. When one considers the dialectical intention that is the guiding force in both Corneille's critical writings and his tragedies, the criticisms Hegel makes of *Le Cid* in particular and French tragedy in general are placed in a highly ironic light: if they are at all just, then they must also apply with equal force to the German or Hegelian version of tragedy.

From the perspective of Corneille, the nature of tragedy can be understood only if it can first be determined whether tragedy is past or present, ancient or modern. An exact appreciation of the ancients and of their theory and practice of tragedy is thus as important for Corneille as for Hegel. Corneille and Hegel diverge, however, in terms of the importance they attach, at least explicitly, to Aristotle's *Poetics*. Corneille reaches his theoretical conclusions concerning tragedy through a detailed commentary and discussion of Aristotle's text, whereas Hegel devotes only a few lines to the *Poetics* in the *Aesthetics*. But though they differ in this respect, in the end, Corneille's discussion of the *Poetics* produces a result—and a dilemma—similar to the one that emerges from Hegel's discussion of modern art and modern tragedy.

Corneille's three *Discours* and even an earlier critical text such as the "Avertissement" of 1648 to *Le Cid* show that his views concerning the importance of Aristotle were not simply imposed on him by a repressive, rule-conscious literary milieu. In the "Avertissement," he rejects the help of those who defend *Le Cid* with the argument that Aristotle's rules for tragedy are no longer applicable in the modern age. They have committed a serious poetic error, one that "is no less injurious to Aristotle than to myself."[6] And yet, important though the *Poetics* is in defining tragedy for Corneille, the most casual reader of his three "Discours" on tragedy and the "Examens" that preface the published versions of his own plays is immediately struck by his ambivalence, both theoretical and practical, in relation to the *Poetics* and to ancient tragedy in general.

Aristotle and the ancients as a group are frequently portrayed, as in the "Avertissment" to *Le Cid*, as occupying a commanding position in relation to tragedy, and the wisdom of the modern tragedian consists only in recognizing their supremacy and trying to work within the boundaries they fixed for tragic poetry. In the same "Avertissement," Corneille goes on to say of Aristotle, "This great man treated poetics with so much skill and judgment that the precepts he has left to us are for all times and for all peoples" (1:725). His position in the three *Discours* is more nuanced, but the dominant tendency is to discover, through a close and judicious reading of the *Poetics*, the true Aristotle, whose precepts properly interpreted are as relevant in the modern era as they were in ancient times.

Corneille's ambivalence toward the *Poetics* is also evident, however, in this more nuanced reading, and it comes to the fore in relation to the Aristotelian concept of catharsis. Corneille admits in his "Discours de la tragédie," a text that could with equal justice be called the *Discourse on Catharsis*, that he does not really understand what Aristotle means by this term. He adds, "I am quite afraid that the reasoning of Aristotle on this point may be no more than a beautiful idea, which never had an effect in reality [*la vérité*]."[7] The purgation of fear and pity by the arousal of fear and pity is not the only aspect of catharsis Corneille cannot fathom. Equally problematic for him is the association of pity and fear in the cathartic process. Neither the examples adduced by Aristotle nor Aristotle's own discussion enlighten Corneille as to how the two emotions can be consistently associated, and he concludes by deciding that Aristotle must have meant that, in certain plays, fear alone is responsible for the cathartic effect, and in others, fear working in connection with pity is responsible. If, in a third type of play, both emotions are aroused, it seems eminently more sensible to Corneille that one, essentially bad character be the focus of the fear of the spectators (a fear of what would befall them if they performed similar deeds) and another, essentially good character be the focus of the spectators' pity ("Discours," 1:38).

This interpretation of catharsis relates to the other major point on which Corneille is ready to depart from Aristotle: the crucial issue of character. By separating fear and pity, Corneille is able to defend the idea that a tragic hero can be all good, rather than neither "altogether innocent" nor "very bad" (1:39), as Aristotle requires. Even if he is all good, the play as a whole can still arouse both pity and fear. The fear may simply be aroused by another character (1:38). "Héraclius and Nicomède pleased the audience, even though they inspired only pity, and gave it nothing to fear, nor any passion to purge, because we saw them oppressed and ready to perish, without there being any fault on their part of which we might correct ourselves according to their example" (1:36–37). The count in Le Cid, in contrast brings on his own downfall through his excessive pride and jealousy and thus can purge these emotions from the spectators (1:37), leaving Rodrigue free to arouse only pity.

The division of labor between good and bad characters is clearly designed to facilitate the rationalization of catharsis. But an equally important function of this division is to defend Corneille's modern concept of the tragic hero and of what, to borrow from Hegel, could be called his firmness of character, his ability to remain one even in the face of the most lacerating contradictions. Taken together, Corneille's arguments relating to catharsis undermine his assertion that Aristotle – and ancient tragedy – is "for all times and for all peoples." They point to what are from his perspective both the limitations of Aristotle's Poetics and the superiority of (Corneille's own) modern tragedies as compared to those of the ancients. They also indicate that for Corneille, the implicit superiority of modern tragedy lies in the way it makes the firm and undivided individual the "ground and cause of everything."

The contradictions in Corneille's reading of Aristotle's Poetics are not accidental, nor do they necessarily indicate that Corneille is a defective critic and theorist of dramatic poetry, as Lessing was to accuse. Instead, they stem from the theoretical situation in which he finds himself, and in this sense neither a Lessing nor a Hegel is more able to escape from or resolve these contradictions than Corneille. What underlies Corneille's vacillations is the tension within his own theory, and practice, between a modern and dialectical conception of tragedy based on character and an ancient or Aristotelian model based on what for him is the murky and self-contradictory concept of catharsis.

Corneille, however, like Hegel, attempts to transcend the opposition between the ancient and the modern, and this is also evident in terms of his comments on Aristotle's concept of catharsis. What these comments show is that Corneille, despite his disavowal of catharsis, nonetheless attempts to salvage what from his point of view is essential in catharsis and in the *Poetics* as a whole. What is necessary is a positive form of identification that permits us as spectators to "correct ourselves according to [the] example of the tragic characters"; that is, to see ourselves in the good hero and reject, through fear, the model of behavior offered by the bad hero. According to the model of tragedy implied in such a positive form of identification, the central character in tragedy would no longer be a contradictory mixture of good and bad qualities, and spectators would be relieved of the corresponding disorientation implied by the mixture of fear and pity in their own feelings. Aristotelian catharsis would be thus be conserved in relation to the tragic drama as a whole but, at the same time, transcended in the figure of the tragic hero.

Corneille's implicit belief in the capacity of the modern hero to provide a satisfactory resolution even to what appear to be the most absolute types of ethical and aesthetic conflict can be seen in his *Oedipe*. So, too, can his desire to use his conception of the tragic hero to resolve the poetic conflict between the ancient and the modern, to sublate these two terms in a virtually dialectical manner. Though Corneille barely mentions the *Oedipus* of Sophocles in the three "Discours," when he does, it is in connection with the central issue of identification. He notes that the character of Oedipus is cited by Aristotle as an example of one that inspires both fear and pity, but he avers that he does not understand why. Oedipus "does not seem to me to commit any fault, even though he kills his father, because he did not recognize him" (1:35). The implication is clear. In a modern *Oedipe*—that is, one that would be based on a positive form of identification—Oedipus would be presented not as a bad or even partly good and partly bad character but, rather, as virtuous. He would thus be an object not of fear and pity but, rather, of pity alone.

Of course, Oedipus is not the only character drawn from ancient tragedy in terms of which Corneille could, and does, make such an argument. Many of his "ancient" characters find the idea of accepting responsibility for the deeds they have unconsciously committed to be repellent,[8] and in this sense they defend both their own virtue and their freedom to maintain their virtue—their own firmness of character—even in the face of a hostile destiny. As Theseus puts it:

> What? the necessity of virtues and vices
> Must follow the capriciousness of an imperious star?
>
> . . . .
>
> The soul is thus wholly enslaved: a sovereign law
> Towards good or evil incessantly drags it.
>
> . . . .
>
> Attached without respite to this sublime order
> Virtuous without merit and vicious without crime.[9]

Theseus cannot tolerate such a contradictory view of character—he asks to be excused from such a blindness, that is, from such an unreasonable belief (l. 1167, p. 580)—and clearly neither can Corneille. That is why, when Oedipus gouges out his own eyes at the end of Corneille's play, he asserts that he is doing it not to punish himself for his criminal albeit unconscious acts, but, rather, to express his defiant attitude toward the gods who have imposed this frightful destiny on him: to symbolize his freedom and autonomy from their despotic laws and simultaneously to affirm his own virtuous, undivided nature. In a passage clearly anticipating Schelling's thesis that the hero of Greek tragedy "manifests his freedom precisely in the loss of that very same freedom,"[10] Oedipe cries out:

> Let us see the cruel sky no longer,
> Take our vengeance upon it by disdaining its light
> Refuse it our eyes, but keep some life
> To show to all its tyranny.
> (Corneille, *Oedipe*, ll. 1991–94, p. 589)

By carrying out the law of the gods to the letter but in a spirit that is all defiance of them, the tragic hero asserts both his moral integrity and his fundamental modernity. His moral equivocity (is he good or bad?

good and bad?) is negated. He emerges with his virtue and his will intact, and the spectator can thus identify positively with him. Corneille viewed *Oedipe* as his most artful play (*Oedipe,* 567), and this view is related no doubt to his sense that it successfully integrates his own modern conception of the virtuous and free hero into a plot and subject matter taken from what was for Aristotle the supreme example of ancient tragedy.

From the perspective of Corneille's sense of triumph in his *Oedipe,* his *Horace* represents a contrasting and highly significant moment in his work. When his critical texts and plays are read together, it is difficult to escape the impression that his ambivalence toward the ancients, and hence the equivocity of his own position as a modern, manifests itself more clearly in *Horace* than even in his theoretical texts and certainly more than in any other play he wrote, regardless of whether he deems the play a success or a failure. In the light both of Corneille's critical comments on the play and of the play itself, *Horace* appears as the point in his work where the logic of catharsis, the logic of a hero who is both good and bad, overtakes the modern hero and deprives him of his dialectical force. It does this essentially because the action of the play, despite Corneille's intentions, thrusts another tragic hero onto the stage, Horace's sister, Camille.

In order to understand how the position of Horace is undermined by the character and actions of his sister, it is necessary to compare the passages in Corneille's play in which Camille figures most prominently with his critical comments in the *Examen* and elsewhere relating to her character. Corneille's sense that *Horace* is a failure is directly related to what he sees as the disjunction between the first and second halves of the play, and this disjunction is created by Camille's death. The second part of *Horace,* in particular, provides one of those very rare occasions when Corneille finds himself in violation of Aristotle's rules but where in his own estimate the artistic results *do not* justify him. "It is rather generally believed that this play could have been accepted as the most beautiful I have written if the later acts were up to the earlier ones. Everyone would have it that the death of Camille spoils the ending, and in this I agree."[11] Corneille hastens to specify that Camille's death does not disfigure the play for the reason usually cited: because its horrible nature makes it *invraisemblable,* that is, something that may in fact have happened but ought not to be represented. The rule that the theatrical scene should not be bloodied does not come down to us from Aristotle, Corneille notes, but is, rather, a more modern usage, which, as such, holds less authority. Corneille then goes on to spell out the true reason why Camille's murder flaws *Horace*: because it breaks Aristotle's rule concerning the unity of action by subjecting Horace to what Corneille calls a second danger.

Corneille's logic in this extremely nuanced defense and critique of *Horace* is even less straightforward than it sounds, however. In fact, his own interpretation of his play is much closer to his critics' than he indicates. Despite his (characteristic) defense of the idea that it is not against the rules to portray horrible acts on the stage (history, he frequently argues, takes precedence even over the *vraisemblable*), Corneille does agree with his detractors that there is something scandalous, morally and aesthetically, about Camille's death. If he argues that retaining the fact of Camille's death in his plot is not contrary to the rules, he also indirectly acknowledges the horror it inspires in him when he asserts that this is one of those facts that should not be represented on the stage. Corneille refuses to draw a line between history and his play. But he does draw a line between what happens on stage and what ought to happen offstage, and the logic of these two lines is essentially the same. In each case, it reflects an ethico-poetic decision whose function is to allay the ambivalence aroused by his play and more specifically by the scene in which Horace kills Camille.

The specific nature of Corneille's ambivalence becomes clearer if one considers the criticisms he makes of the actors in the early productions of *Horace*, in which the death of Camille was represented on stage. It should have been clear to them that the death ought to take place in the wings, according to Corneille, for "when she sees her brother put his sword in his hand, fright, which is so natural to her sex, must make her take flight and receive the deathblow off-stage" (1:830), as he noted explicitly in stage directions added to later printed editions of the play. Even if the actors did not have specific instructions to the effect that the murder was to take place in the wings, Corneille indicates, they should have seen that that was what was required, given the dramatic situation and the sex of Camille.

The contradiction between the interpretation Corneille gives of his play in these lines and the text of his play could not be more flagrant, however. His image of a naturally timid Camille, who would automatically flee when confronted with the sudden and unexpected appearance of her brother's sword and presumably also by the possibility of her imminent death, simply does not correspond to the Camille of his play. In act 4, scene 4, Camille, alone on the stage, reaches a conscious decision to defy her brother when he returns home (and also her father, who has just told her she must now cease mourning her betrothed and focus exclusively on honoring her brother as the savior of his country):

> Degenerate, my heart, from such a virtuous father;
> Be the unworthy sister of such a generous brother;
>
> . . . .
>
> For this cruel victor show no respect;
> Far from avoiding him, rise up against him when he appears;
> Offend his victory, irritate his wrath
> And take, if you can, pleasure in displeasing him.
>
> (ll. 1239–48, vol. 1, pp. 872–73)

So much for Corneille's argument concerning the natural tendency of her sex to be frightened!

Throughout the scene in which she delivers her impassioned monologue and in the following one, in which she is killed, Camille displays a firmness of character that is significant both in itself and in terms of the light in which it places her brother. Corneille's claims in the *Examen* notwithstanding, the scene that follows Camille's soliloquy and ends in her death is, in the terms of the play itself, a direct result of *her* explicit intentions. Horace's actions are all instigated and in that sense controlled by Camille, who has consciously sought to push him over the edge. Camille and Horace are engaged in a psychological duel whose result will be to demonstrate the complete mastery of Camille, for throughout this scene, Camille retains the initiative, and Horace is merely reacting. In other words, Horace's actions in this scene are determined not by his own will but by Camille. Because of the force of *her* character, the character of Horace is robbed of the unity Corneille obviously sought to give it.

Camille, moreover, reveals a superior insight into the pathos of her brother. She knows that he is not animated by mere egotism, and that, in order to offend him to the utmost, it is not enough to insult him personally. She can do the greatest possible injury to him by showing her contempt for Rome; for Horace's actions on the battlefield are justified in his own eyes only because, in killing the Curiaces, he has done his patriotic duty. If Rome is unworthy, if the state is not the supreme authority and value, then Horace is just a murderer. Thus, with her taunting "Rome, unique object of my resentment!" (l. 1301, vol. 1, p. 874), with "Rome" repeated in each of the four following lines, she pushes Horace to the point where he loses control completely and kills her. The result is to negate the sublime virtue he has just demonstrated in his triumph on the battlefield, and thus not only to interrupt the continuity of the action, but also to place the "virtuous" and supremely forceful character of Horace in contradiction with itself.

Camille's firmness in relation to Horace places his character in an ambiguous light for another reason: because of what might be called the law of family resemblance that obtains in the play. The logic of this law is already apparent in the opening scenes. When we are introduced to both Sabine and then her brother, it quickly becomes apparent that they share a distinctive family trait: both are characters who pity—themselves and others. The Horaces (that is, Horace, his father, and Camille) are similarly identifiable as members of a family thanks to the opposite trait: all are essentially immune to pity—for both themselves and others. In this play about the division between man and woman that underlies the ethical community (that is, in the terms of Corneille's play, the entity made up of both Rome and Alba), the feminine principle of pity is represented by the Curiaces and the masculine principle of force or virtue by the Horaces. Camille, then, is a Horace, but a Horace as a Curiace. In other words, she is a man, but she is a man as a woman. As such, she represents what, in Horace's own name and his own character, opposes itself to Horace and lies beyond his control. Their conflict is so intense *because* it grows out of a common identification with their family name and the masculine virtues it symbolizes. Equally important, the absolute intensity of their conflict also reveals that identification is, if not stronger, then at least as strong as the natural difference between the sexes, which according to Corneille should have made Camille flee when her brother drew his sword.

Camille's death is thus troubling not only for the same reasons as any violent act (and Corneille regularly suppresses other violent acts— that is, he relegates them to the wings—but without all the theoretical fuss he makes here). Given the way Corneille himself distorts his play and Camille's character when he argues that the murder ought to have taken place offstage, it appears that, from his own perspective, there is something deeply troubling about Camille's actions and hence about *Horace* itself. It is obvious that her active or even "virile" nature is at least part of the problem. For though one can find other heroines in Corneille's dramaturgy who are similarly active or masculine, Camille exemplifies these qualities with special purity. As a result, her heroism and her corresponding insubordination succeed in revealing what in Corneille's other major tragedies is more successfully obscured. The violence Horace does to Camille at her instigation reveals that *her* (ethical) power—whether one calls it the power of the family, of passion, or of the woman—is the equal of his. The result is that, in *Horace*, conflict appears absolute. That is to say, it divides not only the masculine Horaces from the feminine Curiaces but also the masculine Horace(s) from himself (from each other) and is therefore as much within the family, within the state, and within the masculine (and the feminine) as between them. No (modern) hero, no matter how virtuous or powerful, can overcome such absolute conflict, and thus no hero confronted with such conflict can be the object of a wholly unambiguous, positive form of identification.

But can such a view of the *equality* of Camille and Horace as the representatives of two opposing ethical powers—in effect the "law of woman" and the "law of man"—be applied to the play as a whole? Does not the conclusion to the play successfully vindicate Horace and preserve his virtue and dialectical force? There is an argument to be made according to which, though individual male characters in *Horace* may suffer reversals, the masculine principle exemplified by the Horaces as a family still emerges supreme. According to this same argument, the king of Rome cannot punish Horace any more than the king of Spain can punish Rodrigue—because they have in fact prevailed upon the field of battle, and because in fact only a masculine character could prevail. By the same token, the same argument would have it that the state always emerges as the dominant ethical power, because without it the family must perish.

The always implicit argument concerning the natural difference between the sexes has been used at a crucial moment by Serge Doubrovsky in his reading of the famous scene from *Le Cid* in which Rodrigue comes to Chimène's apartment after having killed her father and offers to let her kill him.[12] According to Doubrovsky, Chimène must herself kill Rodrigue, just as he has killed the count, if she is to be truly his equal. Chimène's failure to do just that, Doubrovsky concludes, shows her inability to measure up to the heroic standard by which Corneille's male characters are judged.[13] But Doubrovsky himself has also supplied another standard for judging the heroism of Corneille's characters, one according to which the distinction that he draws between Chimène and Rodrigue—or the one that could, using his terms, be drawn between Camille and Horace—appears problematic. *Corneille, ou la dialectique du héros* is, of course, informed by Sartrean existentialism, and thus Doubrovsky makes the notion of will, with the complementary notions of subjectivity and responsibility, the key to his interpretation of Corneille's work.[14] But because of what one might call the subjective character Doubrovsky himself ascribes to will, the supreme test it faces, he argues, is not in overcoming an external obstacle but, rather, in overcoming the self. Rodrigue is a hero, a man of will and responsibility, not only because he is able to kill the count and innumerable Moors, but also because he has successfully dominated his own fear of death and, in this sense, has become one with his own will.[15]

From a certain perspective, one could say that this is still a military and in this sense a masculine or virile definition of will. It still assumes something on the order of a state of nature of a Hobbesian type in which each is the enemy of all. But from another standpoint, it totally divorces the notion of will from any natural basis. Will is no longer tied to the reality of natural strength or physical action. What we have is a metaphysical notion of will to which all natural subjects may conform to the same degree. (And in this sense it is also a natural definition of will—*another* natural definition.) From the standpoint of such a conception of will, that Chimène cannot and does not kill Rodrigue is irrelevant. What is relevant is her capacity to surmount her fear of her own death. And if it can be argued that Chimène never really has the chance to prove her heroism according to this second standard, Camille does—as, one might add, Antigone did before her.

Of course, in Doubrovsky's reading of *Horace*, Camille appears in a very different light than Chimène. "The death of Camille is a *heroic death*, insofar as heroism consists in voluntarily putting human values to a mortal test" (166). Whereas Chimène is Rodrigue's inferior, the ethical force of Camille is equal to the ethical force of Horace, at least if they are compared as individual characters. But in *Horace* too,

Horace, who is absolutely unable to defeat his sister, is nonetheless vindicated from the perspective of the play as a whole, according to Doubrovsky, when "the center of philosophical gravity . . . displaces itself from Horace to Tulle, and the king takes over from the faltering hero" (180). Thanks to the king's judgment that Horace's punishment for killing Camille will be to live, Doubrovsky argues that "the failure of heroism, on the individual plane, is redeemed by the success of the system" (182). The hero and the masculine principle thus triumph in a problematic sense, inasmuch as Horace's own status is now equivocal. But according to Doubrovsky they do triumph nonetheless, insofar as they provide the basis for and sustain the interests of the broader community or system. Doubrovsky insists that the triumph of the system over the individual also represents a personal triumph for and vindication of the character of Horace: "It is important to note that at the end of the play, the sacrificial gesture of Horace [his murder of Camille] is not condemned" but on the contrary is accepted as analogous to the act that founded Rome, Romulus's murder of Remus (181).

The importance Doubrovsky attaches to the role of the king in redeeming Horace's individual failure requires, of course, that he reject Corneille's views concerning the flawed nature of *Horace*: "There is no . . . duality of action in *Horace*. . . . Once more, we would defend Corneille the creator against Corneille the critic" (154). But if Corneille himself criticizes *Horace* for its lack of unity, if the terms in which he both condemns and defends it are so contradictory, it is because the play also lends itself to another reading, in which the masculine principle does not triumph, even in the more problematic sense in which Doubrovsky holds that it does when the king takes over from the faltering Horace and the success of the system is affirmed. The point here is not to argue that either of Doubrovsky's very persuasive readings of Corneille's two tragedies is wrong, but, rather, to suggest that both tragedies, and in particular *Horace*, lend themselves equally well to an alternative reading that contradicts Doubrovsky's. There is no question that *Horace*, like *Oedipe* and *Le Cid*, constitutes an attempt to decide the questions it opens and resolve the contradictions it uncovers. The flaw in *Horace* is that another reading of the play, in which Horace's heroic nature is so radically undercut that the system itself is disrupted, now seems equally plausible. In other words, there lurks in *Horace* another play, which would probably be called *Camille*, just as Sophocles' play about the conflict between the family and the state, man and woman, is called *Antigone*.

The preceding analysis of *Horace* borrows the language Hegel uses to discuss ancient tragedy, and it would be difficult to do otherwise. In failing to be the play Corneille wants it to be, *Horace* becomes in effect Corneille's *Antigone*. Of course, the divisions within the ethical substance itself between competing ethical powers—between the power of the family and the state, between the sphere of woman and the masculine sphere of public life—are all clear in the first half of *Horace*, the part of it which, according to Corneille, corresponds to his poetic intention. But in those first acts, the possibility still exists that Horace can overcome these divisions if he displays sufficient firmness of character.

This changes, however, when Horace is exposed to a second danger. Once Camille dies on the stage, the divisions in the ethical substance appear so deep as to be beyond the power of any individual to overcome them, whether that individual be a hero or a poet. The final act is "still another of the causes of the lack of satisfaction given by this tragedy" not only because, as Corneille would have it, "it is entirely composed of speeches for the prosecution and the defense" (*Horace*, 1:833), but, even more importantly, because these various speeches, whether made against or on behalf of Horace, are profoundly anticlimactic in the sense that they cannot fundamentally alter the situation that is revealed at the close of the fourth act. They cannot reestablish the harmony of the woman and the man, the family and the State, any more than they can restore to Horace his commanding position as hero.

In theoretical terms, *Horace*, then, unlike Corneille's *Oedipe*, is not a synthesis of the ancient and the modern but rather a monstrous hybrid: not the ancient and the modern, finally reconciled as and by the modern, but the ancient in the modern—as we might say, the fly in the ointment. Of all Corneille's tragedies, *Horace* is the best example of the radical contradiction fundamental to modern tragedy and the force with which it undermines the dialectical project of the modern playwright and the modern theorist of literature no less than the modern philosopher. The logic of that contradiction, even as it prevents them from imitating the ancient, also prevents both the heroic individual and the poet from fully overcoming the ancient and producing an exclusively modern tragedy. It forces them to obey a logic other than their own, dialectical one, and in doing so, it disrupts the relatively simple opposition between the ancient and the modern in terms of which the modern poet/theorist seeks to overcome the tragic and the ancient.

In one sense, Corneille's failure in *Horace* seems a simple confirmation of Hegel's thesis that there is no modern tragedy—at least not in French. But in another sense, that failure reflects back on Hegel's entire project in his *Aesthetics*. As we have seen, Corneille's commitment to the individual as an aesthetic principle is unquestionable. Thus it is all the more significant that, in *Horace*, Corneille should be unable to vindicate this principle, that he should be forced despite himself to show, if not its dependence on, then at least its inability to overcome wholly the conflict and contradiction that loom so large in Sophocles' *Antigone*. In this sense, Camille's death is not only a flaw in Corneille's play; it amounts to an interruption or suspension of the dialectical progression that leads from the ancient to the modern and also, therefore, from the age of modern art to the age of philosophy. It shows us that the ancient and the tragic are in a sense never overcome, but, rather, that they permanently disrupt the modern and the individual.

This can only mean that they permanently disrupt philosophy as well. The movement through which philosophy ultimately dissolves art by resolving its contradictions is compromised if the terms of the various contradictions themselves cannot be clearly articulated—that is, if the modern is still ancient and therefore the ancient is already modern; if the individual is already dialectical but also still tragic; if feminine pathos is equal to masculine honor and the masculine already feminine. It is because of the way in which Corneille's *Horace* mirrors speculative philosophy that it permits us to see its project in a perspective that is no longer that of speculative philosophy itself— that is, to see philosophy not as the *Aufhebung* of the tragic and the aesthetic in general but as belonging to the age in which it is contaminated by art and tragedy: the age of the modern.

CHAPTER 4

The Uneasy Identification of Psychoanalysis and Tragedy: Freud and Racine

Rational cognition has one critical limit which is its inability to cope with suffering.

—Adorno

What did Racine put in the place of the many beauties [of the Phaedra *of Euripides]? Nothing, absolutely nothing.*

—A. W. Schlegel

Hamlet versus Oedipus in the Work of Freud

Of all the problems with which tragedy has presented theory, none is more difficult than that of tragic guilt. In his *Philosophy of Art* (as earlier in his *Philosophical Letters on Dogmatism and Criticism*), Friedrich Schelling articulates this problem in the following terms:

> People have asked . . . how the Greeks were able to endure these terrible contradictions inherent in their tragedies. A mortal, preordained by fate for guilt and transgression, even—as is the case with Oedipus—struggling *against* fate and fleeing that guilt, nonetheless is frightfully punished for a transgression that was actually the work of fate. Are these contradictions, people have asked, not simply devastating?[1]

By implication, not the least of the merits of Schelling's philosophy in his own eyes lies in its recognition that the idea of freedom is alone capable of resolving the contradictions posed by the guilt of Oedipus and the other heroes of Greek tragedy. For Schelling, the ultimate sense of their guilt lies in what he calls "the most sublime idea and the greatest victory of freedom," which consists in voluntarily bearing "the punishment for an unavoidable transgression in order to manifest . . . freedom precisely in the loss of that very same freedom" (254). In Schelling's version of speculative philosophy, freedom sublates the contradiction tragedy poses for reason; by taking on and making itself the instrument of necessity, freedom negates itself and at the same time raises itself to a higher level. The ultimate purpose of the contradiction of tragic guilt is thus to make manifest human freedom. This knowledge is ultimately what makes it possible for the spectator to endure tragedy and grasp the rational basis of its beauty.[2]

Whatever the scientific and empirical bases of psychoanalysis, its deep historical and theoretical affinity with speculative philosophy can be seen in its own particularly radical attempt to come to terms with the problem posed to reason by tragic guilt and by tragedy generally speaking. In his first published references to the legend of Oedipus and to Sophocles' play, Freud indicates his link to speculative philosophy and also his ambition to surpass it when he explicitly criticizes the explanation of tragedy proposed by Schelling. Neither philosophy nor aesthetics, Freud implies, is equal to the task of understanding the power of tragedy. Psychoanalysis alone is, because only the psychoanalytic concept of the unconscious is capable of accounting for tragic guilt:

> If *Oedipus Rex* moves a modern audience no less than it did the contemporary Greek one, the explanation can only be that its effect does not lie in the contrast between destiny and human will, but is to be looked for in the particular nature of the material on which that contrast is exemplified. There must be something which makes a voice within us ready to recognize the compelling force of destiny in the *Oedipus*, while we can dismiss as merely arbitrary such dispositions as are laid down in [Grillparzer's] *Die Ahnfrau* or other modern tragedies of destiny. And a factor of this kind is in fact involved in the story of King Oedipus. His destiny moves us only because it might have been ours—because the oracle laid the same curse upon us before our birth as upon him. It is the fate of all of us, perhaps, to direct our first sexual impulse towards our mother and our first hatred and our first murderous wish against our father. Our dreams convince us that that is so. King Oedipus, who slew his father Laïus and married his mother Jocasta, merely shows us the fulfillment of our own childhood wishes.[3]

The effect of *Oedipus* on audiences from the days of the Greeks to our own can be explained not in terms of the ideas of freedom and destiny but only by a concept of the unconscious, understood as a region of the psyche cut off from consciousness, a region that harbors the incestuous and murderous wishes that find expression in *Oedipus*.

The horror Oedipus inspires in us and presumably the punishment he suffers are the result of the "repression by which those wishes" have "been held down within us" (4:262–63). The unconscious must take evasive measures in order to circumvent this repression or censorship of its wishes. But the ultimate law governing the unconscious is a pleasure principle, whose aim is to seek the fulfillment of those wishes. Thus, even if a censoring agency imposed punishment on the tragic heroes, much as it imposes distortion and other evasive strategies on the dream process, the Greeks presumably were able to endure the contradictions of their tragedies because unconscious wishes were fulfilled in them.

Freud's sense of the historic importance of the discovery which he first conveyed in published form in this passage from the *Interpretation of Dreams* is evident. Psychoanalysis has at last been able to explain the "profound and universal power to move" of the Oedipus legend and Sophocles' masterpiece (4:261). There is a similar note of triumph in the interpretation of *Hamlet* that immediately follows Freud's remarks on *Oedipus*. Thanks to his theory of the unconscious, he can also provide an explanation of Hamlet's hesitations, whereas the attempted explanations proposed before his, including Goethe's, "have failed to produce a result" (4:265). "After all," Freud writes in his "Psychopathic Characters on the Stage," "the conflict in *Hamlet* is so effectively concealed that it was left to me to unearth it" (7:310).

Freud thus presents himself as the thinker who has finally revealed the ultimate secret of tragic guilt, and no doubt a considerable part of the scientific legitimacy of psychoanalysis stems in Freud's own eyes from the success with which it has explained this age-old mystery. But, as Jean Starobinski has argued in two articles devoted to Freud's work, "Psychanalyse et connaissance littéraire" and "Oedipe et Hamlet," the place that Freud gives to both Sophocles' *Oedipus* and Shakespeare's *Hamlet* is so central that it is difficult to see them only as the most important examples of "dream-work" or the most important confirmations of Freud's theory of the unconscious. Starobinski notes that Freud refers to these two plays early and frequently, even before the publication of *The Interpretation of Dreams*, particularly at moments in his correspondence with Fliess and also in his published work when he is describing a theoretical breakthrough. For Starobinski, these references indicate that the two plays not only serve to illustrate Freud's thought but are in fact a kind of matrix for it.[4] From Starobinski's perspective, psychoanalysis is as much thought by *Oedipus* and by *Hamlet* as they are thought by it. The two plays permit Freud to elaborate the concept of the unconscious which he then uses to reveal their secret.

This general argument leads Starobinski to conclude, in the case of Sophocles' *Oedipus*, that the play is not merely a reflection of unconscious drives; it *is* (the theoretical model for) the unconscious drives as they are understood by Freud. The implication is that *Hamlet*, to which, Starobinski notes, Freud refers as frequently as *Oedipus*, must play an analogous theoretical role. And yet, while Starobinski argues convincingly that the importance of *Hamlet* is as great for Freud as that of *Oedipus*, he does not provide the same kind of analysis of its theoretical significance.

If the concept of the unconscious provides the key to understanding tragedy, then a single model should suffice to exemplify the tragic genre as a whole. The problem, then, is to discover why it is that psychoanalytic theory should require that there be *two* examples of tragedy. The recurring references to the figure of Hamlet in Freud's theoretical texts and the particular set of psychoanalytic concepts to which it is linked indicate that, as Starobinski has argued for *Oedipus*, something in particular is being thought in the figure of this modern tragic hero, a "something" that is not just an element of psychoanalysis but is in some sense constitutive of it. That Freud needs still another model or version of tragedy seems to indicate that the model of the unconscious provided by his interpretation of *Oedipus* is not sufficient, that it must be supplemented in some way by another.[5]

An initial indication as to the theoretical significance of *Hamlet* in relation to psychoanalytic theory itself is to be found in the opening lines of Freud's analysis of Shakespeare's tragedy in *The Interpretation of Dreams*. For Freud, as for Hegel, Shakespeare is unquestionably the preeminent modern dramatist, and *Hamlet* is Shakespeare's most significant work:

> Another of the great creations of tragic poetry, Shakespeare's *Hamlet*, has its roots in the same soil as *Oedipus Rex*. But the changed treatment of the same material reveals the whole difference in the mental life of these two widely separated epochs of civilization: the secular advance of repression in the emotional life of mankind. In the *Oedipus* the child's wishful phantasy that underlies it is brought into the open and realized as it would be in a dream. In *Hamlet* it remains repressed; and—just as in the case of a neurosis—we learn of its existence from its inhibiting consequences. (*Interpretation of Dreams*, 4:264)

While the desire that gives form to the Oedipus complex may be universal, repression has a history. That history falls into two stages: the ancient and the modern. Within the framework of this historical theory of repression, Oedipus represents the ancient, and Hamlet, the modern. Or rather, in terms closer to Starobinski's, *Oedipus* provides us with the interpretive schema that permits us to theorize simultaneously the unconscious and the ancient, and *Hamlet* with the interpretive schema that permits us to theorize repression and the modern.

Very clearly, Freud's conception of the historical relationship between Oedipus and Hamlet, like Hegel's, is not merely chronological but also points to a structural relationship. As Freud puts it in *The Interpretation of Dreams*, *Oedipus* corresponds to the dream in which the child's wishful fantasy is brought into the open and realized. *Hamlet*, on the other hand, corresponds to a neurosis, in which the existence of the wish is learned of through its inhibiting consequences. What is at stake in the contrast between Oedipus and Hamlet is thus not only a distinction between historical periods but also the theme or problem of repression, of its nature and origin.

Freud's discussion of *Hamlet* in *The Interpretation of Dreams* provides the theme—repression—with which the figure of Hamlet is consistently associated throughout his work. What it does not provide is a sense of the continuing problem this theme represents for his theory and in particular for his attempt to understand the psyche in economic terms. Freud's interpretation of Oedipus harnesses the contradictions of tragedy and converts their power into a scientifically and theoretically productive force. But the contradictions posed by tragedy for theory resurface in the modern version of tragedy and more specifically in the figure of Hamlet. What is being indicated despite Freud's intentions in his analyses of *Hamlet* is the disruptive nature of repression in relation to the pleasure principle (or, more broadly, of the psychic economy, whatever its ultimate principle of organization might be); that is, the disruptive nature of repression in relation to the very principle that provided Freud with his original explanation of tragedy. As such, repression is a problem that demands not just an extension or refinement but a constant revision of psychoanalytic theory. And yet repression remains a problem even after such revision has been undertaken. The persistence of the problem of repression and also the uneconomical nature of the displeasure it entails are both indications that *modern* tragedy is not just an object among others for psychoanalysis any more than it is for philosophy. Ultimately, Freud needs to refer not just to an ancient tragedy but to a modern tragedy as well, because the unconscious itself, or at any rate an unconscious, is in some irreducible sense modern.

Freud's *Hamlet* and the Problem of Primary Masochism

Freud makes his earliest and in certain respects one of his most significant attempts to come to terms with the problem of repression in his essay "Psychopathic Characters on the Stage."[6] This essay comments from a psychoanalytic perspective on the view that "the purpose of drama is to arouse 'terror and pity' and so 'to purge the emotions'" (7:305). The general theme of this essay is thus the cathartic suffering of the spectator of tragic drama, and the issue of repression emerges in connection with this suffering. Freud's principal problem in "Psychopathic Characters" (as in slightly different terms in the much later essay "On Repression") is to give an economic account of suffering or displeasure. According to the traditional interpretation of Aristotle, the displeasure of the spectator is of a sympathetic kind, and in this sense is less difficult to reconcile with the pleasure principle. But as Freud proceeds in his analysis, he becomes interested in a more direct form of displeasure, one that results from the spectator's own *resistance* (or the *resistance* of his or her unconscious) to the pleasure occasioned by tragic drama—or at least by certain tragic dramas. Freud interprets this resistance as the direct result of repression, since only repression can explain why what should in principle be pleasurable becomes instead a source of displeasure.

Significantly, "Psychopathic Characters" contains the most extended

commentary of *Hamlet* to be found in all Freud's work, and the importance Shakespeare's play assumes in this essay stems from what in
Freud's perspective is its direct relevance to the problem of repression. Freud calls *Hamlet* "the first of [the] modern dramas" (7:309) and
goes on to explain that the modernity of the play lies precisely in its
provoking in the (neurotic) spectator not merely "an *enjoyment* of the
liberation [or discharge of emotion] but a *resistance* to it as well"
(7:309). Tragedy as a whole does not necessarily present psychoanalysis with a problem, because it makes possible a process of blowing
off steam, and this process is a source of relief or pleasure (7:305). But
the specifically modern component of tragedy – resistance or repression – does pose a problem because it is a direct source of displeasure.[7] The challenge *Hamlet* presents to the model of the unconscious
elaborated on the basis of Freud's interpretation of *Oedipus* is already
being suggested here. Given the terms in which Freud himself has
defined modern tragic drama, it would seem that, at the very least, a
serious revision in the interpretation of the psyche based exclusively
on the *Oedipus* model is called for in order to account for the equally
compelling effect *Hamlet* has on its audiences.

"Psychopathic Characters," however, does not provide such a revision, even though it indicates that one is necessary. In the end, Freud
reaffirms the pleasure principle in strong terms, thus preserving
intact the model of the unconscious – and the interpretation of tragedy – he had already outlined four to six years earlier in *The Interpretation of Dreams*.[8] The exorbitant manner in which he does this,
however, seems to contradict his explicit position – it seems to indicate that once the existence of resistance and repression has become
an explicit problem, then the primacy of the pleasure principle is in
jeopardy. Freud argues that only a neurotic can truly enjoy a work
such as Shakespeare's.[9] The whole problem of resistance is thus rele-
gated to abnormal psychology, in order to protect the authority of
Oedipus.

This argument is implicitly insufficient from Freud's own point of
view, however, inasmuch as he brings forward two more to buttress
it. Clearly uneasy about his first argument, he goes on to make the
equally surprising claim that "the dramatist's business is to induce
the same illness in us" as we see in his neurotic hero (7:310). *Hamlet*
pleases only neurotic spectators, but virtually every spectator becomes
neurotic in the course of the play. But there is more. Freud concludes

"Psychopathic Characters" by asserting that even for the more or less neurotic spectator, the pleasure afforded by *Hamlet* overshadows the displeasure it causes. This is because Shakespeare has successfully provided us with libidinal compensation for our suffering, both by diverting our attention in order to allay our resistance and by offering forepleasure.

The additional arguments brought forward to supplement the initial argument, however, have the effect of weakening rather than strengthening it, and Freud is placed in a position he himself was to analyze in *Jokes and Their Relation to the Unconscious*. A man, A, is accused by another man, B, of damaging the kettle he borrowed from him and defends himself with the "argument of the kettle": "First, I never borrowed a kettle from B at all; secondly, the kettle had a hole in it already when I got it from him; and thirdly, I gave him back the kettle undamaged." (*Jokes and Their Relation to the Unconscious*, 8:62). In the conclusion to "Psychopathic Characters," Freud can be seen to argue in a similar spirit when he states that first, only a neurotic can enjoy the displeasure caused by *Hamlet*; second, *Hamlet* makes virtually all spectators into neurotics; and third, even a neurotic spectator derives a pleasure from the play which overshadows his displeasure.

One could argue that, despite the steps Freud takes to reaffirm the primacy of the pleasure principle in the conclusion of his article, what begins to emerge in his discussion of *Hamlet* is something that could be called a negative concept of tragedy, in which suffering would be the central interest of tragedy and not merely an occasion for a pleasurable discharge of emotion. In short, according to this negative concept of tragedy, suffering would be primary or fundamental rather than derivative or incidental. As Philippe Lacoue-Labarthe puts it, borrowing from Freud himself, suffering would be "anterior to the 'pleasure principle' or beyond it—'independent' in any case, 'and, perhaps, more primitive than it'" ("La Scène est primitive," 203). It would thus be more fundamental, more primary than the pleasure principle, *both in terms of tragedy and in terms of the psyche as well*.

Freud already in this article seems reluctant to pursue the path opened up by such a concept of tragedy, no doubt because it is disruptive both of his economic model of the unconscious and of psychoanalysis itself, insofar as its possibility and the possibility of an economic account of the psyche are one and the same. The tragic still confronts Freud as a problem even once it has helped provide him with the concept of the unconscious. The problem of tragic suffering has not been resolved by psychoanalytic theory: finding a way to account for tragedy still looms as an accomplishment that can decide the question of the scientific status of psychoanalysis. The stakes of Freud's interpretation of *Hamlet* and the solution of the problem of repression are thus high. In both this article and the later ones that pursue the problems it raises, Freud can be seen looking for a path that will allow him to account effectively for the displeasure associated with repression *and* retain the economic principle of explanation (even ultimately at the cost of the pleasure principle).

In the group of essays written by Freud in 1914–15, a group that includes "On Narcissism: An Introduction," "Instincts and Their Vicissitudes," and "Mourning and Melancholia," as well as "On Repression," repression becomes a theme and a problem in its own right. These essays already give a clear indication of the radical turning point in his work which Freud himself was to date from the appearance of *Beyond the Pleasure Principle*, since they already point to the insufficiency of the pleasure principle to account for the whole of psychic processes. When the problems raised in "Psychopathic Characters on the Stage" are considered from the perspective of these later articles, one can discern the radical nature of the question that is only beginning to emerge in that brief, early essay. But one could also argue that these later essays, and even *Beyond the Pleasure Principle* itself, can also be read from the perspective of "Psychopathic Characters." Freud, it can also be argued, never abandons the aim of giving an economic explanation to the disruptive forces uncovered by his consideration of the problem of tragic suffering. As a result, these later essays, like "Psychopathic Characters," imply a view of modern tragedy in which its negative elements continue to disrupt psychoanalytic theory and offer a picture of the modern psyche which is only partly consistent with the one Freud derives from *Oedipus*.

Hamlet is referred to only once in the essays comprised in this important group. And yet that brief reference indicates that the set of problems addressed in these papers can legitimately be seen as an attempt to work through certain of the implications of the theory of modern tragedy which Freud's remarks on *Hamlet* in *The Interpretation of Dreams*, his letters to Fliess, and above all his "Psychopathic Characters on the Stage" had left hanging. The reference occurs in "Mourning and Melancholia," where he is describing the heightened

self-criticism of the melancholic: "There can be no doubt that if any-
one holds and expresses to others an opinion of himself such as this
(an opinion which Hamlet held both of himself and of everyone else),
he is ill." To this reference to Shakespeare's hero Freud appends a quotation from act 2, scene 2 of the play: "Use every man after his desert,
and who shall scape whipping?" ("Mourning and Melancholia,"
14:246). Hamlet is thus the prime example of the melancholic, and his
speech can be quoted verbatim as a model of melancholic discourse.[10]

The psychological situation of the melancholic, Freud goes on to
tell us in "Mourning and Melancholia," can be explained only by the
existence of a critical agency "split off from the ego," even though it
is an "institution of the ego" (14:247). This agency, which is "commonly called 'conscience,'" (14:247) is the origin, if not of all forms of
defense, then at least of repression. It represents the ego ideal to the
ego, and the formation of this ideal, as Freud had already argued in
the slightly earlier essay "On Narcissism," is "the conditioning factor
of repression," not just in neurotics, but in the normal individual as
well (14:94). Conscience, it appears, makes not only cowards but also
melancholics of us all. Thus conscience or the superego is the agent
of what from the economic perspective is the paradoxical phenomenon of repression, this strange "process by which the pleasure of satisfaction is changed into unpleasure" ("On Repression," 14:146).

The melancholia so perfectly exemplified by Hamlet already appears to necessitate at least a revision of the view that psychic phenomena are governed solely by a pleasure principle, inasmuch as it
brings about a situation fundamentally similar to the one described
by Freud in a later essay, "The Economic Problem of Masochism."
And yet only in this later essay is the economic problem posed by this
violation of the pleasure principle clearly articulated by Freud himself. Like repression and melancholia, the problematic character of
masochism derives from its contradiction, at least on the surface, of
the Oedipal law that the satisfaction of instincts is a source of pleasure: "The existence of a masochistic trend in the instinctual life of
human beings may justly be described as mysterious from the economic point of view. For if mental processes are governed by the pleasure principle in such a way that their first aim is the avoidance of
unpleasure and the obtaining of pleasure, masochism is incomprehensible" ("Economic Problem of Masochism," 19:159). In this passage we see Freud confront the possibility that, while psychoanalysis

can offer a theory of pleasure, it may not be equal to the task of providing a theory of pain.

The line of questioning Freud pursued beginning with "On Repression" and including "Mourning and Melancholia" thus leads directly to the problem of masochism, and more precisely, to the problem of a *primary* masochism, that is, a form of masochism that is not simply a projection inward of an aggression originally directed outward: "The death instinct which is operative in the organism—primal sadism—is identical with masochism. After the main portion of it has been transposed outwards on to objects, there remains inside, as a residuum of it, the erotogenic masochism proper, which on the one hand has become a component of the libido and, on the other, still has the self as its object" (19:164). As this passage shows, *Beyond the Pleasure Principle* prepares the way for "The Economic Problem of Masochism," by making it clear that the preeminence of the erotic and life instincts is not self-evident and by providing the concept of a death instinct that would be the motor force accounting for the spontaneous character of primary masochism.

By showing that the erotic and life instincts are no more primary than masochism, "The Economic Problem of Masochism" also places the erotic instincts, in particular, in a new light. They have not lost their primary position in the model of the psyche, but because they now share that position with masochism, the death instinct and the erotic instinct become fused in and through the ego/libido. Erotogenic masochism, according to Freud, "has become a component of the libido and, on the other hand, still has the self as its object" ("Economic Problem of Masochism," 19:164).

The picture of the disposition of the *erotic* or *libidinal* elements of the psyche offered in "The Economic Problem of Masochism" is consistent with the one that had been offered earlier in "Mourning and Melancholia" and in *Beyond the Pleasure Principle*. In both of these, Freud had indicated the importance of narcissism in determining the object-choices of the libido. As he argues in "Mourning and Melancholia," *identification* is the basis on which the object of love is selected in the case of the melancholic. This picture of love was to be sustained in *Beyond the Pleasure Principle* when Freud reached the conclusion "that the ego is the true and original reservoir of libido, and that it is only from that reservoir that libido is extended on to objects" (18:52). The second statement confirms the first by showing us the ego/libido making object-choices that are in effect little more than extensions of itself. But it also represents a refinement and further development of the concept of identification as presented in "Mourning and Melancholia." It shows that identification includes not only the process through which objects lying outside the psyche are chosen but also a more primary process through which the ego itself is chosen by the libido, which as a result is said by Freud to be originally housed in the ego.

But the significance of the originally narcissistic nature of identification changes when the problem of masochism is introduced. Instead of making self-love in the traditional sense the original and natural state of the psyche, ambivalence—a mixture of love and hate that corresponds to the primary character of both masochism and the erotic instincts—becomes primary, and *identification*, therefore, now appears as an ambiguous process that is as much negative as positive.[11] "The Economic Problem of Masochism" thus not only points to the original nature of (tragic) suffering. It also indicates the fundamentally ambiguous nature of identification, which now serves no longer only to unify the subject but also to divide it from itself.[12]

"The Economic Problem of Masochism" does not by any means represent the last in the series of steps by which Freud advances toward and retreats from the implications of the questions that originate in his reading of *Hamlet* and in the necessity that imposes it on him as another model for the unconscious. But *Hamlet* can be seen as the source of the entire theoretical chain extending from repression, to melancholia, to the death drive, to primary masochism and beyond, not only for historical reasons, but, more important, because it is Hamlet who realizes not only the wish that lies at the bottom of the Oedipus complex but also the *repression* of that wish by the neurotic and healthy individual alike. In the simplest, most schematic terms, one could say that Oedipus represents the pleasure principle and Hamlet the death drive, which, though Freud maintains that it is never manifest as such, must be posited in order to make certain enigmatic phenomena comprehensible—phenomena such as primary masochism, repression, and melancholia.

Hamlet is thus the exemplary melancholic, that is to say, the exemplary masochist; and in him modern man can come to understand his own masochistic character, the uneconomic and primary nature of the suffering he endures at the hands of the superego, understood now as "a representative of the id" itself ("Economic Problem of Masochism," 19:167) and not merely of an external authority. One can thus see an irony in the triumphant tone of the passage in which Freud asserts that he *alone* has come to grips with Hamlet. It seems equally or more plausible that *Hamlet* has come to grips with Freud. If masochism and repression are primary, then it does not suffice to claim that Shakespeare's *Hamlet* is a reflection of the psychic apparatus. It now appears that "the play's the thing wherein" conscience and the psyche as a whole are "caught" or mirrored. This is so not just because the content of certain plays evokes the content of repressed wishes, but because the psychic apparatus has been revealed as having the character of a *modern* tragic stage, insofar as pain is as primary or even more primary in it than the pleasure afforded by the realization of the deepest unconscious wish. From the moment the existence of repression and the superego becomes problematic for Freud, his model of the psyche risks being transformed into a structure that resembles the scene of modern tragedy, and suffering appears no longer to be merely the price paid by the psyche for its pleasure but instead quite possibly its primary aim.

Freud's *Hamlet* and (Modern) Theory

What Freud in the essay "Mourning and Melancholia" calls conscience and later, the superego, has another function related to its critical nature, a function he describes in his essay "On Narcissism":

> The complaints made by paranoiacs also show that at bottom the self-criticism of conscience coincides with the self-observation on which it is based. Thus the activity of the mind which has taken over the function of conscience has also placed itself at the service of internal research, which furnishes philosophy with the material for its intellectual operations. This may have some bearing on the characteristic tendency of paranoiacs to construct speculative systems. (14:96)

In this passage and in the essay as a whole, we see Freud operating according to a logic he invokes throughout his work. In order to "arrive at an understanding of what seems so simple in normal phenomena," he has turned once again "to the field of pathology with its distortions and exaggerations'' (14:82). In the case of the paranoiac, we see a spectacular example of the link to be found in every individual between the functioning of conscience or the superego and of intellectual operations.

Jacques Lacan and Jean Hyppolite have both pointed out that the link between the operation of the superego (that is, between repression) and intellectual activity is the subject of another essay by Freud, "Negation."[13] Negation is a very specific form of repression, in which the repressed content is admitted into consciousness but continues to be repressed nonetheless, as when the patient tells the analyst, "You ask who this person in the dream can be. It's *not* my mother'" ("Negation," 19:235). In such instances, Freud tells us, the analyst can safely assume it *is* the mother.

According to Hyppolite, if we want to understand the essay "Negation" in all its "philosophical density," we must note and weigh carefully Freud's use in it of *Aufhebung* as a synonym for *Verneinung* or negation. Hyppolite quotes from Freud: "Negation is an *Aufhebung* of repression, but is not for all that an acceptance of the repressed" ("Commentaire," 881).[14] For Hyppolite this passage from Freud's work raises an obvious question: is it merely a coincidence that Hegel and Freud both use the term *Aufhebung*, or does it point to a deeper link between psychoanalysis and philosophy? His answer is that a deeper link must in fact exist, because the psychoanalytic term *negation* and the philosophical term *Aufhebung* are in fact virtually identical. Both mean "at one and the same time negate, suppress and retain, and fundamentally raise to a higher level" (Hyppolite, "Commentaire," 880–81).

The singularity of negation as compared to other forms of repression lies in that it allows the neurotic to become conscious of the repressed content, even though it continues to be repressed. In this sense it differs from the dream, in which unconscious desires also find expression, but in a distorted form. And yet it could be argued that all expressions of the unconscious that reach consciousness take the basic form of negation, inasmuch as distortion and reversal are only other modes of negation, other ways of saying, "This is *not* my mother." In other words, all repression involves negating, suppressing, and retaining, and raising to a higher level.

There is thus a deep and complex link between psychoanalysis and philosophy because intellectual activity is an extension of the process of negation/repression. As Hyppolite stresses, it is quite true that negation is not yet intellectual judgment in the full sense, just as Freud considers that "repression is [only] a preliminary stage of condemnation" or judgment ("On Repression," 14:146). But we can nonetheless recognize all forms of intellectual and theoretical activity beginning to emerge in negation/repression—including philosophical speculation and psychoanalysis itself.

The broader implication of Hyppolite's reading is clear. Like Hegelian philosophy, psychoanalysis also involves a dialectic, in which repression plays an ambiguous role as both an element of the unconscious and the first step in the emergence of theory. Repression, like the *Aufhebung*, marks a coming into consciousness, in a form appropriate to consciousness, of what was previously unconscious. But the reverse is also implicitly true. The *Aufhebung*, like repression, hides what it reveals; it not only creates consciousness but also simultaneously roots consciousness in an unconscious it can never fully master, and, I would emphasize, in a displeasure it can never fully theorize, that is, make pleasurable.

By linking intellectual and theoretical activity to negation or repression, Hyppolite's commentary points beyond Freud's article "Negation" to the other texts analyzed here in which the question of the origin of repression is pursued. Whatever that origin, it is *also* the origin of intellectual activity, of judgment, of philosophy, and of psychoanalysis itself. Freud's reflections on *Hamlet* thus provide a theoretical matrix within which not only the problem of repression but also the problem of intellectual activity, and ultimately of psychoanalysis itself, emerge. In other words, in the dialectic of psychoanalysis, as in the dialectic of speculative philosophy, Hamlet occupies a similarly pivotal position. He represents the *Aufhebung*/repression of both the ancient by the modern and of the unconscious and tragic by the theoretical. He is the tragic hero as theorist, and the suffering he endures is not merely the price he pays for knowledge and self-knowledge but a fundamental element of it.

Starobinski's argument can now be completed in the following manner: if *Oedipus* is (the model of) the unconscious, then *Hamlet* is (the model of) the theory of the unconscious, but that theory must now be understood as radically and irreducibly implicated in the processes it seeks to analyze. Theory no longer appears spontaneous, or rather, its spontaneity is that of primary masochism, the death drive, and repression. Even as a figure for theory itself, Hamlet remains a *tragic hero*. In this sense he indicates that psychoanalysis itself, and not just this or that psychoanalyst, remains the thing, if not directly of the drives it seeks to theorize, then of the scene that frames—and represses—those drives for the modern spectator.

There is thus still implicitly something negative in *Hamlet* for Freud as for Hegel, something that is being denied as much as admired—as Lacoue-Labarthe indicates when he comments on the perplexing fact that Freud never published "Psychopathic Characters" and seems even to have forgotten the article or at the very least to have relinquished it ("La Scène est primitive," 187). Of course, throughout his work, Freud's explicit posture in relation to art and poetry is one of admiration.[15] Even more, Freud freely acknowledges the convergence of the findings of psychoanalysis and the insights of artists and poets and also what to him appears to be the relatively greater ease and simplicity with which they arrive at their conclusions. Poets, he writes in a typical passage, can "save without effort from the whirlpool of their own feelings the deepest truths, towards which the rest of us have to find our way through tormenting uncertainty and with restless groping" (*Civilization and Its Discontents*, 21:133.) In passages such as these, Freud is affirming the similarity between the truths uncovered by the psychoanalyst and the poet. However, what is still being denied is the deeper similarity between psychoanalysis and art, inasmuch as nothing could be less alike than the effortless recovery of the deepest truths from the whirlpool of the poet's own feelings and the torment, uncertainty, restlessness, and groping of psychoanalysis. What is still being denied, in other words, is the deeper affinity between art and psychoanalysis, between Hamlet and the theoretician.

When the function of the figure of Hamlet in psychoanalytic theory is interpreted in terms of its potentially disruptive implications, it reveals that the identification of psychoanalysis with Shakespeare's play is uneasy at best. The process through which psychoanalysis comes implicitly to recognize itself in Hamlet is potentially painful for psychoanalysis, however, not because it involves a loss of the sense of the superiority of the rational and theoretical in relation to the intuitive and subjective. It is, rather, because the process makes apparent the theoretical character of both art and psychoanalysis—that is to say, the displeasure or suffering they share.

Racine's *Iphigénie* and Modern Tragic Guilt

Though Racine's tragedies were never the subject of a psychoanalytic study by Freud himself, the readiness with which they lend themselves to interpretation from a psychoanalytic perspective is attested to by the works of several literary analysts. Roland Barthes's, André Green's, and Charles Mauron's readings of Racine each, from a somewhat different perspective, confirm the fruitfulness of psychoanalytic criticism, understood as the application of psychoanalytic categories and schemas to the study of works of literature. For Barthes, Racine's tragedies invite a psychoanalytic reading "because only a language such as psychoanalysis, which is . . . capable of registering fear of the world, appeared appropriate" to him for the analysis of the Racinian hero.[16] For Green, whose *Un Oeil en trop* is inspired by Bataille, Nietzsche, and Artaud, as well as Freud, Racine's plays serve to trace the gradual effacement of the emotions associated with the Dionysian ritual in which tragedy originates, in both historical and psychic terms.[17] For Mauron, the psychoanalytic interpretation of Racine's plays provide a particularly rich document of the "temptations or . . . defenses, . . . desires or . . . fears" of its author.[18] After reading the works of Barthes, Green, and Mauron, one gets the strong impression that for them psychoanalytic criticism and Racine's tragedies were made for each other.

And yet, once Freud's concepts of the superego, masochism, and repression are analyzed in their problematic relation to modern tragedy, the whole question of the affinity between Racine's plays and psychoanalysis appears in a different light. We can, of course, like Mauron, Barthes, and Green, still use psychoanalysis to define themes and structures that Racine's plays can then be seen to echo. But we can also view those plays, along with Hegel's *Aesthetics* and psychoanalytic theory itself, as different elements in a more or less continuous theory of tragedy, and their affinities, therefore, as historically determined rather than as a reflection of the way in which Racine's plays embody the truths of psychoanalysis in dramatic form. Moreover, from the standpoint of this broader historical tradition encompassing both psychoanalysis (or philosophy) and tragedy, Racine's tragedies and his critical texts would appear to contribute no less actively than the texts of Hegel and Freud to the elaboration of the problematic concept of modern tragedy, inasmuch as a central, if not *the* central interest in Racine's texts, as in Freud's, lies in how they deal with the "modern" dimension of the problem of tragic guilt.

Racine's reflections on his own work—specifically his prefaces to the published versions of his plays—most often take the form of a comparison between his tragedies and those of the ancients from whom he frequently borrows. In contrast to Corneille, Racine is much clearer in expressing his allegiance to the ancients, and perhaps the best example of his attitude is found in his preface to *Iphigénie*.[19] Yet it can also be seen in this same preface and in other texts as well that Racine's relationship to the ancients is in certain respects as ambiguous and ambivalent as Corneille's.

In the exploration of the complexities of this relationship, however, a second problem, which is inextricably linked to the first, emerges almost immediately. In Freud's terms it could be called the problem of the superego. In Racine's terms it is the problem of tragic guilt or destiny. All Racine's plays and most of his prefaces also refer more or less directly to this second, crucial problem. In Racine's terms any clear definition of the relationship between ancient and modern tragedy must simultaneously find the rationality underlying the contradiction posed by tragic guilt.

The preface to *Iphigénie* is particularly instructive not only in indicating the nature and importance of these two problems but in showing their interdependence as well. As André Green notes (*Un Oeil en trop*, 167), this tragedy is very different from what it was initially projected to be—little more than a translation of Racine's ancient model, Euripides' *Iphigenia in Aulide*. While the preface to Racine's *Iphigénie* contains one of his strongest affirmations of the authority of the ancients and the classical (or neoclassical) nature of his own work, it also acknowledges and discusses in detail the changes he has made in Euripides' tragedy. Racine is forced into an uncharacteristic admission that he has departed from his ancient model because of the problems presented by the treatment of the theme of guilt in *Iphigenia in Aulide* and also in other ancient versions of Iphigenia's story. In his preface, Racine can be seen attempting to resolve the question of his relation to the ancients through a critical reflection on the subject of ancient guilt—a reflection apparent in the play as well.

Racine states in his preface that, though he has borrowed heavily from Euripides' play, he finds the conclusion unacceptable for the modern stage. According to that conclusion, Diane, having taken pity on Iphigénie, has her transported to Tauride by supernatural means, and a doe is sacrificed in her place. Racine also notes that in other versions of her story found in the work of other ancient playwrights, including Aeschylus and Sophocles, Iphigénie is actually sacrificed. These he finds equally unacceptable. However respectful Racine may be of the authority of the ancients, he feels he can no longer accept it completely when confronted with these two possible conclusions:

> What chance was there that I would defile the stage by the horrible murder of a person as virtuous and lovable as Iphigénie had to be represented as being? And what chance was there of [successfully] concluding my tragedy through the help of a goddess and a machine, and by a metamorphosis that could indeed be believed in the time of Euripides, but which would be too absurd and too incredible to us? (*Iphigénie*, 670)

We moderns would find it outrageous if an innocent Iphigénie were sacrificed. The version in which Iphigénie is rescued by Diane is implicitly even more unacceptable, however, because it solves the problem posed by the sacrifice of a "virtuous and lovable" victim through supernatural means.

Racine's aim is of course not to defy the authority of the ancients but, rather, to devise a conclusion that can satisfy both the ancient and the modern sense of justice. Iphigénie must be saved from an unjust punishment, but she cannot be saved by supernatural means. The substitution of Eriphile for Iphigénie at the conclusion of the tragedy thus represents Racine's attempt to resolve the opposition between a modern conception of ethics based on a conscious sense of responsibility and an ancient conception of punishment and guilt which to "us" appears irrational and unacceptable but still carries much authority because it is ancient. Iphigénie does not die, but Eriphile (whose name, significantly, is also Iphigénie) does. Moreover, Eriphile, like Iphigénie, is innocent in the sense that she has committed no crime that clearly merits her sacrifice. But she is not so "virtuous and worthy of love" as Iphigénie. Thus her character in itself represents an attempt to reconcile the ancient and the modern, because she must be imperfect enough so that her sacrifice appears less outrageous than would that of Iphigénie, but she must be innocent enough so that her death has *some* of the horror that Iphigénie's would have had for the modern audience, had she been sacrificed.

The principle according to which Racine seeks to reconcile the ancient and the modern is thus exemplified in Eriphile's character, understood as neither good nor bad. Though the poetic justification for this principle is articulated with particular clarity in relation to Eriphile, it can, however, be shown to constitute the essence of Racine's view and practice as concerns the construction of character[20] in all of his plays. His preface to *Andromaque*, for example, gives another justification of the mixed nature of his heroes and heroines. To those who criticize his characters for their moral defects, Racine responds:

> I beg them to remember that it is not for me to change the rules of the theater. Horace recommends that we describe Achilles as fierce, inexorable, and violent, such as he was and such as his son was described. And Aristotle, far from asking that our heroes be perfect, on the contrary wants tragic characters, that is to say, those whose misfortune is the catastrophe of the tragedy, to be neither altogether good nor altogether bad. He does not want them to be extremely good, because the punishment of a good man would excite the spectator's indignation rather than his pity; nor that they be excessively bad, because one has no pity for a scoundrel. (*Andromaque*, 242)

Racine happily finds a conception of the tragic hero that is very similar to his own in the highest of all ancient authorities—Aristotle's *Poetics*. He can thus deviate from Aeschylus, Sophocles, and Euripides and still claim to be respecting the authority of the ancients. But his finding support for his own position in Aristotle should not be allowed to obscure the modernity of his uneasiness with the contradictory nature of tragic guilt as presented in the plays of the ancients and the way he attempts, through his conception of character, to rationalize and in this sense modernize tragic guilt.

The idea that the tragic hero or heroine should be neither good nor bad is also invoked by Racine to explain the character of Phèdre— even more, to explain that aspect of Phèdre's character which Hegel finds so objectionable in both artistic and ethical terms.[21] Phèdre, according to Racine, is "neither altogether guilty nor altogether innocent" (*Phèdre*, 745), and an aspect of this mixed character is evident in her relation to Oenone:

> I even took pains to make her [Phèdre] a bit less odious than she is in the tragedies of the ancients, where she resolves on her

own to accuse Hippolyte. I felt that calumny was too low and too black to be put in the mouth of a princess whose sentiments are in all other respects so noble and virtuous. This baseness appeared to me more appropriate to a nurse, who might have more servile inclinations, and who in any case only initiates this false accusation in order to save the life and the honor of her mistress. (745)

Here too, the principle followed by Racine is the same. Phèdre must be neither good nor bad if she is to be a tragic heroine and if she is to exemplify the character of tragic guilt. What to Hegel appeared as vacillation and lack of firmness appears to Racine as the essence of tragic character.

Racine's insistence that the hero be neither good nor bad is thus a step that forms a part of his reflection on the enigma of tragic guilt; and it would be a mistake to interpret that insistence as some kind of commonsense interpretation of Aristotle based on the idea that the hero should be average or not perfect in order to foster the spectator's identification with him. The notion of being neither good nor bad is meaningless in relation to Racine's characters (and in relation to those of Sophocles, Aeschylus, and Euripides as well) if it indicates a moral mediocrity.

Though Hegel has very little to say about the problem of tragic guilt, what little he does say is helpful in understanding the next step Racine takes in his attempt to come to terms with it. Hegel's most important allusion in the *Aesthetics* to the problem of tragic guilt concerns precisely the issue of what he calls the plasticity of the ancient tragic heroes—in the terms of Racine and Aristotle, the idea that they should be neither good nor bad. Basing his remarks on the character of Oedipus as he is portrayed in the two Sophoclean tragedies recounting his life, Hegel defines plasticity as the coexistence in him of the bad and the good, the intentional and the unintentional, the conscious and—the unconscious:

> What is at issue here [in *Oedipus Rex* and *Oedipus at Colonnus*] is the right of the wide awake consciousness, the justification of what the man has self-consciously willed and knowingly done, as contrasted with what he was fated by the gods to do and actually did unconsciously and without having willed it. . . . On the [modern] presupposition that a man is only guilty if alternatives are open to him and he decides arbitrarily on what he does, the

> Greek plastic figures are innocent: they act out of this character
> of theirs, of *this* "pathos," because this character, this "pathos"
> is precisely what they are. . . . It is just the strength of the great
> characters that they do not choose but throughout, from start to
> finish, *are* what they will and accomplish. (*Aesthetics*, 1214)

Though it would be an exaggeration to say that in this passage Hegel
invents the Freudian notion of an unconscious, he at least can be seen
to take a step in its direction in order to come to terms with the
"guilty innocence" of the Greek heroes. Without at least a pre-
Freudian notion of an unconscious, there is no way to describe the
Greek heroes and even begin to account for their simultaneous guilt
and innocence. The Greek hero is plastic—that is to say, in other
terms, he is neither good nor bad because he is *both* good and bad,
because though he is consciously good, he is unconsciously bad.

Thus, though Racine's heroine Phèdre is criticized by Hegel as
defective, in fact Racine, in a manner initially like Hegel but increasingly like Freud, also focuses on the *unconscious* nature of tragic crime
in order to clarify the peculiar nature of tragic guilt. Racine's first tragedy, *La Thébaïde*, already spells out this central preoccupation and
indicates that for him, as for Hegel, the notion of unconscious or involuntary crime offers the only explanation for the punishment
suffered by the heroes of tragedy. As Jocaste puts it:

> O heaven, your rigors would not be so deadly
> If the thunderbolt crushed the guilty straightaway!
> . . . .
> And yet, oh gods, an involuntary crime
> Should it incur all your wrath?
> Did I recognize, alas, this unhappy son?
> You yourselves led him into my arms.
> (*La Thébaïde*, act 3, scene 2, pp. 137–38)

Only if the Gods punish unconscious crimes with the same severity
as conscious ones can tragic destiny and tragic guilt be understood in
rational terms.

But at this point, Racine takes a step that leads him beyond the
logic of ancient tragedy and ancient guilt as exemplified in *Oedipus*
and as understood by Hegel, a step that amounts to a radical attempt
to grasp its fundamental nature. It is as if Racine's plays were telling
us, "But if the Gods punish unconscious crimes—crimes that from

the modern perspective are not crimes at all—with the same severity as conscious ones, then it is not really any more surprising that they punish even when there is apparently no crime." Indeed, while Jocaste's crime was unconscious in the sense that it was involuntary, the "crimes" for which Racine's other characters suffer are often even more obscure—unconscious in a deeper sense. Very frequently, Racine's characters are punished without having committed a deed that either they or the spectator can identify as even an involuntary or unconscious crime; in *Andromaque*, Oreste is the character who articulates this paradox:

> My innocence begins at last to weigh on me.
> I know that an unjust power always
> Leaves crime in peace and pursues innocence.
> Wherever I turn my eyes upon myself
> I see naught but misfortunes that condemn the gods.
> Let us deserve their anger, let us justify their hatred
> And may the fruits of the crime precede the punishment.
>
> (Act 3, scene 1, p. 271)

In a bitterly ironic outburst, Oreste declares himself ready to commit a crime in order to rationalize his suffering.

But of course, the crime never precedes the punishment in Oreste's case or in the case of many other Racinian heroes and heroines. Oreste not only never wins Hermione's love, but he never succeeds in taking her by violence; and yet he suffers as if he had. He is punished by something even worse than the loss of his life when he is forced to recognize what for him is the unthinkable: that he does not even exist for Hermione, who has only used him as a means in her struggle to gain recognition (love) from Pyrrhus. The madness Oreste experiences in the closing lines of *Andromaque* reflects the radical, utterly self-negating consequences of his failure to gain the recognition of the other, but it also reflects the unthinkable nature of Oreste's punishment and of the punishment of the other characters as well. It simply cannot be fully rationalized, and our very attempts to understand it rationally only lead to an inconceivable paradox—that of a punishment without a specific crime.

The case of *Iphigénie* provides perhaps the most spectacular version of this situation in all of Racine's work, and in this sense it can be considered the exemplary Racinian play. For the Gods to demand the sacrifice of Iphigénie is more unthinkable than the punishment of an Oreste or even an Hyppolite—though Hyppolite's fate too deserves special scrutiny. In Iphigénie's own words: "Heaven! for so much rigor, of what am I guilty?" (*Iphigénie*, act 3, scene 5, p. 706). In the words of Agamemnon: "I do not know for what crime / The anger of the gods demands a victim" (act 4, scene 4, p. 716). For the gods to demand her sacrifice is in effect to punish the innocent, or else to affirm the existence of a primary guilt from which no one escapes. Even though Racine's chosen conclusion to the play averts the monstrosity of Iphigénie's sacrifice, the possibility of just such a primary guilt is clearly posed in *Iphigénie* as well as in Oreste's speech in *Andromaque*.[22]

The tragic world of Racine thus appears to be governed by a primary masochism, inasmuch as many Racinian heroes and heroines are punished despite having committed no crime, even a distorted crime of the type found in Shakespeare's *Hamlet*. Their guilt has no history, and the suffering they endure is thus spontaneous and original. We have seen how, in his interpretation of *Oedipus* and the culture that produced it, Freud argues that in the ancient tragic world "the child's wishful phantasy"—in other words, his wishful crime—is "brought into the open and realized as it would be in a dream" (*Interpretation of Dreams*, 4:264). The world of the Racinian characters seems to be the antithesis of the world of Oedipus, and it bears some resemblance to the world of Hamlet only insofar as Shakespeare's play also raises the issue of the primary nature of repression and guilt.

Thus, it could be argued, in Freud's terms, that Racine's plays mark *two* steps in the advance of repression, the first of which takes them beyond *Oedipus* and the second beyond even *Hamlet*. In the logic of Freud's distinction between the ancient and the modern, the unconscious and the neurotic, Racine's plays could be seen as offering an image not just of neurosis but of madness, inasmuch as the Oedipal situation is no longer simply distorted and repressed but to a great extent "forcluded." But, as with *Hamlet*, Racine's portrayal of character can serve both to illustrate certain aspects of psychoanalytic theory and to question critically other aspects of it. Racine's plays can be seen both as case studies relating to specific categories of psychic disorder and as an active, critical mirror in which Freudian theory can be confronted with its *own* hesitations and contradictions, especially as concerns the fundamental problem of primary masochism.

As we have seen, the possibility of such a masochism is constantly

indicated by Freud but never fully accepted. Though he acknowledges its existence, he nonetheless seeks to derive primary masochism from the child's well-founded fear of punishment. In doing so, he
betrays his determination to find an economic explanation that would
in the last instance deny masochism its primacy.[23]

With the exception of the *New Introductory Lectures*, which recapit-
ulates the conclusions of *Beyond the Pleasure Principle*, and "The Economic Problem of Masochism," Freud's later essays develop the line
of reflection opened up there not in terms of the problem of masochism per se but, rather, in terms of conscience and the superego. There
is a good reason for this. A central aspect of Freud's argument concerning the superego is that it is the last of the psychic instances to
emerge. If the punishment meted out by the superego is the cause of
the displeasure of the ego, and if the superego is, as he argues at
length in *Civilization and Its Discontents*, the principal cause of (unconscious) displeasure, then pain and displeasure are also, at least by
and large, secondary or late developments, and the existence of a primary form of masochism or suffering appears less significant. Freud
thus shifts from a primary to a defensive masochism adopted by the
ego as a reaction to the cruelty of the superego: "The fear of this critical agency [the super-ego], which is at the bottom of the whole relationship [between the super-ego and the ego], the need for punishment, is an instinctual manifestation on the part of the ego, which
has become masochistic under the influence of a sadistic super-ego"
(*Civilization and Its Discontents*, 21:136). "'Thus conscience does make
cowards of us all,'" Freud writes in a note at the beginning of chapter
8 of *Civilization and Its Discontents*, but this parting nod to Hamlet
acknowledges the guilty hero rather than the melancholic or masochistic one.

Yet one could argue that there is in fact a deep link between the primary phenomenon of masochism and the much later emergence of
the superego and even the emergence at some intermediate stage of
the sense of guilt, which according to Freud predates the superego
per se. What Freud identifies as primary masochism in "The Economic Problem of Masochism" can be seen as serving as a primary
guilt—that is, a displeasure that already has the character of the displeasure caused by the superego and the sense of guilt, but without
being related to any of the specific events to which Freud ties their
emergence. According to Freud himself, primary masochism brings

together the death instinct and the ego—the psychic forces from which the superego will be formed—and places them in the same relation to each other that they will be in once the superego is instituted. Primary masochism, as we have seen, is comprised of that portion of the death instinct which is not transposed outward onto objects but "remains inside, as a residuum of it." This remaining portion of the death drive "still has the self as its object" ("Economic Problem of Masochism," 19:164). The situation produced by conscience and, more spectacularly, by melancholia, is essentially the same. As Freud puts it in "The Ego and the Id," "In melancholia, the superego [becomes] a kind of gathering-place for the death instincts" which it then directs against the ego (19:54). With the emergence of the superego, the death instinct is (once again) directed against the ego, just as it was in the case of primary masochism. Thus in effect, primary masochism is a proto- or an archi-superego, in which the superego as such is grounded.

The idea that primary masochism is an archi-superego in turn explains the paradox of the innocence of Racine's tragic characters, as well as the version of that same paradox that confronts Freud when he examines the problem of guilt. In Racine's plays, as we have seen, tragic destiny treats innocent and guilty characters with the same severity. Freud comes up against the same problem when he acknowledges the seemingly unaccountable severity of the superego of those who, in his words, "have carried saintliness furthest" (*Civilization and Its Discontents*, 21:126). If the superego emerged from the ego as a reaction to the moral infractions of the subject, it would be least developed in those who are (consciously) blameless. But, on the contrary, observation shows us that the saintly are most apt to "reproach themselves with the worst sinfulness" (21:126). The implication is obvious, paradoxical though it may be: "Instinctual renunciation creates conscience, which then demands further instinctual renunciation" (21:129). Though he retreats from it in the passages of *Civilization and Its Discontents* that follow this one, Freud's argument here is that the origin of instinctual renunciation is . . . instinctual renunciation, and that conscience is the creation of . . . conscience. According to this logic, guilt appears, once again, not as a response to events but, rather, as a structure as primary or even more primary than the crimes for which the superego punishes the ego.[24]

The primary nature of guilt would account for or at least square better with a second, crucial characteristic of the superego, intimately related to the fact that the severity of the superego only increases with instinctual renunciation. The superego, Freud repeatedly reminds us, though it represses instincts, is nonetheless derived from them: it is an institution of the id as much as of the ego.[25] As such, the superego conforms to a law of the unconscious which Freud established very early: the unconscious carries within it no "indication of reality."[26] The superego accordingly reveals itself to be wholly unconcerned with whether or not the ego has in fact committed the crimes for which it is punished. It treats unconscious thoughts, unconscious acts, and conscious thoughts all in the same manner as it treats conscious acts (and may in fact even treat unconscious thoughts with the greatest severity).[27] The superego, in other words, behaves exactly like tragic destiny, and the psyche appears to have the character of the stage on which modern tragedy plays itself out.

In the tragic universe of Racine's plays, we can also see that the superego/destiny is indifferent to the question of whether or not the moral law has in reality been broken, and thus it punishes thoughts as severely as actual crimes. In his preface to *Phèdre*, Racine writes: "What I can assure you is that I have written [no play] in which virtue is thrown into greater relief than in this one. In it the slightest faults are severely punished. The mere thought of crime is regarded with as much horror as crime itself" (747). Racine might have added, in commenting on his own play, that the absence of even the thought of crime is treated in the same manner as the thought of crime, as we see in the fate of Hippolyte. Roland Barthes is certainly right not to contrast the characters of Hippolyte and Phèdre, but to treat them instead as doubles (*Sur Racine*, 116). If the totally innocent Hippolyte suffers a fate as terrible as or perhaps even more terrible than that of Phèdre, it can be only because from the standpoint of "the gods"–that is, from the standpoint of guilt–their status is the same.

The relative absence or at any rate the deemphasis of action is another characteristic of Racinian dramaturgy which can be seen as a logical consequence of the view that guilt is primary rather than a later development in the history of the psyche. In Racine's theater, because more often than not no criminal deed is committed to warrant punishment, the action often appears slight or nonexistent. One of Racine's most cryptic but also most revealing statements about his work can be interpreted in terms of a modern conception of the problem of guilt. The "simplicity of action" of the ancients cannot be carried too far, he argues in a celebrated passage: "In tragedy, only the plausible ["le vraisemblable"] touches us. And how plausible is it that there happen in one day a multitude of things that could hardly have happened in several weeks? There are some who think that . . . simplicity is the indication of a lack of invention. They do not imagine that, on the contrary, invention consists in making something of nothing" (Bérénice, 466).

Of course, Racine (like Corneille) was to be repeatedly criticized for his interpretation of the three unities, and much of eighteenth- and nineteenth-century theater criticism can be, if not reduced then at any rate linked to this anti-Racinian strain.[28] As we have seen, Hegel's criticisms of French dramatic poetry in the Aesthetics concern chiefly the issue of portrayal of character. But his distaste for French drama finds additional confirmation in what he, like Lessing and many others, sees as a too rigid interpretation of the rules concerning the unities of action, place, and time.[29]

Racine's radical interpretation of the unities, however, is perfectly consistent with the idea that tragic guilt is primary in nature. Dramatic invention consists in making something of nothing, at least in part because the true nature of tragic guilt is apparent only when its primary character is revealed; and its primary character becomes apparent only when we see guilt operating in the absence of any act or crime. The restrictive interpretation of the unity of action, time, and place embodied in Racine's theater is thus most appropriate to (modern) tragedy because, in its ideal form, the form that would fully realize or express the nature of (modern) tragic guilt, the tragic action is the "nothing" of which Racine speaks in his preface to Bérénice.

Many of the features of Racine's overall dramatic style thus relate to the primary character of modern tragic guilt, but so do the characteristics of individual tragic heroes and heroines. This is especially true of the character of Eriphile in Iphigénie, whom critics have long identified as one of the most important and most tragic of Racine's heroines. Despite significant differences in their interpretations, Barthes, Green, and Goldmann, for example, all agree that without Eriphile there would be no tragedy of Iphigénie. For Barthes, she is the one genuinely tragic character (and the one non–family member) in what would otherwise be a family comedy or romance (Sur Racine, 114). For Goldmann, "there is no link between the tragic universe of Eriphile and the providential universe of Iphigénie" (*Le Dieu caché*, 404). For Green, Eriphile is the one Racinian character who truly represents the authentic, Dionysian spirit of (ancient) tragedy: "With the sacrifice of Eriphile, *horror religiosus* reigns once again on the stage and the sacred with which ancient tragedy was suffused resurfaces after having appeared to have been effaced" (*Un Oeil en trop*, 214).

For each of these critics, Eriphile is thus preeminently tragic not only in the sense that hers is a particularly moving or pathetic fate, but also in the sense that she incarnates the very essence of tragedy itself. This view of her character can be understood in even more depth when it is analyzed in terms of the problem of modern tragic guilt. As nearly every modern commentator of *Iphigénie* has noted, by far the most striking element in the character of Eriphile is her masochism. The term is explicitly employed by Green in connection with his interpretation of her character. But even when the term itself is absent, those who analyze Eriphile are virtually unanimous in seeing the lines in which she describes the origins of her love for Achille as the key to her character and in underscoring the self-destructive nature they reveal. It is not, she confides to her *suivante* Doris, his specious expressions of sympathy for her plight that have made her love Achille. On the contrary, it is her enemy and captor whom she loves (*Iphigénie*, act 2, scene 1, pp. 689–90). There is always a possibility that the audience will give an "economic" interpretation to this declaration and see it as an admission that she loves Achille *despite* his being her abductor. Racine, however, ensures that the audience will understand these lines correctly—he uses Iphigénie to make it implacably clear that Eriphile loves Achille *because* he is her abductor. In response to Eriphile's protestation that she could not possibly love the man who has devastated her former home of Lesbos, Iphigénie replies:

> Yes, you love him, perfidious woman
> And this same furor that you describe to me,
> These arms that you saw bathed in blood,
> These dead, this Lesbos, these ashes, this flame
> Are the arrows with which love has engraved him in your soul.
> (Act 2, scene 5, p. 697)

Of all Racine's heroines, Eriphile is the one who perhaps best exemplifies the tragic and destructive character of Racinian love, a love in which pleasure and pain are indistinguishable.

Though the masochism of Eriphile is particularly striking, this psychological trait—but of course it is more than that—is not confined to her. Green and Mauron, for example, both argue against distinguishing in too rigid a manner between Eriphile and the other characters of *Iphigénie*, and between Eriphile and Iphigénie in particular. As they point out, Eriphile and Iphigénie are in fact similar in a profound way—what is explicitly indicated at the end of the play when we learn that Eriphile's real name is also Iphigénie is implicitly indicated throughout the play. As Green puts it, Iphigénie's quick and correct interpretation of the signs of Eriphile's (masochistic) love can signify only that she herself is experienced in such matters (*Un Oeil en trop*, 192-93)—that, as I would say, she identifies with it. The scene in which Iphigénie recognizes Eriphile's love for Achille is thus also a recognition scene (albeit a tacit one) in another sense. It indicates that Iphigénie is able to understand Eriphile's love for Achille because of a similarity in their situations. That similarity lies not only in her love for Achille but also, and even more importantly, in her steadfast—and masochistic—love for her father, a love that persists even though, or rather, inasmuch as he is ready to sacrifice her on her marriage altar (192). Iphigénie's ability to understand Eriphile is thus a sign to the audience that Iphigénie's own character must be understood in terms of Eriphile's masochism. Though we learn at the end of the play that Eriphile is literally another Iphigénie, according to Green's interpretation we can see in this scene that Iphigénie is another Eriphile.

But if there is an Eriphile lurking inside the pure and virtuous Iphigénie, one could argue that there is an Iphigénie (an Eriphile) within all the Racinian characters who are portrayed as being in a masochistic relationship to a parent—that is, who continue to revere a parent who punishes them. There is an Iphigénie in Phèdre, who imagines her father, the god Minos, forced to invent a new punishment for her, his child, as she enters the underworld (*Phèdre*, act 4, scene 6, p. 791); but there is also an Iphigénie in many of Racine's male characters. In his other plays, the situation of the sons who are in conflict with their fathers often mirrors that of Iphigénie, in the sense that Racine underscores their love and respect for the father and at the same time the terrible punishment the father is ready to mete out to the son: Xipharès in *Mithradate* and Hippolyte are two obvious examples.

Roland Barthes has argued that Oedipal conflict is the true basis of every Racinian tragedy.[30] If this is so, then one would have to add that in his portrayal of the Oedipal situation, Racine indicates that a certain masochism is its fundamental element. In Freud's terms, the superego is erected on the ground prepared by the Oedipal complex, and, Racine would add, the Oedipal complex has itself sprung from the terrain of primary masochism. The idea that the masochistic situation of Eriphile and Iphigénie can serve as the model for a Racinian Oedipus is supported by a very important parallel between the hero of Sophocles and the heroine of Racine. In the words of Barthes, Eriphile "fervently wishes to die from knowing herself ("veut pleinement mourir de se connaître"), thus accomplishing the fundamental tragic contradiction, that of Oedipus" (*Sur Racine*, p. 110). Like Oedipus's, Eriphile's tragic destiny is accomplished in the same moment in which she learns her true identity.

When Barthes describes the fundamental conflicts depicted by Racine as so many versions of the Oedipus complex, he tells only part of the story of Racinian tragedy, however. For what is striking about the Oedipal situation in Racine's tragedies generally, and especially in *Iphigénie* (and *Phèdre*), is that it is so often interpreted from the perspective of the female characters.[31] And when it is interpreted from the standpoint of the male characters, their masochistic relation to the parent is highlighted. Charles Mauron formulates the issue in the clearest and most succinct terms when he writes, "Why *Phèdre*, and why not *Oedipus*?" (*L'Inconscient*, 146). Racine's own contemporaries frequently commented – often negatively – on the femininity or effeminacy of Racine's characters, especially when they are contrasted with the heroes and "virile" heroines of Corneille.[32] This impression, it can be argued, is rooted in the deepest levels of Racine's works and is one more sign of the predominance of a psychology of masochism in his theater, at least if, following Freud, one postulates masochism as being in some sense inherently feminine ("Economic Problem of Masochism," 19:161–63).

Here again, however, one can speak of Racine's interpretation of ancient tragedy, in this case of the figure of Oedipus, as a distortion of the initial ancient (unconscious) situation. *Or* one can see it as providing the basis of an analysis and critical reflection on it. From the second perspective, Racine's decision to treat the Oedipal situation in terms of women characters relates to one of the most problematic aspects of Freud's theory of the Oedipus complex and his concomitant theory of the emergence of the superego—the whole question of the "dissolution of the female Oedipus complex."

According to Freud, the dissolution of the Oedipus complex, though complicated, is nonetheless relatively understandable in the case of the boy ("Dissolution of the Oedipus Complex," 19:177). It is as a result of this dissolution that the superego is instituted, through the interiorization of the idealized imagos of the parents. In the case of the little boy, these developments occur when he is forced, by the threat of castration, to renounce—or repress—his love for his mother and his hostility toward his father. But, as Freud himself readily acknowledges, when the psychoanalyst turns to the case of the girl, "our material—for some incomprehensible reason—becomes far more obscure and full of gaps" (19:177). What causes her to renounce her love for her father is not clear. It is self-evident for Freud that fear of castration cannot be an inducement for her, because she must *already* see herself as castrated—indeed, this recognition of her castration is her entryway into the Oedipus complex (19:178). She has, in effect, been "punished" *prior to* her Oedipal crime, so that now she cannot be punished *for* it.[33] As a result, the answer to the question of how the little girl is to surmount the Oedipus complex remains "unsatisfactory, incomplete and vague" (19:179), and Freud, in "Some Psychical Consequences of the Anatomical Distinction between the Sexes," acknowledges—in an unusual and highly apologetic series of prefatory remarks—the correspondingly tentative nature of his reflections on the subject (19:248–49).

In the end, Freud is left without any explanation for the existence of a feminine sense of guilt; but he makes a virtue out of necessity by arguing that women simply do not have a developed conscience or sense of justice (19:257–58). In a passage that clearly recalls Hegel's interpretation of Antigone as the embodiment of the natural (as opposed to rational) ethical principle, Freud writes:

> For women the level of what is ethically normal is different from what it is in men. Their super-ego is never so inexorable, so impersonal, so independent of its emotional origins as we require it to be in men. Character-traits which critics of every epoch have brought up against women—that they show less sense of justice than men, that they are less ready to submit to the great exigencies of life, that they are more often influenced in their judgements by feelings of affection or hostility—all these

would be accounted for by the modification in the formation of their super-ego which we have inferred above. (19:257–58)

In his discussion of the female Oedipus, Freud thus remains faithful to the current of his thought that tries to derive guilt from the threat of a specific punishment. That is, he retreats before the problem of feminine guilt, because in order to be able to account for it, he would have to entertain the possibility of a punishment—or a sense of guilt—without a crime. This means he would have to entertain the possibility that the masculine sense of guilt can be seen as derivative of a deeper and more primary feminine sense of guilt, rather than feminine guilt being a (defective) form of masculine guilt. In other words, he would have to accept the hypothesis that the Oedipus complex itself is played out on a psychic stage that is instituted, framed, and described by just such a feminine sense of guilt. Eriphile's masochism and her femininity—but are they different in Racine's (Freud's) terms?—thus make her an exemplary Racinian character, and, moreover, perhaps the tragic character par excellence. When Freud's interpretation of Hamlet is read from the perspective of the primary masochism of the Racinian characters, we can see, in other words, that Shakespeare's *Hamlet*, or at any rate, Freud's interpretation of it, may well be a distorted version not of *Oedipus* but of Racine's *Iphigénie*.

Modern Tragedy and Theory: The Drive for Knowledge

Eriphile's masochism is not her only striking trait, however. Or perhaps one should say that her masochism has a second aspect to it. Her masochistic love for Achille is consistently intertwined with another motif: her search for knowledge and, more particularly, her quest to learn her true identity. The scene in which Eriphile, through a long dialogue with her *suivante* Doris, is introduced to the audience makes this point, albeit obliquely (*Iphigénie*, act 2, scene 1). Like the other portions of the play directly concerning Eriphile, this scene as a whole has an ironic quality, as does the oracle contained within it. The scene describes Eriphile's character and fate, but in a sense that will become clear only as the play progresses. This is the scene in which we learn that Eriphile loves Achille and also that he was her abductor from Lesbos. Only later, however, in the celebrated exchange between Iphigénie and Eriphile, is the relation between these two elements fully clarified, when the audience learns that she loves him *because* he is her captor.

Similarly, the audience learns in this initial scene between Eriphile and Doris that Eriphile cannot know her identity without giving up her life, for, she admits, an oracle has told her, "Unless I perish, I cannot know myself" (act 2, scene 1, p. 688). Doris responds that Eriphile must try to learn her identity nonetheless, for the oracle surely means only that she will die in the sense that she will gain a new name and a new identity as a result of her search. Like the audience, Doris supposes that the risk of death will discourage Eriphile from trying to learn of her origins. But once we have understood, thanks to Iphigénie, that Eriphile's love for Achille derives from her masochism, we can see the relationship between her quest for self-knowledge and the peril she faces in that quest in a new light also. As a result of Iphigénie's insight, we can see that if suffering is an inducement for her to love Achille, then it must be the same with knowledge. If Eriphile must suffer or even die in order to gain the knowledge she seeks, this will not deter her but, on the contrary, only spur her on. Death will not be her punishment for knowledge or self-knowledge, it will be the culmination of that knowledge.

The interrelationship between Eriphile's masochism and her desire for knowledge is also apparent in the words with which she is described for the audience prior to her first appearance onstage. According to Eurybate, Eriphile has come to Aulide to question Calchas concerning her "destiny, which she does not know" (act 1, scene 4, p. 685). This description of her also has the same ironic quality as the oracle's pronouncement that unless she perishes, she cannot know herself. It clearly alludes to her ignorance concerning the identity of her parents, but it is phrased in such a way that it refers simultaneously to the fate that awaits her in Aulide—her sacrifice/suicide. The full meaning of these lines, then, becomes clear only with the conclusion of the play: what she has sought all along is self-knowledge/death. In other words, her quest for self-knowledge is motivated by the same masochism that expresses itself in her love for Achille and in her suicide, and it is this fundamental masochism that propels both her quest for knowledge and her love for Achille toward the same tragic conclusion.

Knowledge and masochism are thus intertwined in Eriphile's character much as they appear to be in psychoanalytic theory itself from the moment the displeasure associated with repression and the superego emerges as a constitutive element in intellectual activity, judgment, and philosophical speculation. The will to knowledge is so powerful because it, too, springs from, or at any rate is originally fused with, the masochistic trend whose primacy is revealed in Eriphile's fate. The image of Eriphile both as an exemplary masochistic and as a modern Oedipus engaged in a quest for knowledge and self-knowledge gives new force to the by now familiar idea that the theorist is of necessity always implicated in his or her theoretical object. Tragic suffering and judgment do indeed have a common root; tragedy and theory, whether psychoanalytical or philosophical, are grounded in the same, archaic sediment.

Iphigénie is not simply an anti-*Oedipus* or an anti-*Hamlet*, but like *Antigone*, though for somewhat different reasons, it can be used to raise fundamental questions about the models of theory, art, and sexuality derived from Shakespeare's and Sophocles' plays. Once the primary nature of masochism is revealed, then theory can no longer self-confidently approach the tragic work of art with the certainty that it can resolve the contradiction posed by tragic guilt and thus vindicate both the principles of reason and pleasure. Nor can theory any longer assume that the *sexual* conforms to those principles. Freud's interpretation of *Oedipus* represents an attempt to overcome the contradictory logic of tragedy through a theory of sexuality and the unconscious, but in the end, that contradictory logic proves to be the logic of the unconscious and of sexuality themselves. Theory cannot be the arbiter of the conflict within the field of sexuality and thus cannot overcome it, because the model of the psyche in which guilt would be original has as strong a claim to represent the true picture of the psyche as the model in which guilt is a secondary or later development—and because theory itself is deeply implicated in that conflict by its own affinity with masochism.

The answer to the question, Why *Phèdre* (or why *Iphigénie*) and why not *Oedipus*? is clear. The feminine characters are central in Racinian tragedy because of the deep link between femininity and masochism, and because of the central role of masochism in relation to Racinian theater and tragic drama as a whole. That is, a common relationship to masochism links the feminine and the tragic and makes the women characters particularly crucial, not just in terms of the action of the plays but as figures of tragedy itself. The picture of the woman as resentful both of the "defect" that prevents her from fully participating in an economy of pleasure and of the man as finding pleasure where she cannot is thus if not negated then transformed. Both the masculine and the feminine now appear as parts of a much more open or mixed economy, in terms of which the identity each assumes in Freud's Oedipal scenario appears to be based on a deeper identification that in each case is not only positive but also negative, that is, not only pleasurable, but painful as well.

CHAPTER 5

The Sexual Interruption of the Real:

Auerbach and *Manon Lescaut*

*Aesthetic historism, followed by general historism, practically orig-
inated in the second half of the eighteenth century, as a reaction
against the European predominance of French classicism.*
—Erich Auerbach, *Mimesis*

Tragedy and the Real in Auerbach's *Mimesis*

Erich Auerbach's best-known work, *Mimesis: The Representation of Reality in Western Literature*, stands out as an eminent—if not the most
eminent—example of the theory of literary realism. It is a theory that,
in Auerbach's own words, traces its origins to "the German intellectual development during the second half of the eighteenth century
which laid the aesthetic foundation of modern realism," a development that "is currently known as Historism."[1] This text has lost very
little of its critical force and relevance in a contemporary setting in
which the concept of mimesis has been systematically reexamined
and criticized. This is no doubt because Auerbach's concepts of the
historical and the real provide a critical perspective on the dominant
ideologies and theoretical systems of the various historical periods
analyzed in *Mimesis*, a perspective that can also be used to reveal
effectively the dogmatic nature of many contemporary theories of history and the real as well.[2]

Though Auerbach's theory of literary realism and the philosophy of
Hegel have their origins in the same historical period, the same national soil, and in several instances, the works of the same writers,
many today would argue that they are essentially opposed. Auerbach's thesis that the highest aim of Western literature lies in the representation of reality puts him directly at odds with Hegel, who
criticizes the notion of mimesis in the introduction to the *Aesthetics*.[3]
But this opposition is in the final analysis relatively superficial and
concerns terminology more than the substance of their interpreta-

tions of literature. It could be argued that what opposes them in a much deeper way is their respective understandings of "the historical" and "the real." Auerbach appears to reject an essential—if not the essential—aspect of Hegel's philosophy when he repeatedly condemns theoretical systems on the grounds that they are incompatible with the random character of the real. For Auerbach, as for many modern or new historicists, historicism is not systematic and totalizing but is concerned, rather, with preserving the unique, the specific, the contingent, and the diverse and with arguing that the real and the historical are to be found in them rather than in an overriding system or totality.

Such a view of the relation between Auerbach and Hegel and more broadly between historicism and speculative philosophy is, however, an oversimplification. In the first place, it neglects the crucial role played by specific historical cultures and historical periods, or, in the aesthetic domain, by specific works of art representative of particular historical contexts, in Hegel's philosophy generally and his *Aesthetics* in particular. It is significant that the *Phenomenology* and the *Aesthetics*, the one from the early and the other from the late stages of Hegel's career, both exhibit the same deep concern with history and the same conception of the fundamental task of philosophy. For Hegel that task is to find its reason in history, thus bringing history into the sphere of reason but, equally important, bringing philosophy into the sphere of history. That the real is historical, that history is the overriding framework within which all other entities must be placed to be understood (by philosophy), that the particular is not just to be subsumed by the general but is instead a necessary mode of the general itself—these arguments had already been made by Hegel before being made by Auerbach.

Equally important, the view that Auerbach and Hegel represent antithetical intellectual tendencies is also an oversimplification of historicism in general and of Auerbach's work in particular. Given the emphasis Auerbach places on randomness in defining the real, it comes as no surprise that he defends the random character of *Mimesis* itself, particularly in the epilogue.[4] Nonetheless, his narrative of the history of Western literature is in fact highly structured, and the criteria according to which works are chosen and treated in it highly consistent. Foremost among the elements determining that structure and those criteria is what should be called a hidden dialectic, which shapes *Mimesis* no less than an explicit and open dialectic shapes the philosophy of Hegel. The difference is that, unlike Hegel's dialectic, Auerbach's must remain hidden. Were it to emerge explicitly, his own narrative would lose its random, contingent appearance – its own literary-historical realism.

The dialectic underlying Auerbach's realism is evident in the triad, or series of triads, that structures his narrative. In these triads, the third term represents the other two and, as in Hegel's dialectic, thereby reconciles them. The triadic structure of *Mimesis* is elaborated in subtle and varied ways: one of the terms of an antithesis may be supplied long after the other, and the resolution of a given antithesis is not always immediately revealed. Nonetheless, this structure is clearly discernible in Auerbach's work, and once set in place, however discreetly, it becomes "a conceptual machinery that nothing is capable of withstanding," to borrow a phrase Heidegger uses to describe the opposition between form and content[5] – or, as I shall argue, that *almost* nothing is capable of withstanding. Just as Hegel's dialectic hits a snag with the "age of modern tragedy," so Auerbach's more subtle and supple dialectic stalls or is interrupted in the eighteenth century. In *Mimesis*, the literature of the eighteenth century represents a false step on the path that leads both to the "serious realism" of the nineteenth-century French novel and to historicism, the conceptual mimesis of serious realism.

Like Hegel's dialectic, the dialectic of realism recognizes no genuine other: in principle *all* literary examples are for Auerbach examples of realism, and all have their place in the history of realism. Still, literary realism does have its antitheses, and one of the most important is found in the chapter of *Mimesis* devoted to an analysis of French neoclassical drama, especially the plays of Molière and Racine. Auerbach considers the conventions of the neoclassical stage both from the standpoint of the ethos of Molière's *honnête homme* and from that of Racine's heroes, whose awareness of their princely rank is so strong that it never leaves them for a moment. But though he refers to both comedies and tragedies in making his argument in this chapter, the essence of Auerbach's argument concerns tragedy. What neoclassical comedy and tragedy have in common, according to Auerbach, is that they empty dramatic poetry of its reality, and this anti-realist tendency is exemplified in its purest form in neoclassical tragedy: "The classic tragedy of the French represents the ultimate

extreme in the separation of styles, in the severance of the tragic from
the everyday and real, attained by European literature" (*Mimesis*, 341).

Auerbach of course never defines the real systematically but instead
adduces qualities to it as his narrative progresses. Nonetheless, a series of characteristics emerges in the chapter on French neoclassical
drama as central to that realism. The everyday, the natural, and the
"creatural," Auerbach argues, are all missing to a great extent from
the plays of Corneille and Molière and are entirely lacking in Racine's
work, and the absence of these specific qualities is for Auerbach indicative of their lack of realism. As he uses them, the concepts of the
everyday, the natural, and the creatural appear to overlap to some
extent, but each nonetheless captures a specific tendency of the real
as he understands it. By the everyday, Auerbach means especially the
practical business of daily life, which is missing both in Molière's
comedies (324) and in Racine's tragedies, where the "actual function
of rulership" is never made apparent "except through the most general allusions" (332) to the activities of the princely heroes. By the natural, he means the complex, multilayered character of reality, as we
learn when he contrasts Shakespeare, whom he considers to be not
so much a preeminent tragic poet as a preeminent realist, with the
French and Greek dramatists.

In the chapter of *Mimesis* devoted to Shakespeare's *Henry IV*, Auerbach spells out further the opposition between the real and the
tragic. Whereas he consistently compares Racine and Euripides, he
just as consistently contrasts Shakespeare with Euripides in particular and the Greek tragic poets in general. Shakespeare's crucial place
in Auerbach's *Mimesis* stems not from his importance as a poet of the
tragic but, rather, from the way he subverts the tragic genre and sal-
vages it for realism. He does this, of course, through a "mixture of
tragic and comic elements" (275), thus ignoring the separation of
styles. But there is more. His plays also capture the real and history
in the sense that his "ethical and intellectual world is much more agitated, multi-layered, and, apart from any specific dramatic action,
more dramatic than that of antiquity" (285). This statement alludes
back to something Auerbach has told us in the opening chapter,
namely that "the historical event which we witness or learn about
from the testimony of those who witnessed it runs much more vari-
ously, contradictorily, and confusedly" than in legend (16)—or, he
might have added, than in Greek or French neoclassical tragedy.

The everyday and natural aspects of the real are united in the third, the creatural, by which Auerbach means the concrete existence of the literary characters, including their bodily existence, with its attendant vicissitudes. The creatural is characteristic for Auerbach of "Christian anthropology," which "emphasizes man's subjection to suffering and transitoriness" (218). Other early examples of it are found in bourgeois literature of the late feudal age. In the farces of this period, human sexuality enters onto the literary stage, and in the historical narrative, human mortality enters as well (216). The creatural thus unites several aspects of the real that come into conflict in other periods of the history of Western literature. By encompassing both the bodily and sexual, on the one hand, and the suffering of mortality, on the other, the creatural brings together the preeminent themes of both comedy and tragedy, and it thus implies the need for a mixture of styles, which for Auerbach is typical of all great works of literary realism. The creatural, he argues, is by and large missing from neoclassical drama, and insofar as one can cite examples of it, they appear only "on the comic stage, and even there only within certain limits" (339).

The "classic tragedy of the French" is thus for Auerbach the antithesis of the real and the historical, understood as the natural, the everyday, and, above all, the creatural. This assessment should not lead one to conclude that Auerbach, like Hegel, views French neoclassical tragedy as a degraded version of an older and purer model. It is particularly striking that Auerbach's history of "the representation of reality in Western literature" contains few references to the Greek tragic poets, whose names and works loom so large in Hegel's narratives of the Western tradition. Auerbach's history of realism begins instead with Homer and the Bible: Greek tragedy, he stresses in an aside, developed only much later, as a result of the separation of styles, which left no room for realism (19). He does not feel the need to discuss Greek tragedy because, like neoclassical tragedy, it too separates the tragic from the real, albeit not in such an extreme manner as French tragedy (326). As a result, its role in the history of Western literature can be performed or represented just as well by French neoclassical tragedy.

At bottom, then, Auerbach's assessment of French neoclassical tragedy is no more positive than that of Hegel. If it nonetheless has a more important place in *Mimesis* than Hegel gives it in the *Aesthetics*,

it is for an eminently Hegelian reason: because, for Auerbach, its negativity still participates in the common substance of creatural realism.
French tragedy is retained and raised to a higher level by what Auerbach calls the "modern tragic realism" (404) of Stendhal, Balzac, and
Flaubert (424–25). Modern tragic realism or "objective seriousness"
(432), as he also calls it, subjects the tragic as Racine understood it to
the operations that constitute the dialectical process. The tragic is first
negated: Stendhal, Flaubert, and Balzac present concrete historical situations and characters and their concrete bodily existence rather than
the disembodied and abstract princely heroes and heroines of neoclassical tragedy. But rather than treating these situations and characters in the manner of classical comedy—which represents the creatural to an extent, but at the cost of giving it any tragic or serious
significance—objective seriousness raises the creatural to the higher
level of modern (nineteenth-century) realism. In this sense, it retains
the tragic along with the creatural and elevates both to the level of an
absolute or pure form of realism.

Auerbach's account of the movement that culminates in nineteenth-
century realism thus reconciles the conflict between the aesthetics of
the seventeenth and the nineteenth centuries. In doing so, it also reconciles what is implicitly a deep and prolonged conflict, extending
from ancient times to the seventeenth century, between the tragic and
the creatural or between tragedy and realism. Though Auerbach repeatedly reminds us that each age in the history of realism is incom-
parable and unique, the opposition between realism and the tragic is
not confined to one age but is in effect transhistorical. The history of
the representation of reality is not just divided into different historical
epochs; it is also even more deeply divided "down the middle" by the
opposition between the tragic and the real. The importance Auerbach
attaches to nineteenth-century realism is all the more understandable
when one considers that without such a pure form of realism, in
terms of which all the other historical forms of realism can be unified
and understood, the history of realism would not be a history at all.
It would instead be something more closely resembling a neoclassical
drama about an irreducible, "tragic" conflict between historical realism and tragedy.

Eighteenth-Century French Literature:
The Intermediate Genres "before" Realism

When Auerbach is read critically, the search for a resolution to the underlying conflict between the real and the tragic appears as a powerful motor force driving his interpretation of Western literature. Profound though this conflict appears, however, it can be—and is—overcome in Auerbach's terms. In this sense, the age of neoclassical tragedy constitutes a negative term, but one that can nonetheless be recuperated by the dialectic of realism. In and of itself, the tragic is not disruptive of the dialectical pattern structuring Auerbach's history of Western literature, but instead gives it a dynamic and complex character without detracting from its ultimate, overall unity and continuity.

And yet there *is* a dead space in the narrative of *Mimesis* that coincides with eighteenth-century French literature. Unlike neoclassical tragedy, eighteenth-century French literature does not constitute a dialectically recuperable opposite of the age of realism. In the eighteenth century as described by Auerbach, we see a coming together of the real and the tragic that is neither altogether different from nor the same as what we see in his analysis of nineteenth-century realism (or neoclassical tragedy). Like the modern tragic realism of Stendhal and Balzac, this eighteenth-century literature links the tragic and the real. Nonetheless, in a manner that totally contravenes the dialectical spirit in which Auerbach otherwise approaches the various historical versions of realism and reality, the eighteenth-century version of realism is excluded by Auerbach from the real. As a result, eighteenth-century literature as a whole is also excluded from the dialectical narrative of the history of Western literature, or—what amounts to the same thing—it comes to represent an interruption of it.

There are five representatives of the literature of the eighteenth century in Auerbach's *Mimesis*: Saint-Simon, Voltaire, Prévost, Schiller, and Goethe. Significantly, Auerbach claims that Saint-Simon, whose work is the only wholly positive example of realism that he finds in this period, "did not fit into his age" (366). Voltaire, Schiller, and Goethe are all in the end dismissed because, in one way or another, their literary works betray the essence of literature and literary realism by mixing literature and politics, either directly, as in the case of Voltaire and Schiller, or indirectly, as in the case of Goethe.[6] Prévost's *Manon Lescaut*, however, does not suffer from this defect, but it too,

Auerbach asserts, represents a failure to attain realism. Among the works of the period treated in *Mimesis*, the special significance of Prévost's novel is that, from Auerbach's own standpoint, its failure is properly literary. In this sense it represents what are in his eyes the properly literary failings of eighteenth-century literature as a whole.

The irony of the portrait of the literary art of the eighteenth century that emerges in Auerbach's analysis of Prévost is that it should be so negative. As Auerbach himself shows, its aims are very close to those of both modern tragic realism and historicism itself.[7] We do not have to wait for Balzac or Flaubert—their sense of detail and their use of observations from everyday life are already found in *Manon Lescaut*, as Auerbach points out in a passage where Prévost's own profusion with details is mimed: "When the occasion permits, clothes, utensils, furnishings are described or evoked with coquettish meticulousness and great delight in movement and color. . . . We hear a great deal about money; there are lackeys, inns, prisons; officials appear; a scene outside a theater is carefully delineated, even to the name of the street; . . . there is realism everywhere" (351).

Manon Lescaut exemplifies Auerbach's own notion of realism not only from the standpoint of these details drawn from everyday life, however, but also from that of the fusion of genres or styles. "There is no question of any strict separation of styles" in *Manon Lescaut* (351). The everyday is present and furthermore so is the tragic, that other crucial element of modern tragic realism. Present, that is, in what Auerbach considers to be a degraded form. "The story even ends tragically," he notes in passing (353). Moreover, the language of the characters is often the language of tragic heroes, but given the situations into which it is transposed by Prévost, it evokes not neoclassical tragedy but, rather, the *comédie larmoyante*, that is, the (melo)drama of Prévost's own day (352). Even for Auerbach, to put the lofty language of tragedy in the mouths of characters depicted in concretely historical terms is clearly an example of the mixture of styles, which is a crucial element of realism. But instead of judging Prévost's mixture to be a synthesis of the tragic and the everyday, Auerbach considers it to be one sign among others of the "tearful sentimentality" and "ethical frivolity" of *Manon Lescaut* (351).

Though the defects of *Manon Lescaut* stem in large measure, according to Auerbach, from the shallowness of its author (352), in the last analysis, he argues, they nonetheless also exemplify the weaknesses of the literature of the entire age:

> The tragic exaltation of the classical hero loses ground from the beginning of the eighteenth century. Tragedy itself becomes more colorful and clever with Voltaire, but it loses weight. But in its stead the intermediate genres, such as the novel and the narrative in verse, begin to flourish, and between tragedy and comedy we now have the intermediate *comédie larmoyante*. . . . In its intermediate level the erotic and sentimental style of *Manon Lescaut* coincides with Voltaire's style in propaganda. . . . And so we must conclude that, in contrast to classicism, a mixing of styles now occurs once again. But it does not go far or very deep either in its realism or its seriousness. (362)

Instead of a genuine realism, which blends together the creatural and the tragic, *Manon Lescaut* offers us a shallow realism, which results from a mixture of mere sentimentality in the place of tragic seriousness, and eroticism in place of the creatural.

Eighteenth-century literature thus appears to be guilty of two failings. Its failure to depict the creatural is the graver one, however, because it is ultimately the erotic character of eighteenth-century literature that degrades its seriousness to sentimentality, thus eroding any claim it might have to be either the legitimate heir of an earlier tragic literature or the progenitor of ninetheenth-century realism. In *Manon Lescaut* we see, according to Auerbach,

> an undistinguished sort of corruption; it lacks all greatness and dignity; but the author does not seem to feel this. There is something exemplary about the Chevalier's frenzied sexual thraldom and Manon's almost ingenuous amorality, precisely by virtue of their lack of distinction. . . . With the lack of distinction in vice goes an equally undistinguished conception of virtue. It is concerned entirely with sex, with order or disorder in conducting one's sex life, and hence is itself steeped in eroticism. What is meant by virtue in this instance cannot be imagined detached from the whole apparatus of erotic sensations. (352)

Whereas the creatural admits the sexual into the real by subordinating it to what for Auerbach are serious, ethical concerns, in *Manon Lescaut* we see a form of the sexual that has overpowered the ethical and the serious and given them *its* character.

The degradation of the tragic by the erotic, moreover, is not confined to *Manon Lescaut* but is, rather, as Auerbach goes on to argue, characteristic of much eighteenth-century literature:

> The pleasure which [Prévost] endeavors to evoke in his readers by his representation of his lovers' childishly playful and unprincipled corruption, is in the last analysis a sexual titillation, which is constantly interpreted in sentimental and ethical terms while the warmth it evokes is abused to produce a sentimental ethics. This mixture is often found in the eighteenth century. Diderot's ethical attitudes are still rooted in an enthusiastic sentimentality in which the erotic plays a part; and even Rousseau still shows traces of it. (352–53)

Thus it is not just Prévost (or even Voltaire) who is being condemned in "The Interrupted Supper," but rather the major literary figures of an entire age. What is "interrupted," according to Auerbach's reading, is not just des Grieux's supper with Manon but the unfolding of the history of realism itself, the dialectical process by which even the negative moments in that history participate in the movement that leads to the full realization of realism. And the element that interrupts that dialectical process is the erotic, understood as an "excessive" form of sexuality that does not remain within the bounds prescribed for it by the creatural.[8]

Once the systematic nature of Auerbach's concept of realism is made explicit, it becomes possible to question the presuppositions that sustain it. Moreover, because of the special place he gives it, *Manon Lescaut* may be viewed as a crucial testing ground for the assumptions underlying the system of aesthetic values and assumptions structuring Auerbach's dialectic of realism, and in particular his exclusion of the erotic or the sexual from the real. In *Manon Lescaut*, the sexual emerges not as a degradation of the tragic but, rather, as a crucial element of it. And because of the role the sexual plays in relation to the tragic, the tragic itself takes on a disruptive significance in relation to Auerbach's notion of the real. A tragic in terms of which the sexual plays a decisive role is not dialectically recuperable in the same sense that Auerbach's conception of the tragic is. In the form they take in *Manon Lescaut*, the sexual and the tragic cannot be integrated into the dialectic of realism, but at the same time they now no longer can be used to represent a defective vision of reality as Auerbach would have it.

Manon Lescaut as Tragedy

The search for one or more intermediate genres, as Auerbach states, is a driving force in much of the literature of the Enlightenment. The intermediate genre that many of the leading literary figures hope to create would be a synthesis of comedy and tragedy. But, with the possible exception of Beaumarchais, what they seek is not a less tragic or more "comic" tragedy, but rather a tragedy that provides a more serious treatment of historical materials and whose subjects are drawn from the everyday lives of the members of a society that is increasingly bourgeois in its outlook. That is to say, what they want, above all, is to modernize tragedy.[9]

Though the abbé Prévost wrote no extended critical text or critical appreciation of his own work, his novels contain literary references that can be used to situate them within the group of literary works exemplifying a self-conscious search for an intermediate genre, understood as a modern version or modern form of tragedy. *Manon Lescaut* itself contains only one overt literary reference, but it is, significantly, to Racine. When des Grieux asks Manon if she isn't tempted by the gifts offered to her by the son of a man who had her incarcerated in the *Hôpital*, she responds "by tailoring two verses of Racine to her thought."[10] In this passage, Manon herself mixes the styles of tragedy and realism, but in a self-conscious and ironic manner.

Another passage, not from *Manon Lescaut* itself but from the larger work of which it is a part—the *Mémoires et avantures d'un homme de qualité*—refers to Racine in a similar manner. In it the characters amuse themselves by recreating one of Racine's tragedies in a setting in which its conventions appear out of place and even ludicrous. The *homme de qualité*, his friend the marquis de Sévigné, and the marquis's mistress, an actress, decide to amuse themselves at the expense of a friend, a hapless *abbé*:

> We carried out the project of the marquis, which was to have the *abbé* de Cogan recite a scene from Racine; he agreed to do it. We put him in a wig and a beribboned costume, etc. to play the role of Titus. I have never laughed so wholeheartedly. The actress was enchanting as Bérénice. The poor *abbé*, who had never exercised his speaking talent except in some miserable sermon, expressed the agitation of Titus in a perfectly ridiculous manner.[11]

Despite the differences in the two situations and casts of characters, Prévost's general thrust is the same, whether Manon cites *Iphigénie* or the *abbé* plays Titus. Prévost's evocation of Racine underscores the distance that separates his characters' world from that of tragedy, but at the same time it indicates that the ideal of tragedy is still relevant to understanding what happens in *Manon Lescaut*. He warns us that his work is a modern tragedy whose relationship to those of *le grand siècle* is ironic, but at the same time he invites us to compare his works with those of Racine.

Prévost's construction of character is an important feature of his work which can be better understood when it is compared to the tragedies of Racine than to the novels of Stendhal or Balzac, at least as Auerbach interprets them. The concreteness and wealth of detail in *Manon Lescaut*, as Auerbach notes, pertain to the world in which des Grieux and Manon live but not to the characters themselves. Manon's physical image is totally abstract. We are told she is beautiful, but the narrator never describes her in detail, any more than he does des Grieux. And Manon is equally abstract in psychological terms. The nagging question that has occurred to every reader of the work and is also the focus of much criticism of the novel—Does she really love des Grieux?—is so persistent precisely because of this abstractness, because the personality or individuality (to use Hegel's term) in which the puzzle might resolve itself, the psychological essence of her character, remains hidden from the reader.[12]

If Manon and des Grieux appear as frivolous, it is in large measure because of this abstraction. Because of their remoteness, it is always possible, in terms of a realism such as Auerbach's, to fill the void created by their lack of individuality with hypocrisy and a self-serving attitude. Recent feminist interpretations of *Manon Lescaut*, however, provide a different perspective on Manon's character in particular. According to these readings, Manon's remoteness is a necessary consequence of the narrative perspective, that of the *homme de qualité*, which privileges des Grieux's voice exclusively. Manon's inscrutability as a character is not a sign of her superficiality, according to this view, but, rather, of the radical alterity of the feminine with respect to discourse, which is in some fundamental way imprisoned in masculinity and unable to reach out beyond itself. This perspective has an undeniable critical force in relation to the general problems of narration, language, and sexuality, and it opens up the problem of the construction of character in *Manon Lescaut* closed off by Auerbach's theory of literary realism. From the standpoint of such a critique, it appears that Auerbach must of necessity treat Manon's character as superficial and frivolous because his concept of the subject is unproblematic, and therefore he can interpret only as defective a form of subjectivity that does not conform to his own idea of it.

The feminist reading places the question of Manon's character in a new light, but it is equally important in terms of the way it opens up the question not just of feminine subjectivity, but of subjectivity or individuality in general. In terms of *Manon Lescaut*, the opacity of Manon's character leads almost immediately to the problems posed by des Grieux's equal remoteness. Does he really love decency and honor as much as he claims, or are his protestations merely the hypocritical mask worn by his passion for Manon? The character of Tiberge is problematic in a similar sense. Is his devotion to religion as wholehearted as he claims, or does not the continual aid he offers to des Grieux in the name of friendship indicate his continuing attachment to and fascination with the secular world? Questions such as these, however, imply that we are dealing with characters in a novel by Stendhal or Balzac (and interpreted by Auerbach), characters with a unifying, psychological principle that informs, if it does not dictate, their behavior and in terms of which any conflicts manifested in that behavior can ultimately be overcome. This is, of course, not necessarily the case.

In his *Aesthetics*, Hegel tells us that tragedy offers a very different model for the construction of character, and he points to *Antigone* in support of his assertion. For Hegel, the difference between the characters of *Antigone*, the supreme tragedy, and the characters of other, essentially comic dramatic and literary works is the difference between character conceived as the concrete and individualized representation of the moral substance and character conceived as a unique and specific individual:

> In tragedy the whole treatment and execution presents what is *substantial* and fundamental in the characters and their aims and conflicts, while in comedy the central thing is the character's *inner* life and his *private* personality. (*Aesthetics*, 1205)

> The true content of the tragic action is provided, so far as concerns the *aims* adopted by the tragic characters, by the range of

> the substantive and independently justified [ethical] powers
> that influence the human will. . . . A similar excellence belongs
> to the genuinely tragic *characters*. (1194)

From the perspective that Hegel provides in these two passages, it would thus be utterly foolish to ask what Antigone's true feelings are about the ethical power or the aspect of the ethical substance of which she is a concretization, for she has little or no feeling and little or no individuality independent of that ethical power.

To an important extent, Manon, des Grieux, and Tiberge, like Antigone, can be understood as the embodiments of elements of the ethical substance, that is, of the larger society conceived of as a creation of human will. But the conflicts among the ethical powers of the society of Tiberge, des Grieux, and Manon cannot be reduced to the conflict between state and family, the law of man and the law of woman, which Hegel finds in *Antigone*. In the case of Tiberge, the ethical power in question is that of religion. In the case of des Grieux, it could be considered to be love. And in the case of Manon, it is the sexual or the erotic as such, an ethical power denied ethical status by the dominant forces of the society, as it is denied realistic status by Auerbach, but present nonetheless. The character of Manon offers a challenge to Auerbach's concept of realism, not only because of its lack of depth and individuality, which he condemns as superficiality and frivolousness, but also because the ethical power that provides her character with its substance is excluded by him from the real.

As we have seen, Hegel holds that the different aspects of the ethical substance are realized and individualized as *conflict*, albeit a conflict that is superficial with respect both to the indivisibility and harmony of the ethical whole and to the firmness of each individual tragic character. In *Manon Lescaut*, too, the conflicts that divide and unite the various characters reveal both the different aspects of the ethical substance and their common, ethical nature. But what differentiates Prévost's characters and their world from those of *Antigone*, as Hegel interprets it, is that in their world and in their individual characters we can also see the fundamental nature of the division between the different ethical powers. The conflict between the different ethical powers—or, in more modern terms, between the different values and codes of conduct of society—is irresolvable because each is equally ethical or—what amounts to the same thing—is equally unethical from the perspective of the others.

Before considering the characters of des Grieux and Manon, it is useful to look at Tiberge in order to understand the logic of conflict that structures the ethical world of Prévost's characters and gives each its relative distinctness. At first glance, the character of Tiberge appears far less important than that of Manon or des Grieux, and the religious values he constantly affirms appear largely irrelevant to the action of the novel. Nonetheless, when one considers the work of Prévost as a whole, the importance of the theme of religion is self-evident. One has only to think of the passage quoted earlier in which an *abbé* plays the role of Titus to become aware of one of the most important conflicts structuring Prévost's work in general and *Manon Lescaut* in particular: the conflict between religion and the secular world. Underlying the laughter of the *homme de qualité* when he sees the *abbé* declaiming lines written for Bérénice's lover is the acknowledgement of a deep separation between the two. The recurring allusions to Jansenism throughout the *Mémoires et avantures*, but especially in the early sections of the novel, are another indication not only of the importance Prévost attaches to religion generally speaking but also of the specific role religion plays in his novels. All the spokesmen for Jansenism who appear in the novel—and they include Arnauld and even Racine—reduce it to a single, crucial feature. For them religion is above all an opposition to and a retreat from the secular world. The life story of the *homme de qualité*, who narrates des Grieux and Manon's story, exemplifies the ethical power and significance of religion when he retreats more than once from the world.

Religion is equally important in determining the character of des Grieux's world, where it is personified by his friend Tiberge. If, in terms of the unfolding of the narrative, this character could be considered to have only secondary importance, he is a character of the first order for understanding the tragic dimension of the novel as a whole. In the broadest terms, the novel can be read as a struggle between Manon and Tiberge, between love and religion, for the allegiance of des Grieux. It could be argued, of course, that Tiberge's hold on des Grieux is extremely weak, and that as a result the ethical force of religion is being undermined rather than affirmed by the novel. But if des Grieux never does what Tiberge would like him to do, neither is he willing to accept many of Manon's suggestions, despite the intensity of his attachment for her. In this sense, Tiberge's moral authority represents a limitation of the authority of Manon.

The figure of des Grieux presents a greater challenge to the interpretation of *Manon Lescaut* from the standpoint of tragedy. Certainly from the perspective of Auerbach, there is nothing particularly ethical about the power he represents, and des Grieux's attempt to give dignity to his love appears to be sheer bad faith. The objection Auerbach raises, which of course does not apply to Prévost alone, is a theme of the literary criticism of Prévost's own period, of which Voltaire's prefaces to his own tragedies offer a good example. Central to a number of those texts is the question of whether or not love is a proper subject for tragedy. This discussion relates directly to Voltaire's assessment of the importance of Racine's work, for if tragedy and love do not mix, then Racine and French theater generally can no longer claim to be the preeminent literature of the modern age: "Our nation is reproached with having made theater soft by too much tenderness."[13] Voltaire's answer to the question is thus predictable in its major lines. He argues that, in Racine's plays at least, the tragic is not degraded by love, but, rather, the two are perfectly synthesized.[14] And yet even Voltaire seems at times to question his own position on the issue of love—and on the excellence of Racine's work. In a letter to Mademoiselle Clairon, he writes, "I dare say that in general the tragedies that can subsist without this passion [love] are without question the best."[15]

If, despite his admiration for Racine and French theater generally, Voltaire makes such an admission, it is because there *is* for him a risk associated with the dominance of the theme of love, a risk of effeminacy. "To want to put love in all tragedies seems to me to be an effeminate taste" ("Discours sur la tragédie," 323), and thus, implicitly, any play in which love is the dominant interest may end up emasculating tragedy. A similar view underlies A. W. Schlegel's critique of Racine's *Phèdre* in his "Comparaison entre la Phèdre de Racine et celle d'Euripide."[16] Racine's play has several defects in Schlegel's eyes: the decision to treat Phèdre as the principal character, to show Hippolyte to be in love with Aricie, and correspondingly, to degrade the purity of Hippolyte's character. But all of these converge in his judgment that "the French poet, by denaturing and giving less weight to ("émoussant") the character of Hippolyte, destroyed the beautiful contrast that existed between him and Phèdre" (360).

Prévost's affinity with Racine is especially evident in terms of the weight and character of love in his novel. Prévost's novel does in part

confirm the picture of the effeminization of the tragic by the predominance of love that Voltaire indirectly and Schlegel directly attribute to
Racine's plays. In *Manon Lescaut*, des Grieux's need for money soon
causes him to turn to Manon's brother, Lescaut. Among other things
Lescaut proposes to him is that des Grieux himself should let Lescaut
introduce him to "some old and generous lady" who would make his
fortune in the same manner that Manon's rich lovers have in the past
made hers (*Manon Lescaut*, 68). Prévost also "destroys the . . . contrast" between des Grieux and Manon in the scene describing
Manon's escape, with the help of des Grieux, from her imprisonment
in the *Hôpital*. He brings with him, hidden under a large outer garment, the clothes she will need to disguise herself with in order to
facilitate her getaway—all except a pair of pants. His solution is to give
his own pants to Manon and hope that his outer garment will cover
him sufficiently (108). In another episode, des Grieux is placed in an
effeminate position by Manon herself, when she rejects the offers of
an Italian prince who seeks to make her his mistress. She does this in
a spectacular manner, by confronting the prince with the image of the
handsome young man whose hair and attire she has spent the better
part of the day arranging as coquettishly as possible in preparation
for the visit of the prince.

Though a certain effeminization of the characters can be seen in
both Racine's plays and Prévost's novel, both nonetheless indicate
that this effeminization cannot be simply equated with degradation.
Prévost's references to *Bérénice* are particularly relevant in this regard,
since this play is about the dual nature of love—that is, about the tension between love and duty, but also about the ethical power of love.
For Racine, as for Prévost, love is not merely an expression of individual will or desire. It also channels or forms desire, giving it direction
and discipline. As a youth, Titus, "raised in the court of Nero," was
little more than a pleasure seeker. All that changed when he met
Bérénice, and both his military successes and his good works stem
directly from his love for her.[17] Though his sense of obligation to
Rome eventually causes him to renounce Bérénice, the ethical nature
of his love has already prepared him to fulfill the even higher ethical
demands of the state.

Such an interpretation clearly opens the door for a sentimental exal-
tation of love which endows petty emotion with a false tragic grandeur,
as is indirectly acknowledged in an earlier section of the *Mémoires*

et avantures. Auerbach criticizes Prévost for his "tearful sentimental-ity," but Prévost himself criticizes Racine in essentially the same vein when, through the mouth of a Spanish nobleman, he characterizes Racine as a *pleureux* and praises Corneille as the true tragic play-wright (*Mémoires et avantures*, 1:394).

Nonetheless, *Manon Lescaut*, like *Bérénice*, focuses on the ethical nature of love, by opposing it to merely sensual passion. Very early in the novel, we see des Grieux rejecting the substitutes for Manon offered to him by his father, who is convinced that his son has a weak-ness for women in general. Later on, we will see him reject the pros-titute Manon sends to him as her replacement when she is unable or unwilling to leave G— M— *fils*. The ethical nature of des Grieux's love is also evident in that it places him in conflict with his society and religion. No one in des Grieux's world thinks of condemning B—, G— M—, or G— M— *fils* for having a mistress, any more than they would condemn des Grieux himself, if Manon were only a mis-tress. Just as, in Hegel's reading of *Antigone*, the conflict between An-tigone and Creon stems from the ethical nature of the claims of each, so des Grieux's love brings him into conflict with the dominant, pater-nal, ethical powers of his society precisely because it is also an ethical power, but of another sort.

Behind the question of the ethical nature of des Grieux's love for Manon, however, stands the question of the ethical nature of Manon herself. In her case, it seems even more difficult not to come to the same conclusion as Auerbach, for whom she represents a counter-force to the ethical: that is, pleasure, the erotic, the sexual. But Auerbach's reading of *Manon Lescaut* overlooks the points that form the basis of the ethical claim of pleasure and sexual passion in the novel. One of the most important of these is that the pleasure in ques-tion is primarily Manon's.

It is easy to see that the society of des Grieux and Manon views their love as a scandal, that it represents a challenge to the very struc-ture of a society that permits the moneyed classes to buy women of a different class, to marry women of the same class, but not to love women of a different class. What is perhaps less obvious is that the same mechanisms that censor des Grieux's love for Manon also cen-sor passion and pleasure in general, and specifically the passion and pleasure of the woman. The existence of this not-so-hidden censor-ship accounts for the fact that in this world there are only two stable positions the woman can occupy, wife or prostitute. In each of these, the woman is cut off from spontaneity and pleasure and subjected to an extra dose of repression over and above what men experience. For the respectable woman, marriage is *in principle* a renunciation of pleasure, insofar as she has nowhere to turn should the marriage be an empty one. For the man, marriage may entail the renunciation of pleasure, but not as a matter of principle, since respectable society nonetheless tolerates prostitution—as is attested when des Grieux's father offers to provide him with a mistress in order to take his mind off Manon. However, the prostitute is also denied pleasure, inasmuch as her desire is subordinated to that of a paying customer, or, just as bad, to a panderer or madam.[18]

Thus, while des Grieux finds himself in conflict with a series of father-figures who embody the repressive force and hypocrisy of society, Manon is involved in a perhaps even more intense conflict with paternal authority. Indeed, in Prévost's novels, where conflict between father and son looms so large, the only example of patricide occurs in his *Campagnes philosophiques,* when a father is killed by his daughter, mademoiselle Fidert, a heroine who stands out in Prévost's *oeuvre* along with Manon on account of the intensity and force of her sexual passion.[19] In the context of a hypocritical society, which denies pleasure to women and makes them—whether through marriage or prostitution—the property of men, Manon's persistent quest for pleasure does in fact take on an ethical dimension. Only a love or marriage that would reconcile itself with her pleasure could claim to represent ethical values.

The notion that *Manon Lescaut* is constructed to an important extent according to the principles of tragedy accounts for the relative abstractness and remoteness of Prévost's characters. It also accounts for a second striking characteristic of the novel: the dramatic series of reversals that structure its action and the character's behavior. Like so many classical and neoclassical tragedies, Prévost's novels contain any number of abrupt about-faces, in which the character or situation shifts from one extreme to another—in direct contrast to the historical principle favored by Auerbach according to which the action and the characters evolve gradually and continuously. Using the example of Racine, one could argue that these reversals are only possible and believable because both the initial situation and the sudden reversal of it are in a deeper sense identical, and their function in the drama is to point up that identity. At one moment Hermione can wish aloud that Pyrrhus be killed and in the next want to kill his murderer, Roxane can offer Bajazet a place on the throne or in the grave, because in their universe love and hate are fundamentally one, two sides of a single passion that enslaves one subject to the other and thus creates the profound ambivalence felt more often than not by Racine's heroes toward those they love.

In a similar fashion, des Grieux can be a novice at Saint-Sulpice, on the point of taking his final religious vows, and at the next moment leave Saint-Sulpice behind with no thought other than of Manon, because religion and love are structurally similar. Both are absolute values demanding total commitment from the individual character. Because both are absolute, they are of necessity antagonistic, so that a character cannot be faithful to one without betraying the other. The structural similarity of the conflicting ethical powers thus explains more than one paradox in the novel. Des Grieux's aptitude for religious life—his achievements at Saint-Sulpice, his gifts as a student of theology, and his religious feeling—is the *same* as his aptitude for love. Similarly, Manon, when she comes to Saint-Sulpice to see des Grieux, will abruptly renounce pleasure for love, just as she will abruptly renounce love for pleasure in other sudden reversals of character. Like des Grieux, who experiences love and religion as structurally similar and hence competing absolute values, she will experience pleasure and love as irreconcilable but will remain attached to each for the same reason.

Of course, not all of *Manon Lescaut* can be interpreted from the standpoint of *Antigone* or *Bérénice*. There is a whole side of the novel that relates much more clearly and immediately to *Oedipus*, as has often been noted by Prévost's interpreters. From this standpoint, what appears most important in the novel is the figure of des Grieux and the series of conflicts in which he is pitted against his own father and several additional father-figures: B—, G— M—, the lieutenant of police, and Synnelet *père*, characters whose paternal function is in almost every case underscored by the presence in the novel of a son: G— M— *fils*, M. de T—, and the younger Synnelet. Another unmistakable sign of the Oedipal nature of much of the conflict in *Manon Lescaut* is the scene in which des Grieux is introduced to G— M— as Manon's brother. It is thus by sleeping with her fictive brother that Manon plans to teach G— M— a lesson. Still another

sign is provided when des Grieux is apprehended in bed with
Manon by G— M— and is thus taken away by the police for having
been on the verge of doing exactly what both G— M—and his own
son had proposed to do.

The Oedipal principle also explains what has always been a central
enigma for the critics of *Manon Lescaut*: des Grieux's passionate attachment to his faithless mistress. Prévost's solution to the enigma implies that realism alone cannot account for love, because love is not
based on unique qualities that inhere in each specific character. It can
be accounted for only by fate—that is, by a sexual conflict central to
the family and society, a conflict that defines each character and over-
rides the significance of any purely individual character traits. In the
terms of *Oedipus*, the conflict is one between the father and the son,
but it is an unconscious conflict, which, as a result, manifests itself
not as such but, rather, in a displaced fashion. Thus on the one hand
des Grieux finds himself in conflict with his own father, but not
because both desire the same woman. On the other hand, he finds
himself in conflict with G— M— because both desire the same
woman, but G— M— is not des Grieux's father, only a father-
figure.

Manon's character can also be interpreted in terms of the conflict—
the unconscious conflict—between fathers and sons. She teeters on
the brink of the line separating respectable society from the society of
common prostitutes. Were she a common prostitute, she would not
be the object of any conflict, because she would belong to all men (to
the sons) indiscriminately. Were she a member of respectable society,
she would not be the object of conflict, because she would belong, as
it were, to the father (her father or a husband). Manon, however,
belongs to neither the son nor the father; she is neither wholly rep-
utable nor wholly disreputable. Des Grieux's desire for her is thus
not explicitly and consciously a threat to his father, but it is implicitly
a threat to his father in a way it would not be if she were a common
prostitute. Des Grieux's choice of Manon is thus understandable only
in Oedipal terms—it mirrors the law of the father as the (unconscious) formative force of society.

Finally, the conflict between Manon and des Grieux, on the one
hand, and their society as a whole, on the other, is also Oedipal in
nature, in the sense that it is the result of their sharing, to a large
extent, the values of that society, and, more specifically, of the aristo-

cratic class, which dominates it. They are typically presented to the reader not as degraded or degenerate but, rather, as the true representatives of aristocracy. The reader is disposed to believe that the degraded condition of Manon and des Grieux in the opening pages of the novel is at odds with their true ethical/social quality thanks to Prévost's use of the general narrator of des Grieux's story, the *homme de qualité*. The disruption Manon and des Grieux cause when the convoy of prostitutes reaches the small village where the *homme de qualité* first meets them is immediately interpreted for the reader. They are not, the *homme de qualité* tells us, what their situation suggests— common criminals. The image of Manon is especially important in conveying this, because it stresses the contrast between her beauty, which is invariably interpreted in moral/social terms as a sign of nobility, and her degraded condition as a prostitute. Similarly, the cause of the initial impression made by des Grieux on the *homme de qualité* is that, despite his extremely modest garments, one can nevertheless discern "at first glance, a man of good breeding and education" (*Manon Lescaut*, 35).

If they share the ethical claims and ideals of the aristocratic class (the class of the fathers), they also share in its self-serving attitudes and its hypocrisy. This is particularly true of des Grieux, whose defense of himself is so frequently simply a defense of his prerogatives as a nobleman. When G— M— catches des Grieux on the verge of sleeping with Manon in the bed of G— M—'s son, des Grieux, who is unable to counter with his épée, offers the following verbal riposte: "Be apprised that my blood is nobler and purer than yours" (149). Similarly, in justifying himself to his father, he is careful to cite the examples of men of rank, in order to diminish his crimes (157). When, in the course of his escape from Saint-Lazare, des Grieux kills a prison guard, the father superior of the prison will hide the fact from the authorities. If the father superior does not report this crime, and if, moreover, des Grieux is not particularly astonished by this fact (he views it as a stroke of luck), it can only be because in his eyes, as in those of his society, it is not a serious crime for an aristocrat to kill a man of common birth. The father superior's silence makes him and the society whose values he represents accomplices in des Grieux's crime. Des Grieux is thus in conflict with his society, and/but he reveals his deep attachment to it and its values at every turn.

Des Grieux's choice of Manon, the nature of his feelings for her, and even the hypocrisy of his actions and speech are thus explained by the figure of Oedipus. Des Grieux finds himself in conflict with his society and with his father-figures because he is like them. The father-figures condemn him, not just because he rebels, but also because he does what they do. "Be like me/don't be like me"—this is a law des Grieux cannot fail to respect and cannot fail to transgress. To conform to the law of the father is to break it; to break it is to conform to it. The most fundamental expressions of this law are the prohibition of incest and a corresponding sexual license in regard to those women who are not objects of the sexual desire of the father (the son). As a result, the most serious challenge to it can take only a sexual form.

On one level, it could be argued that the many elements of *Manon Lescaut* which can be accounted for from the standpoint of *Oedipus* merely provide additional evidence of the deep connection between the sexual element in *Manon Lescaut* and the tragic, and hence of the seriousness of the sexual—in direct contradiction to Auerbach's thesis. But on another level, the novel clearly indicates that, disruptive though des Grieux's love for Manon may be, Manon herself is the more disquieting figure. It is she who is incarcerated at the infamous *Hôpital*, while the authorities content themselves with subjecting des Grieux to a much less humiliating and more comfortable detention at Saint-Lazare. Toward the end of the novel, it is Manon who is sent to America, while des Grieux is set free. In the end, it is Manon who dies, while des Grieux lives to tell their (her) story.

What is most disquieting in the figure of Manon is the excessive sexuality that gives the novel the erotic character Auerbach condemns. That element of her character cannot be accounted for in terms of *Oedipus*, because the logic of Oedipus can account for her being desired but not for her desires. In terms of *Oedipus*, the conflict that exists between her pleasure and her love for des Grieux remains enigmatic, as does the correspondingly excessive nature of her sexuality.

What might be called the Antigone complex can account as well for des Grieux's love: it is the manifestation of one of the competing ethical powers in the world of *Manon Lescaut*, but it can also explain Manon's intractable "attachment to pleasure." The excessive nature of her sexuality is a direct correlate of the ethical character that sexuality takes on in the social context depicted in *Manon Lescaut*, in spite of or really because of the dominant, paternal, that is, Oedipal values of that society. Like the other ethical powers, (her) sexuality is an imper-

ative, and it cannot be subsumed or combined with other, equally absolute, ethical imperatives. The tragic realism of Prévost is not a creatur-
alism in which the sexual exists but is subordinated to the other aspects
of human existence. It is one in which the sexual, in the figure of
Manon, plays a central role in the conflicts that define and structure the
ethical and social world and the characters that inhabit it. Auerbach
reproaches *Manon Lescaut* because it contains "not a trace of the problematic. The social milieu is an established frame of reference, which is
accepted as it happens to be" (*Mimesis*, 353). But in terms of the disruptive sexuality of Manon, it is more accurate to say that the social
appears, on the contrary, to be defined by irresolvable conflicts—
between the world of prostitution and respectable society, between the
"law of the woman" and the "law of the man," between *Antigone* and
Oedipus. Despite what Auerbach says, these conflicts give the social
world of *Manon Lescaut* a radically problematic character.

The excessive sexuality of Manon is equally disruptive of a histori-
cized literary realism. It disrupts the dialectic uniting the sexual—in
the form of the creatural—with the tragic or the serious, and in the
process, it redefines the tragic in a manner that shows its deeper link
to the sexual and more specifically to the feminine. From the perspective of *Manon Lescaut*, the sexual is the source of conflict in the novel
and is also what gives conflict its tragic, irresolvable nature. For Auerbach, the tragic can always be subsumed by modern tragic realism; or
in other words, the divorce effected by the tragic between itself and
the real can be overcome by the real itself. Provided the real is random, multilayered, and complex enough, it can always unify all
heterogeneity under a concept of *the* real. But in the light of *Manon
Lescaut*, the dialectic of realism now appears to be interrupted, suspended somewhere between des Grieux's dinner with Manon and
Julien Sorel's dinner with Mathilde, between this eighteenth-century
representative of realism and the literary realism of the nineteenth
century. Equally important, Auerbach's real, however flexible and critical it at first seems, appears now as *a* systematic, dialectical real,
alongside which subsists another, tragic real, one shaped by irresolvable conflict and contradiction between competing ethical powers,
one whose critical power is exemplified most clearly in the figure of
Manon.

CHAPTER 6

The Dialectic and Its Aesthetic Other:

 The Problem of Identification

in Diderot and Hegel

More than a century before the emergence of psychoanalysis the French philosopher Diderot bore witness to the importance of the Oedipus complex . . . in his famous dialogue, Le Neveu de Rameau.

—Freud

Catharsis and the Dialectic

In terms of the issue of the uneasy relations between art and philosophy, few texts are of greater interest than the section of Hegel's *Phenomenology* that consists of an interpretation of Diderot's *Le Neveu de Rameau.* In it, Hegel exposes in great detail the workings of speculative discourse in relation to a work of art that is at the same time explicitly a dialogue on art. Hegel's stance in relation to this text is remarkable when one considers his overtly critical view of neoclassical (French) aesthetics in general and even of those texts by Diderot himself relating to the project for a *drame sérieux,* or what Hegel calls the introduction of "direct and natural expression" into the theater.[1] It is even more striking when one compares it to his assessments of the poets and aestheticians whom he at least in part admires and whose works and theories he attempts to incorporate into the dialectical movement of the *Phenomenology of the Spirit* or his *Aesthetics.* His reading of Kant, as we have seen, emphasizes as much the shortcomings of Kantian philosophy as its positive contribution to the history of reason and aesthetics. In the case of the Schlegels, Hegel's admiration for their critical talent is more than tempered by his contempt for the "miserable philosophical ingredients" of their work (*Aesthetics,* 63). Very few poets (Goethe, Schiller, Shakespeare) and even fewer works of art openly receive the kind of praise implicit in Hegel's treatment of *Le Neveu.*

Hegel, of course, does not directly express admiration for the *Neveu* or its author. He does much more than admire or praise—he *identifies* Rameau's Nephew as *the* manifestation of reason in his age. This privilege is so striking and unusual in Hegel's work that a question naturally arises as to its basis. Only in the case of Hegel's reading of *Antigone* does one find a similar identification of the spirit with a particular work of art. And yet, at least on the surface, the significance and character of his readings of *Antigone* and *Le Neveu de Rameau* appear so dissimilar that the fact the two texts enjoy a similar status seems to be a mere coincidence, without any deeper implication.

Dissimilar though the two works appear to be, both in themselves and in Hegel's interpretation of them, there is, from the perspective of the *Phenomenology* and the *Aesthetics*, a profound link between them. Though Hegel's reading of *Le Neveu* appears in a section of the *Phenomenology* devoted to a stage of spirit in which it takes the form of culture and more specifically of what Hegel calls "disrupted consciousness," the central place of *Le Neveu* in the *Phenomenology* corresponds not only to Hegel's philosophical interest in this stage of the history of consciousness but also implicitly to his interest in art in general and tragedy in particular.

What captures Hegel's attention in *Le Neveu* is, of course, the figure of the Nephew himself. The Nephew is significant because of the way he figures the dominant tendencies of a particular, modern stage of consciousness, but also because he personifies a process central to tragedy and to the theory of tragedy, the process Freud will designate by the term *identification*. Though in the *Aesthetics* Hegel criticizes Lessing along with Diderot for their advocacy of naturalism, Hegel's own relation to Diderot is in crucial respects similar to that of Lessing, and his reading of *Le Neveu* implicitly raises anew the central question of Lessing's *Hamburg Dramaturgy*: Is there a modern form or version of the *catharsis* effected, according to Aristotle's *Poetics*, by tragedy?

In its broad lines, the framework in which Lessing considers the question of *catharsis* is very similar to that in which Hegel approaches the problem of art. Lessing's interest in criticism—his defense of Aristotle's *Poetics* and more broadly of the importance of a proper understanding of "the rules" in the cultivation of artistic genius (or, in the absence of genius, in creating an approximation of genius)—is the key element in a clearly articulated project: to transform the theater into a place where the philosopher-critic can go to laugh, and shed tears, but laughter and tears accompanied by and under the control of reason.[2] Though Lessing reiterates this project in many passages of the *Hamburg Dramaturgy*, nowhere is it expressed more clearly than in the description he gives of the friendship between Euripides and Socrates:

> Socrates was the master and friend of Euripides and hence how many might imagine that the poet owed to this friendship with the philosopher all the wealth of splendid maxims that he has scattered so profusely throughout his plays! I think that he owed far more to him; he might have been just as rich in maxims without him, but he would scarcely have been as tragic. . . . To know man and ourselves; to be observant of our emotions; to search for and to love the smoothest and shortest paths of nature; to judge each matter according to its intention; this was what Euripides learned from Socrates and what made him the first in his art. (154)

Despite rejecting the neoclassical interpretation of Aristotle, Lessing attaches supreme importance to Aristotle's *Poetics* because of his sense of the need that art has of a philosophical friend and master.[3]

The same can be said of Lessing's interpretation of Aristotle's text. Catharsis is the central theme of his reading of the *Poetics* for exactly the same reason that philosophy is for Lessing the best friend of art. The core of the cathartic process as it is presented in the *Hamburg Dramaturgy* is the act of putting oneself in the place of the other, or what we have been calling identification. In his discussion of the meaning of the Aristotelian term *fear*, Lessing asserts it should not be confused with *terror*, because, he argues, without fear, pity (or compassion) does not induce the spectator to put himself in the place of the character. Terror is an emotion that relates only to something or someone perceived as external to ourselves, whereas fear is one that works with pity to create an immediate link between spectator and character: ''It is the fear that arises *for ourselves* from the similarity of our position with that of the sufferer'' (179). From Lessing's perspective, catharsis/identification is the central element in tragedy and in poetics, because it serves as the incontrovertible piece of evidence that the hero of tragedy is another version of ourselves and that as a result we can, through tragedy, ''know man and ourselves.''

Unlike the *Hamburg Dramaturgy*, Hegel's *Aesthetics* contains few allusions to Aristotle's *Poetics*, and much separates Hegel from a perspective on art that places emotion or the affective state of the spectator at its center—as Hegel clearly feels Aristotle in important respects does.[4] Nonetheless, in his one detailed reference to the *Poetics*, Hegel spells out what is at stake in the concept of catharsis in terms very similar to those of Lessing:

> Aristotle, as every one knows, laid it down that the true effect of tragedy should be to arouse pity and fear and accomplish the catharsis of these emotions. By "emotions" Aristotle did not mean mere feeling, my subjective sense of something corresponding with me or not, the agreeable or disagreeable, the attractive or the repulsive. . . . In the case of Aristotle's dictum we must therefore fix our eyes not on the mere feelings of pity and fear but on the nature of the subject-matter which by its artistic appearance is to purify these feelings. A man can be frightened in face of, on the one hand, something finite and external to him, or, on the other hand, the power of the Absolute. What a man has really to fear is not an external power and oppression by it, but the might of the ethical order which is one determinant of his own free reason and is at the same time that eternal and inviolable something which he summons up against himself if once he turns against it. (*Aesthetics*, 1197–98)

Hegel indicates in this passage that the tragic emotions are not the "mere" emotions aroused by something external to the spectator. They are what might be called emotions of reason, inasmuch as through them the spectator is confronted by an ethical order that is indistinguishable from his own free reason. These emotions thus have the power to identify the spectator with tragedy—that is, they oblige the spectator to see himself in the drama or, what is the same thing, to see the ethical order of tragedy in himself. Because of the special character Hegel attributes to the fear and pity associated with tragedy, he is able in this passage to rescue catharsis from the realm of mere feeling, which he calls "the indefinite dull region of the spirit [where] what is felt remains enveloped in the form of the most abstract individual subjectivity" (32). The process of identification effected through the tragic emotions can thus now be interpreted in the terms of reason and philosophy as a process of self-knowledge rather than as one occurring in or involving a region lying outside of reason.

For both Lessing and Hegel, then, catharsis is a process that converts tragedy into self-knowledge and confirms that philosophy is the friend and master of art. In the confrontation between the self as spectator and the self as spectacle, tragedy in particular and art in general reveal their essence and meaning and take on their (philosophical) significance. It is all-important that tragedy should reveal itself to be a form of self-knowledge, for such knowledge is not just one form of knowledge among others: for speculative philosophy, it is knowledge itself. In this sense, the possibility of attributing a philosophical significance to tragedy hinges on the concept of identification and on the nature of the relationship between the spectator and tragic action. One could say that just as, from a dramatic standpoint, identification permits the spectator to see himself in the hero of tragedy, so, from a theoretical standpoint, the concept of identification permits philosophy itself to identify with tragic art. Philosophy can find itself in tragedy and in art in general insofar as their nature is defined by and revealed in the process and concept of identification.

For Lessing, Diderot stands out as the modern dramatist and critic whose work (along with that of Shakespeare) best exemplifies the spirit of Aristotle's *Poetics*, and his project for a *genre sérieux*, in particular, represents the truest and most forceful contemporary interpretation of catharsis. Diderot therefore occupies a position virtually as eminent as that of Shakespeare in the *Hamburg Dramaturgy*, not so much because of the quality Lessing attributes to his plays but, rather, because of the way the concept of catharsis/identification informs his dramatic practice and makes him at once a Euripides and a Socrates. Similarly, for Hegel, Diderot's *Le Neveu de Rameau* implicitly appears as the most powerful modern expression of identification, understood as a process linking not only the characters in the work of art with one another or with the spectator, but also art with philosophy. A theory of tragedy and art as (self-)knowledge subtends Hegel's reading of *Le Neveu* and gives it its significance, not only in relation to a particular stage of consciousness, but also in relation to Hegelian philosophy as a whole.

Hegel, Rameau's Nephew, and the Dialectic of Art

> *The attacks hitherto made against the French forms of art, first by De la Motte, and afterwards by Diderot and Mercier, have been like voices in the wilderness. It could not be otherwise, as*

> *the principles on which these writers proceeded were in reality*
> *destructive, not merely of the conventional forms, but of all poeti-*
> *cal forms whatever.*
>
> —A. W. Schlegel

As in the case of his reading of *Antigone*, Hegel's lack of reserve in relation to *Le Neveu* suggests that he views his reading of it as another particularly strong point in the "history of reason." Clearly, however, it
also has the potentially opposite significance: Hegelian philosophy is
as vulnerable in relation to Diderot's text as in relation to Sophocles'
play. Once Hegel has accepted *Le Neveu* as an exemplary illustration
of the progress of reason, any disagreement concerning his interpretation of Diderot's dialogue goes to the very heart of speculative philosophy itself. Roger Laufer's thesis that Diderot's great merit in *Le
Neveu* is to have anticipated perfectly Hegel's *Phenomenology* can be
turned, if not upside down, then inside out: in this dialogue, the
entire *Phenomenology* (and the *Aesthetics*) is, as it were, staged before
the fact, that is, put into a form in which the *scène* and the *hors-scène*
become distinct and, as a result, the limits and presuppositions that
permit the philosophical stage to exist are made apparent.[5] Like any
reader, Hegel is confronted with certain choices in his interpretation
of Diderot's text. The choices he makes reveal fundamental ethical-
theoretical decisions at the basis of his philosophical system, that is,
the assumptions that allow him to distinguish between the aesthetic
and the philosophical and to privilege the latter as a higher stage of
the former.

If one is to read Hegel's interpretation of *Le Neveu* critically, however, the first thing that should be emphasized is how persuasive and
powerful it is—so persuasive and powerful that it has prefigured the
great majority of subsequent readings of Diderot's text, at least in
their major lines. The key to Hegel's reading of *Le Neveu* is in a sense
quite simple. It lies in the idea that the Nephew, *Lui*, is the hero of the
dialogue, not *Moi*. Much—if not all—of the force of Hegel's reading
stems from the alacrity with which the philosopher of reason embraces this virtually Dionysian figure as the embodiment of reason in
his age. The few readers who offer a counterreading of the dialogue
have stressed that the Nephew constitutes an essentially negative,
albeit at times seductive portrait of the cultural parasite. They have
reminded us that Rameau the Nephew was part of a group of anti-

philosophes, which included Palissot, another "parasite" and man of letters who had authored a play that in Diderot's view libeled the Encyclopedists and himself in a particularly scandalous way.[6] But such a response to Hegel's interpretation fails to address itself to its real strength, which lies in the link Hegel establishes between the exorbitant figure of the Nephew and the speculative itself.

The link between the Nephew and the speculative is provided by the process or logic of identification, and the privilege Hegel attaches to the perspective of *Lui* in his reading of Diderot's *Le Neveu* derives from the speculative or dialectical function of this process. Hegel's reading of *Le Neveu* repeatedly underscores the ability of the nephew to occupy *all* positions in his society, and the corresponding inability of *Moi* to say anything to the Nephew "that [he] does not already know and say,"[7] despite their antithetical nature in moral terms. *Moi*, the honest consciousness, is already in *Lui*, and the objections *Moi* makes to *Lui* are objections he makes to himself. The character of his relationship to *Moi* and to his society as a whole is what makes the Nephew a figure of the dialectic. The Nephew has such an important place in Hegel's interpretation not only of Diderot's dialogue but of the entire eighteenth century because, thanks to what Hegel sees as an unlimited capacity for identification, he becomes the dialectic itself, that is to say, he becomes the embodiment of that discourse within which all other critical positions and discourses are situated.

For Hegel, Rameau's Nephew is the example of a stage of the phenomenology of the Spirit in which it takes the form of culture and, more specifically, of a consciousness disrupted by an awareness of the general contamination of all opposites—good and bad, nobility and servility—in and by culture:

> It [the Spirit] is this absolute and universal alienation of the actual world and of thought; it is *pure culture*. What is learnt in this world is that neither the *actuality* of power and wealth, nor their specific *notions*, "good" and "bad," or the consciousness of "good" and "bad" (the noble and ignoble consciousness) possesses the truth; on the contrary, all these moments become inverted, one changing into the other, and each is the opposite of itself. (316)

The Spirit must pass through this stage of the disruption of its consciousness of itself, of the inversion of opposites, in order to emerge unified and at one with itself, having placed all distinctions on the firm ground of reason. Culture is the stage of the negation and alienation of reason that the Spirit has to negate and assume into itself in order to be fully rational, fully itself.

It is important to stress that in Hegel's view the Nephew dominates the *Moi*, the "honest consciousness," not because the bad dominates the good or servility dominates nobility but, rather, because the Nephew incarnates the consciousness of the contamination of these opposites by each other, their universal perversion:

> The [Nephew's] disrupted consciousness . . . is *consciousness* of the perversion, and, moreover, of the absolute perversion. What prevails in it is the notion, which brings together in a unity the thoughts which, in the honest individual, lie far apart. . . . The content of what Spirit says about itself is thus the perversion of every notion and reality, the universal deception of itself and others; and the shamelessness which gives utterance to this deception is just for that reason the greatest truth. (317)

The basis of the implicit privilege of the Nephew in relation to other figures of consciousness presented in the *Phenomenology* can be articulated in the terms of this passage. Other antagonists—that is, other forms of consciousness—are condemned to fail to identify with the other against which they stand opposed, and, as a result, it is only *for us* that the reconciliation of the opposing terms, their synthesis and sublation, is actual. But the Nephew is both an antagonist in a struggle with a noble consciousness *and* the consciousness of the fundamental identity underlying that struggle and opposition. For Hegel, then, there is nothing in this stage of the *Phenomenology* that cannot be accounted for from the perspective of the Nephew. The *Moi* is powerless in relation to *Lui* because, once again, *Lui* occupies not only his own perspective but that of *Moi* as well.

The ability to occupy all positions also implies a radical estrangement from all positions, including one's own. The Nephew is characterized by a radical alienation of the type Diderot argues, in the *Paradoxe sur le comédien*, is typical of the great actor, who is a master of identification. For Hegel, such radical alienation is the source of a power to transcend the social scene, which this disruptive consciousness constantly observes from a distance, even as he plays a role in it. In Hegel's text, the Nephew *transcends his society precisely because he is at one with it.* Hegel indicates the merging of the Nephew and his society when he equates the Nephew's consciousness with (witty) conversation or talk, which he treats as the expression of the totality of the society of the *ancien régime.* Having established this equivalence, Hegel writes: "In such talk, this particular self . . . *is* the self-disruptive nature of all relationships and the conscious disruption of them; but only as self-consciousness in revolt is it aware of its own disrupted state, and in thus knowing it has immediately risen above it" (321). This description of the Nephew as a witty conversationalist makes it particularly clear that he — and hence identification — are implicitly figures for the dialectic itself. For, like the Nephew, the dialectic also transcends each stage in the phenomenology of the Spirit by becoming one with it. It is in their common ability to occupy *all* positions and hence no single position that the self-disrupted consciousness of the Nephew, like the dialectic itself, immediately *transcends* each and every particular position and becomes absolute (317).

In his article on Hegel's interpretation of Diderot, H. R. Jauss notes that it is a montage of a very select group of quotations from Diderot's text, and he argues that this montage "betrays the point which Hegel's questions want to get at."[8] Thus, Jauss states, Hegel refers to the passage in which the Nephew "heaped upon each other and mixed up thirty arias." But, whereas in Diderot's text this passage describes the musical pantomime of the Nephew, Hegel makes it describe his moral character: the uncommon frankness with which he lumps together the high and the low, the good and the bad. In another instance, Jauss argues, the reverse is true. Hegel takes a quotation whose subject in Diderot's text is the moral depravity of the Nephew and makes it apply to the Nephew as a musician. In both instances, "Hegel completely ignores the rules concerning quotation" (173). According to Jauss, these transgressions of the rules of quotation are necessitated by Hegel's desire to depict the Nephew as uncommonly frank and, ultimately, as fundamentally lucid in the way he mixes up what *Moi* struggles to keep separate.

At first glance, Jauss's reading appears so literal as to be hard to credit. He never seems to entertain the idea that Hegel takes the passages describing the Nephew's musical pantomime to be figures or metaphors of his immorality and his correspondingly cynical lucidity. But, despite its literalness, Jauss's commentary raises a crucial point. For Hegel does indeed read *Le Neveu* as though what is said in it about art can be immediately translated into moral terms; as though what is said about morality can be immediately translated into aesthetic terms, and as though what is said about both art and music is immediately mirrored in the consciousness of the Nephew. The problem is not so much, as Jauss would have it, that Hegel ignores the protocols of quotation (whatever they might be); he seems rather to assume that different protocols are not required to treat the different domains referred to by the various quotations. He does, then, what *Moi* argues that the Nephew himself does: he ignores or denies the incommensurability of the moral, aesthetic, and cognitive orders: "I began to tolerate only with pain the presence of a man who discussed a horrible action, an execrable atrocity, as a connoisseur of painting or poetry examines the beauties of a work of taste, or a moralist or historian underlines and illuminates the circumstances of a heroic action."[9] At the deepest level, however, it would be more accurate to say that Hegel, rather than ignoring these distinctions, is totally preoccupied with justifying his lack of regard for them.

In this sense too, Hegel's interest in the Nephew is consistent with his interest in tragedy in particular, for, as we have seen, Hegel treats *Antigone* as at once the immediate expression of the ethical community and a work of art. Sophocles' tragedy, in other words, authorizes a similar amalgamation of the ethical, the aesthetic, and, ultimately, the philosophical. Hegel's reading of *Le Neveu* thus relates once again to his interpretation of tragedy. Moreover, like his interpretation of tragedy in the *Phenomenology*, it also sets the stage for his treatment of art as a whole in his *Aesthetics*. It leads directly to the argument he makes there: that the rules that apply to speculative discourse also apply to art and morality. Because it reveals the power of identification to overcome all relationships of alterity or opposition, Hegel's reading of *Le Neveu* amounts to a dress rehearsal for the sublation of morality by art and of art by philosophy in the *Aesthetics*.

The mediating power of art, as we have also seen both in Hegel's critique of Kant and in his interpretation of *Antigone*, is what makes art "higher" than morality, that is, what brings it closer than morality to philosophy. Hegel's criticism of (Kantian) morality—his argument that the great stumbling block of morality is its lack of what he calls *actuality*, by which he means the impossibility of moral law ever corresponding to concrete, practical behavior—is also clearly indicated in his reading of *Le Neveu*. Hegel portrays *Lui* as lucid in his sense of the actual contamination of all opposites, including the good and bad, whereas he portrays *Moi* as struggling, unsuccessfully, to keep these opposites from collapsing one into the other, to maintain the distinction between what ought to be and what is.

Hegel's critique of morality in fact echoes that of Rameau's Nephew, who also criticizes moral law for its lack of actuality in his debate with *Moi* over morality and more specifically over the moral value of literary examples. The Nephew has read all the works that purportedly give moral instruction to the reader, but, he argues, their content never conforms to the moral law that they are supposed to illustrate. It could just as well—for the Nephew it does—illustrate his own, perverse principles:

> I have read and ceaselessly read and reread Théophraste, La Bruyère, and Molière. . . . I glean from them what one should do and what one should not say. Thus, when I read *L'Avare*, I say to myself: be a miser, if you wish; but avoid speaking like a miser. When I read *Tartuffe*, I say to myself: be a hypocrite, if you wish, but don't talk like the hypocrite. Keep the vices which are useful to you; but dispense with the tone and appearances which would make you appear ridiculous. (115)

Just as Hegel will repeatedly argue that the concrete actions of the subject never correspond to abstract moral law, so the Nephew indicates that there is always a disjunction between stories and their supposed moral lessons. When one compares the relevant passages from the *Aesthetics* and the *Phenomenology* to this passage from Diderot's *Le Neveu*, it is clear that, from Hegel's point of view, the Nephew's amorality or immorality could very easily be interpreted as emblematic of the dialectic and of art, of the dialectic *as* art—of its freedom with respect to any merely abstract moral aim, and of the corresponding ability of spirit to identify with or comprehend within itself both the good and the bad, both the ideal and the real.

There is another affinity between art and Rameau's Nephew that, from Hegel's standpoint, follows from their shared ability to mediate opposition: both are also reflections of consciousness and hence represent forms of knowledge. Hegel argues that man needs art because he is, above all, a thinking being endowed with consciousness. But consciousness, unlike animal intelligence, requires that man "*duplicate* himself" (*Aesthetics*, 31), become double, himself and an exteriorization of himself. For example, man rises above his animal nature by recognizing and exteriorizing himself as an animal and, in the process, comes to know himself as human. Similarly, in Hegel's analysis of *Le Neveu*, the Nephew's privilege stems from his being double, both a parasite and the consciousness of the perverse relationship of reciprocity between the parasite and the honest consciousness. His identification, like his perversion, is thus without limitation of any kind. It embraces itself in the same way as it includes everything and everyone else, and in this sense his consciousness is a consciousness of his society as a whole. And just as man's consciousness of his animal nature is a sign that he has transcended the animal, so this identification between the Nephew and his society is the sign that he has, in consciousness, already transcended it and has come to know it and himself.

It is thus clear why for Hegel the Nephew's characteristics as a musician can immediately be translated into the terms of his moral cynicism and why, more generally, Hegel does not recognize the necessity for different rules when dealing with the aesthetic, the moral, and the cognitive. In fact, the only distinctions between the moral, aesthetic, and cognitive spheres allowed by Hegel are those determining their relative privileges and subordination. The aesthetic is the *Aufhebung* of the moral because it effects an identification between terms that, from the perspective of (an abstract) morality, can be thought only in terms of opposition. The cognitive is in turn the sublation of the aesthetic, because identification converts art into a source of self-knowledge, and in the process it transcends art itself. The essential themes of the *Aesthetics* — the triumph of art over morality and the essentially conceptual and hence philosophical nature of art — are already implicit in Hegel's reading of *Le Neveu*. *Le Neveu de Rameau* is a crucial text for Hegel not only because it can be termed a philosophical work of art but also because the figure of the Nephew stands for the overcoming of art itself by philosophy, an overcoming effected in and through identification and hence within art itself.

Diderot's *Le Neveu* and the Limits of Identification

> *You were here before coming in, and you will still be here when you go out.*
>
> —Diderot

When one considers the way Hegel's reading of *Le Neveu* and his philosophy reinforce each other, the difficulty of challenging his interpretation becomes clearer. This is especially so if one takes the view, expressed by many of his modern critics, that his philosophy is ineluctable even for those who reject it. Even the writer who successfully "refutes" Hegel on a specific point seems condemned to be overwhelmed by the coherence and force of the logic uniting his interpretation of *Le Neveu* with speculative philosophy as a whole.

Nevertheless, a central point in Hegel's interpretation is clearly open to question: his assumption that the point of view of the Nephew is the most comprehensive in Diderot's dialogue, that, like the dialectic, it encompasses all the others. The question of whether or not the Nephew is the hero of the dialogue has long constituted the focus of literary-historical debates concerning *Le Neveu*. Those who have come after Hegel have most frequently translated his reading into biographical terms. According to one such reading, Diderot, despite his actual dislike for Rameau's Nephew, was unconsciously fascinated by his force and talent and thus unwittingly gave the musician the central role in the dialogue. Roland Desné, a rare dissenter to the view that the Nephew is the work's central figure, has sought to refute it on competing literary-historical grounds (Desné, Introduction).

But beyond the question of Diderot's intentions (assuming this question has validity), beyond even the question of the correctness of Hegel's interpretation with respect to this or that detail in the text, is the question of the link between Diderot's text and Hegel's system. If there are indeed points on which the critic may disagree with Hegel's interpretation, the critical task does not end when those points are simply identified. If there is to be a genuine discussion with and critique of Hegel, then the philosophical implications of those points of disagreement need to be elaborated. The question is, then, Does the perspective of the Nephew really command all others in *Le Neveu de Rameau*? That is, is his identification with the other total and his corresponding ability to transcend his society absolute? Equally important, what are the philosophical and critical implications if they are not?

We have seen how the Nephew's critique of morality, like Hegel's *Phenomenolgy* and his *Aesthetics*, attacks both its abstract character and the resulting contradictions between it and actual practice. From the Nephew's perspective, these contradictions disqualify morality and justify his own view of society, a view that substitutes aesthetic for moral criteria. Like Hegel, the Nephew in effect "completely ignores the rules of quotation"; he fails to respect the boundaries between the ethical, aesthetic, and cognitive spheres. When carried to the extreme, the Nephew's lack of regard for these boundaries fills *Moi* and the reader with horror—as when he tells the story of the renegade of Avignon and his atrocious (but, for the Nephew, "aesthetically" admirable) betrayal of a Jew who had generously befriended him. However, when the Nephew's essentially aesthetic outlook is extended to his relationships with other parasites like himself, the effects are comic. But who really laughs last in such instances?

According to the Nephew's aesthetic conception of life, not evil but rather ridicule is to be avoided at all costs.[10] The Nephew seeks to make others appear ridiculous in order to make manifest his own superiority to ridicule:

> I have no other merit here than to have done systematically and out of a spirit of rigor, out of a reasonable and true view of things what most others do by instinct. That is why their reading does not make them better than I am; but they remain ridiculous, despite themselves. Whereas I am ridiculous only when I want to be, and on those occasions I leave them far behind me; because the same art that teaches me to avoid ridicule on certain occasions teaches me also on other occasions to be ridiculous in a superior manner. (*Le Neveu*, 115–16)

In "being ridiculous in a superior manner," the Nephew once again reveals his affinity with the figure of the great actor as described in Diderot's *Paradoxe sur le comédien*. Like the actor, who supposedly can represent passion precisely because he is, at least as an actor, totally without passion, the Nephew claims to be a master at being ridiculous precisely because he is himself above ridicule.

Equally important, in "being ridiculous in a superior manner," the Nephew adopts the strategy or ruse that Hegel will adopt for the dialectic. Like the Spirit, the Nephew affirms himself and his absolute mastery through an identification with the other to which he is apparently opposed—the other being in this case the abject role he plays in society. According to the speculative logic of identification, the more completely one identifies (or appears to identify) with the other, the greater the resulting lucidity and transcendence of the other. Similarly, according to the Nephew, by choosing how and when he will appear ridiculous, he can ultimately avoid ridicule. To be ridiculous is the greatest sin in the Nephew's eyes; to elevate himself above the contempt of *Moi* and society as a whole is his highest "moral" aim.

But though Rameau's Nephew incarnates the dialectic most clearly at those moments when he both appears ridiculous and thereby affirms his invulnerability to ridicule, he also, paradoxically, becomes subject to the critique that Hegel the dialectician makes of Kant the moral philosopher. The Nephew's lucid critique of morality does not prevent him from committing sins of his own, that is, from being caught in a contradiction between his aesthetic law, "Avoid ridicule," and actuality or practice. He is happy to appear undignified or ridiculous, but only when he *chooses* to appear so. The distinction, however, between those instances when he chooses to be ridiculous and those when he is simply and unintentionally ridiculous is not and cannot be actual: it resides only in the intentions of the Nephew. To the Nephew's boast, "I am ridiculous only when I want to be," *Moi* wryly retorts, "You did well to reveal these mysteries to me; otherwise I would have believed you to be in contradiction with yourself" (116). In this instance, at least, *Moi* has said something to the Nephew that he "does not already know and say." *Moi*'s irony is completely lost on the Nephew, who quite simply *is* in contradiction with himself.

The Nephew's situation is thus identical to that of the moral subject, who cannot actually or effectively distinguish between instances where he intentionally commits good (or bad) actions and those where he inadvertently commits good (or bad) actions. Like morality, the Nephew's aesthetic principles reside ultimately in intentions and consciousness alone. These are the very grounds on which Hegel criticizes Kant: "For morality is only *consciousness*, a negative essence, for whose pure duty sensuousness has only a negative significance, is only *not* in conformity with duty. But in that harmony, *morality qua consciousness*, i.e., its actuality, vanishes. . . . The consummation, therefore, cannot be attained, but is to be thought of merely as an *absolute* task, i.e. one which simply remains a task" (*Phenomenology*, 368). The avoidance of ridicule is an infinite task for the Nephew, and the point at which he will be beyond the reach of ridicule is infinitely deferred.

Even in the moments when the Nephew is supreme as an artist, he does not escape from ridicule:

> And then he began to pace, murmuring in his throat some of the airs from the *Island of Fools*. . . . He started becoming passionate and singing to himself. . . . He heaped one upon the other and confused thirty arias. . . . Everything was there, the delicacy of song and the force of expression; and suffering. . . . Did I feel admiration? Yes, I admired! Did I feel pity? I was touched by pity; but a shade of ridiculousness was fused into these sentiments, and it denatured them. (*Le Neveu*, 149)

In Diderot's *Neveu*, as in the philosophy of Hegel, morality is constantly undermined by its own contradictions and lack of actuality. But this does not mean that Rameau's Nephew successfully sublates morality and raises it to a higher level. In Hegel's reading, *Moi* is blind to contradictions that structure his morality and his corresponding perceptions of the world, but the Nephew has his own "morality" and thus, according to Hegel's own logic, his own blind spots. His aesthetics of power and mastery is also a "morality" in which weakness or ridiculousness are sins, and the contradictions in his position with respect to this other morality are no clearer to the Nephew than those in his position are clear to *Moi*.

When read this way, Diderot's dialogue does not lend support to the conclusion that the consciousness of the Nephew is a "confusion which is clear to itself." Though the Nephew has clearly expressed for himself his own vileness, he has not clearly expressed for himself the contradictions in his aesthetic morality. The aestheticism that perverts him morally thus limits him artistically and intellectually as well. The failure of the Nephew to recognize the contradiction in his own position is not just the sign that this particular character or figure is a defective example of the power of identification. It is the sign of a defect in identification itself, a limitation of identification—and of the dialectic—that affects them from within. It seems, then, that the Nephew is not the central figure that Hegel makes him in the sense that there is a supplementary irony in his situation that reveals a limitation inherent in (his capacity for) identification. As figured by the Nephew, absolute consciousness proves not to be absolute, because only when law and practice coincide has this status been achieved. The Nephew has failed to attain what Jean-François Lyotard has called the primary aim of the dialectic: "to express oneself for oneself."[11] Like morality, the Nephew/the dialectic is plagued by a lack of actuality.

Ostensibly, nothing could be more damaging to the claims speculative discourse makes on its own behalf than such a revelation. And yet, as Lyotard has argued, even it fails to invalidate the paradoxical logic of the dialectic. To express oneself for oneself

> is the end that guides the rebounding of the self in the dialectical phrase. This end is "the reconciliation of reason conscious of itself with reason, that is, with actuality." . . . This aim is unceasingly attained, and thus is never attained. If it is attained, it isn't. When it is not attained, it is attained nonetheless. . . . You don't get out of the speculative. (144)

The logic of the contamination of opposites – the logic of identification – is so powerful that failures can always be turned into successes once they have been expressed by Spirit for itself, or in other terms, once the Spirit has identified itself with them. The opposition between actuality and nonactuality, like any other opposition, turns out in part to be false; there is always actuality where we thought there was a lack of it. As Lyotard says, "you don't get out of the speculative," nor can the process of identification ever be said to fail. And yet, though its terms remain Hegelian, this description of the dialectic and of identification is certainly never explicit in Hegel's work. We may not have gotten out of the "system of identification"; but once it has been described in such terms, it is no longer the same.

The lack of actuality of identification or, rather, the peculiar form taken by its actuality, the fact that it is to be found in its purest form as something implicit in inactuality, has repercussions at every level of Hegel's highly coherent system. Because of this lack of actuality, the end of the system is compromised, but so are all its intermediate stages, insofar as their ultimate existence is fully realized only in the end. Hegel, as is well known, inverts the ordinary language meanings of the terms *abstract* and *concrete*, so that the abstract corresponds to the phenomenal or the empirical and the concrete to the philosophical or conceptual because for him reality lies in the concept or, at any rate, in the mediation of experience by the concept. But if the end of the system, the ultimate form of identification that exists fully both in itself and for itself, is compromised, then the question of the concreteness and actuality of the entire system of identification is also left open, unresolved.

For Philippe Lacoue-Labarthe, Hegel's claims concerning the concreteness of his philosophy—a concreteness that is at the basis of the privilege he gives to the Nephew as the figure of absolute identification—are directly linked to his lack of openness both to the philosophy of Kant and, at the same time, to the question of art. In Lacoue-Labarthe's words, Hegel's philosophy is opposed to Kant's as "a philosophy of the *as such* (of the *als soche*)" is opposed to

> a philosophy of the *as if* (of the *als ob*). . . . Philosophy of the *als ob*, with all that it implies, that is to say, with the radical consequence that Nietzsche drew from "Kant"—but before which, at bottom, Kant himself shrank: to wit, that philosophy itself is essentially artistic (or artifactitious) and that it is worth exactly what art is worth (and so philosophy will have to pay the price of its own depreciation of art).[12]

If the attainment of its end by the dialectic is put into question, that is, if its claim to have attained actuality is in doubt, then the entire dialectical system is opened to the *as if* rather than to the *as such*. By the same token, if the attainment of its end by the dialectic is put into question, then the sense of identification is also altered. It no longer permits philosophy to find itself in art; or at any rate, the fact that philosophy can always find itself in art takes on a new, ambiguous meaning. Identification becomes not just a confirmation of the philosophical character of art but also a process that situates philosophy itself within art, within a series of identifications that it can no longer claim to dominate as the preeminent, absolute form of identification.

Given the close links between the Hegelian perspective on identification and the philosophy of art, Diderot's dialogue cannot provide the basis for a questioning of identification without also raising serious questions about Hegel's philosophy of art. As we have seen, the consciousness of the Nephew is the active force behind identification as it is presented by Hegel, inasmuch as the process through which the Nephew is said to transcend his culture to become absolute is one in which that culture as a whole is mirrored by (his) consciousness. Just as Hegel sees the consciousness of the Nephew as the central element of *Le Neveu*, so in the *Aesthetics* he presents consciousness itself as the central element of art. The centrality of consciousness to art is what makes art a form of knowledge and also what makes it possible for there to be such a thing as a philosophy of art. The (beautiful) work of art is above all the mirror in which the rational subject recognizes itself, and it is thus the rational, knowing subject who commands both art and the process of identification.

In contrast, *Le Neveu* as a whole and also the specific character of the Nephew cannot be understood without reference to a fundamental conflict between the rational subject and the work of art, a conflict that makes the concept of beauty appear problematic. It is difficult to know exactly what vocabulary should be used to analyze the nature of the conflict in terms of which Diderot's work presents the problem of art. Hegel provides little help in describing conflicts within the aesthetic field. Those he does describe are almost immediately resolved in a higher phase of art and ultimately, with respect to art as a whole, in philosophy. As has already been noted, for Hegel, the essence of art is not conflict but mediation. By contrast, for Kant, or at least for the version of Kant which emerges from Jean-François Lyotard's interpretation of his work, conflict plays a crucial role.

Lyotard argues that a specific form of conflict which he calls *le différend* is central to Kant's philosophy as a whole and particularly to the section of the *Critique of Judgement* devoted to the sublime.[13] According to Lyotard, a *différend* is "a case of conflict between (at least) two parties which cannot be decided equitably because of the lack of a rule of judgment applicable to the two arguments" (*Le Différend*, 9). Lyotard thus defines the *différend* as a dispute between two parties, but the notion is equally pertinent for him when one considers aesthetic experience, even though nominally only a single party is involved. Implicitly, for Lyotard, aesthetic experience as Kant defines it is best exemplified by the sublime, and the effect of the sublime, Lyotard argues, is to create a *différend*—that is, a radical division or cleavage—in the contemplating subject. Following Kant, Lyotard defines the experience of the sublime as

> a pleasure mixed with pain, pleasure that comes from pain. In the event of an absolutely immense object . . . which like all absolutes can only be considered outside of reason, the imagination and the ability to present fail to provide appropriate representations. This frustration of expression kindles a pain, a kind of cleavage within the subject between what can be conceived and what can be imagined. . . . From any vantage point around this cleavage, infinity, or the absence of the Idea, is revealed in what Kant calls a negative presentation, or even a non-presentation.[14]

Without obscuring the important differences between the aesthetics of Diderot and Kant, it seems clear that, in *Le Neveu de Rameau*, Diderot's aim is to reflect upon the capacity of art to problematize the identification of the rational subject with the work of art, and in the process to produce, or reveal, a cleavage in the subject. For Diderot, as for Kant, this capacity is evident inasmuch as there are certain circumstances under which aesthetic contemplation produces pain, a lack of ease, discomfort. In Diderot's text, these states, which are potentially those of the reader of the dialogue, are projected into it and exemplified by *Moi*, who articulates his own conflicting pain and interest for the reader.[15] The displeasure experienced by the subject reflects a fundamental conflict concerning *Le Neveu* as a whole. The dialogue is certainly a work of art, but the reader's or spectator's perceptions or experience of it do not harmonize to produce a sense of its beauty. *Le Neveu*, like the Nephew, is at once repulsive and beautiful: "You have sometimes seen, in a brilliant concert, Ferrari, or Chiabrun, or some other virtuoso in the same convulsions, offering the image of the same torture, and causing more or less the same pain [as the Nephew]. For is it not a painful thing to see torment in the one who is occupied with depicting pleasure for me?" (*Le Neveu*, 60). Implicit in these lines is a "paradox of the spectator," according to which the spectator is divided by the conflicting feelings that the art of the Nephew inspires in him or her—not united with him- or herself and the work of art by the bond of a positive identification but simultaneously attracted to and repelled by it and by his or her own feelings.

Thanks to its ability to produce both pleasure and displeasure, art thus has the power to create a cleavage in the subject, whether the subject in question is the actor or the spectator. Diderot's reflections on the affective states of the subject of art link up with a long and distinguished philosophical tradition extending back to Aristotle's *Poetics*. Hegel, however, dismisses this type of investigation in a few lines in the introduction to the *Aesthetics*. In the first place, sentiments, he argues, are subjective, whereas art is objective and universal in its appeal. In addition, "'what feelings should be aroused by art, fear, for example, and pity? But how can these be agreeable, how can the treatment of misfortune afford satisfaction?' Reflection on these lines dates especially from Mendelssohn's time. . . . Yet such investigation did not get far" (*Aesthetics*, 32). By implication, only an irrational subject would tolerate this mixture of pleasure and displeasure. But, for Hegel, an irrational subject would not really be a subject at all.

Hegel's sense of the relative unimportance of sentiment in relation to art is directly related to his view that art is an expression of consciousness. If sentiment were more important than Hegel acknowledges, then the grounds for a (rationalist) philosophy of art would be much more difficult to establish, and Hegel could not legitimately claim to understand art even better than the connoisseurs or men of taste. Hegel does not, of course, suppose that the artist, for example, must be a philosopher in order to produce a work of art. From his perspective, the artist quite clearly is not a philosopher and thus should not be expected to be capable of providing a rational explanation of his work, although an exceptional artist such as Schiller has managed to do just that. But even if the artist remains by and large unconscious of the sense of his work, that does not mean it is not susceptible of being fully elucidated, brought to the light of consciousness. Hegel speaks of the "ruse of reason" in connection with history, but he could as easily speak of such a ruse with respect to art. The artist may not know what he is doing, but reason makes use of him for its own ends. He may not be conscious in the moment of creation, but the consciousness realized in the work of art is still what, in implicit form, guides its creation. This is the sense in which reason or consciousness is the true source of art, and the process of identification that links artist and work or spectator and work is essentially rational.

The picture of art that emerges from Diderot's work as a whole is significantly different, inasmuch as it presents art as having two sources, which are never fully reconciled or harmonized. One of these sources Diderot calls sensibility or passion. The other he calls reflection, the absence of sensibility. These two terms play a fundamental role in most, if not all, of Diderot's aesthetic writings, but they are especially prominent in his texts relating to the theater and specifically to the art of the actor. For Diderot, as for Hegel, the theater is not one genre among others, however—it is the genre that best exemplifies art as a whole. The special status Diderot attaches to the theater in relation to other *poetic* forms is evident in the privilege he consistently accords to the actor as contrasted to the poet.

The special status of the theater as compared to music is indicated in *Le Neveu* itself, when *Lui* argues that gesture and inarticulate sound, which according to Diderot's texts on the theater are the preeminent materials of the actor, are the models for music (*Le Neveu*, 141). The special status of the theater in relation to *painting* is indicated in the *Salons*, where through his successive judgments of the works of contemporary painters, but above all those of Greuze, Diderot reveals that the ideal painting is one that freezes an essentially dramatic situation, catching it when it has evolved to its climatic moment, the moment that can be rendered only by the gestures and the most expressive and energetic accents of the actor.[16] In Diderot's work as a whole, the theater is thus the model for the other arts, and what those texts say about the relationship between passion and reflection applies not only to the theater but to art as a whole.

Significantly, identification—that is, in Diderot's terms, the ability to put oneself in the place of another and take on his or her language and, even more importantly, his or her gestures and expression—is the essence of the art of the actor according to Diderot, and the Nephew is thus a master artist not so much because of his musical talent but perhaps even more because of his talent for pantomime. When interpreted within the context of Diderot's aesthetics, the figure of the Nephew appears to have, at least in this respect, the same significance as he does for Hegel: he represents a particularly radical or pure form of identification. But Hegel and Diderot appear to diverge on the question of the nature and significance of identification—and hence of art—itself. The question is, Is identification a matter of reflection or passion? In those moments in which the actor reaches the height of his art, does his consciousness or do his feelings dominate? Though in certain of Diderot's texts the emphasis is on passion as the basis of identification (particularly in the *Entretiens sur le Fils naturel*), while in others (particularly the *Paradoxe sur le comédien*) reflection and an absence of sensibility or passion are emphasized, neither term is ever completely abandoned—and in *Le Neveu*, both are very much present.

The importance of the theme of reflection in *Le Neveu* is evident in the similarities, noted by many critics, between Rameau's Nephew and the ideal actor described in the *Paradoxe sur le comédien*. Like the ideal actor, the Nephew is devoid of a sense of pity and compassion for others. Also like him, he is capable of changing his expression from one of despair to one of joy, to one of boredom, all within a matter of seconds, ostensibly because he, like the great actor, experiences none of these emotions but only mimes their exterior signs.[17] These traits, it is argued in the *Paradoxe*, characterize men of reflection—those who think in situations in which other, sensitive individuals feel.[18] But one could, without betraying Diderot in the slightest, translate these traits into Hegel's terms: the actor is able to take on all sorts of roles because he is nothing in himself or, rather, because he is nothing more or other than the capacity to identify himself with all other roles and positions; as actor he is nothing more or less than an absolute form of reflection or consciousness, which mirrors its situation and in the process immediately transcends it.

Despite the many elements of *Le Neveu* that relate to the role of reflection in art, an equally important preoccupation in this text is passion. The Nephew himself argues that all art imitates passion: "Song is an imitation, by the sounds of a scale invented by art or inspired by nature, as you like, either by the voice or by an instrument, of the physical sounds or accents of passion; and you see that by making the appropriate changes in this definition, it would apply perfectly well to painting, eloquence, sculpture, and poetry" (*Le Neveu*, 141). But though all the arts derive from passion, not all are by nature equally close to it. The entire range of art forms, which extends from declamation to song, to symphonic music, derives from what Diderot, with *Lui*, calls the accents of passion, that is, the spontaneous sounds produced by men and women when they are moved by passion. But declamation nonetheless mirrors passion more immediately than song or symphonic music. This is evident inasmuch as we judge *declamation* by how it transposes *accents of passion* into its own rhythms and prosody, but we judge (or we ought to judge) *song* in relation to *declamation*, that is, by how well it transposes the rhythms and prosody of declamation into its own melody and rhythms. The symphony, in its turn, imitates and transposes song (141–142). Declamation is thus closer than song or symphony to the (a) source of art.

There is, however, an art even closer to passion than declamation, and that is pantomime. In the *Entretiens sur le Fils naturel*, Dorval argues that the most natural expressions of joy or despair are gestures made with the body and also "gestures" made using the voice, inarticulate vocal sounds and the intonation and accent with which the written lines are spoken.[19] It is because of the importance of gesture that "the worst picture would paint [actions of particular dramatic interest] better than the best discourse" (104). It is also because of the importance of gesture that Dorval holds the actor in even greater

esteem than the playwright, because the actor, not the writer, sup-
plies a given role with the gestures and accents that make it convincing and moving even beyond the spoken dialogue (104–5). In his
mastery of gesture, the actor reveals his absolute proximity to the
(other) source of art. Rameau's nephew may not be a genius like his
uncle, but insofar as he is master of pantomime, he is a more exemplary artist than even the great geniuses he detests. Similarly, *Le
Neveu* may not be a great novel or play, but it can legitimately claim to
be exemplary, that is, closer to the source of great literature, than even
the great plays of Racine and Voltaire, because it includes not only dialogue but also gesture – the detailed description of the pantomime of
the Nephew.

It is, of course, true that pantomime and gesture, like declamation,
song, and symphony, are expressions or representations of passion
and therefore implicitly mediated by reflection. But the reverse is also
true: symphony, song, and declamation are, like gesture, still expressions *of passion*, from which the artist never fully liberates himself.
Thus the Nephew's art may indeed have its source in reflection, but
it is just as likely that passion is controlling him. Passion may indeed
be an unconscious reason, as Hegel would have it; but it is just as
likely that reason is an unconscious passion.

The same logic applies to art as well. It may indeed be an unconscious philosophy, as Hegel would have it; but it is just as likely that
philosophy is an unconscious art. Of course, such assertions obey the
logic of the dialectic: "You don't get out of the dialectic." But the dialectic now no longer achieves its resolution in philosophy, and philosophy itself has become one term in a dialectic that continues beyond
or to the side of philosophy. Philosophy is confronted once again
with accomplishing the end of art that it thought it had already
accomplished, with accomplishing the end that is its own end.

Given Diderot's views on the importance of reflection in art and in
the process of identification, it is not surprising that Hegel should
have been drawn to *Le Neveu de Rameau*. Moreover, to the extent that
Le Neveu can be interpreted as a work of reflection, Hegel's decision to
treat it as a vehicle of knowledge is legitimate. But the knowledge, or
rather, the self-knowledge that philosophy gains when it identifies
itself with the figure of the Nephew is clearly being problematized in
the work in which he appears. In this sense, *Le Neveu* also represents
a trap set for a future Hegel, who could not fail to see the Nephew as

a particularly radical figure of the rational nature of identification and of the sublation of art by philosophy, but for whom the way in which Diderot situates and relativizes the consciousness of the Nephew would of necessity remain invisible. What Hegel "doesn't want to hear anything about" in the complex field of eighteenth-century aesthetics (Lacoue-Labarthe, "L'Imprésentable," 81), of which *Le Neveu de Rameau* is an important element, is clearly profiled in Diderot's text: art as a destabilizing force, art as the double of philosophy, neither different nor the same. The subject who reads and writes *Le Neveu* cannot be assumed to be the essentially rational subject who is posited as the reader and writer in Hegel's *Aesthetics* or *Phenomenology*, where the intended result of the dialectic is always unity.

It should be stressed that the destabilizing force of art as it is presented in *Le Neveu* derives not from its irrationality, but rather from its being not a matter simply of sentiment or reflection, beauty or ugliness, pleasure or displeasure. Thus it eludes the grasp of the philosopher who seeks to distinguish between a (rational) essence of art and the irrational or sentimental element that for Hegel remains inessential to art. Philosophy could not identify itself with art if reflection were merely extraneous to art in general and to *Le Neveu* in particular—if identification were not positive as well as negative. But from the perspective offered by *Le Neveu*, the significance of identification is not only that it permits the philosopher to "take his reason to the theater." It also situates his reason in the theater; it reveals reason to be an element of a process that it does not necessarily dominate or command. In this sense, Diderot's text undeniably testifies to the existence of a friendship between philosophy and art which is of fundamental significance to each. In the process, however, it not only opens art to philosophy but also opens philosophy to what is most alien to it, both in art and in itself.

CHAPTER 7

The Tragic Matrix
of Speculative Philosophy:
Generalized Mimesis
and the *Paradoxe sur le comédien*

Germans and French, although constantly at odds politically and socially, can no longer be presented pictorially in combat. We have adopted too many of their customs, too much of their military attire for us to be able to see a clear difference between almost identically uniformed members of the two nations.

—Goethe

There where sobriety abandons you, there is the limit of your enthusiasm.

—Hölderlin

Art beyond Aestheticism: Lacoue-Labarthe and Nietzsche

Among contemporary philosophers, the work of Philippe Lacoue-Labarthe—from his earliest essays on Nietzsche to his most recent work on Heidegger—stands out in terms of the central place it assigns to the problem of the relationship between art and philosophy. Lacoue-Labarthe's analysis of this relationship emphasizes the critical value of art, its power to undermine the claim of philosophy to be the summa and the truth. In this respect, Lacoue-Labarthe's essays both individually and collectively invite comparison with Nietzsche's *Birth of Tragedy*. His concept of art recalls Nietzsche's concepts of the tragic and the Dionysian not so much because Lacoue-Labarthe's version of art is Dionysian in character but, rather, because art, and particularly literature, has for Lacoue-Labarthe the same capacity to confront philosophy with something with which it cannot confront itself and in this sense to place philosophy in a context in which it appears radically problematic.

Lacoue-Labarthe's critique of philosophy also recalls Nietzsche's in another respect. Though it deals critically with philosophers from the entire philosophical tradition, the tradition as a whole is frequently condensed into a single figure—in Lacoue-Labarthe's case, not Socrates, but Hegel—and a single form of philosophy—speculative philosophy. *The speculative* is a term with two somewhat different meanings for Lacoue-Labarthe. In its narrower sense, it designates above all the philosophy of Hegel and those aspects of modern German philosophy from Kant up to, and even to some extent including, Nietzsche which confirm or are consistent with Hegelian philosophy.[1] In its broader sense, however, the speculative stands for philosophy itself insofar as it can be assimilated to an essentially Hegelian model of philosophy. Modern speculative philosophy makes explicit a tendency that is ultimately an essential—if not the essential—component of philosophy as a whole. It is a tendency on the part of philosophy to speculate, that is, to find itself in its opposite, to find that the other, in particular art, is a mirror image of (the subject of) philosophy. The speculative, therefore, is not just philosophy but also the system of relations regulating the shifting boundary between philosophy and art and determining art itself as an element or form of the speculative.

But though, in the broad lines of his analysis of the relation between art and philosophy, Lacoue-Labarthe appears to have followed Nietzsche in seeking to exploit a critical potential in art, in a very crucial respect he departs from Nietzsche. His interpretation of art appears to exemplify a much more critical and rigorous attitude in relation to aestheticism—or what Nietzsche himself, in criticizing his early work, calls the "artists' metaphysics" in the background of *The Birth of Tragedy*.

Whereas Nietzsche entertains only in an occasional digression or in an indirect manner the possibility that tragedy and philosophy might have a deeper affinity, this view of their relationship is central for Lacoue-Labarthe, who, besides indicating the critical value of art, also insists on its philosophical or metaphysical character. It is significant that, while Lacoue-Labarthe explicitly attaches the greatest possible critical value to art, he nonetheless repeatedly portrays himself as seeking a "minimum of lucidity" in his writing concerning the problem of art and philosophy, rather than any sweeping reversal or upheaval of established philosophical values.[2] This modesty corresponds to an important component of his analysis of the relation between art and philosophy: art is not absolutely other than philosophy, at least not in the usual sense, Lacoue-Labarthe repeatedly stresses. Lacoue-Labarthe's insistence that the era that is constituted and recapitulated by Hegelian philosophy is still ours is another sign of the emphasis he places on the metaphysical character of art. It implies that any question we ask of Hegel, any critical strategy we use to read him is already to some extent implicit in Hegel's philosophy. Even in approaching Hegel from the standpoint of a critical concept of art, we are in a sense under his power.[3]

Lacoue-Labarthe thus maintains that the question of literature belongs to philosophy as a whole and Hegelian philosophy in particular, but only as long as certain suspicions about its mode of belonging are put aside:

> When . . . we ask the question of the relationship between literature and philosophy, when, at least, the *question* is that of literature, when treating literature as a *philosopheme*, we put aside, dispel, or deflect the nagging, paradoxical, and obscure suspicion that there is a possible literary *filiation* of philosophy, we doubtless do nothing more than pose in a Hegelian mode (but not in Hegelian terms) a question that Hegel himself never asked as such. (54)

Literature is a question *for philosophy*, a "philosopheme," but only when the question of what philosophy has in common with literature is not pursued, because it is precisely this "nagging, paradoxical, and obscure" sense of what it might have in common with literature that most threatens philosophy, according to Lacoue-Labarthe. That is, if philosophy is from the start affiliated with and contaminated by literature, an other that can no longer be seen as completely other, then philosophy cannot ever be the same, even as it claims to define its relation with literature, delimit it, and incorporate it into itself.

Implicitly, then, Nietzsche was not wrong to attribute a critical potential to art in relation to philosophy. He himself became a metaphysician, however, when he defined the Dionysian as the opposite of the Socratic, and in the end his critique succeeded only in producing another form or version (the reversal) of Socratic philosophy. What is much more destabilizing in terms of philosophy is the possibility of an art that is not the other of philosophy, even though it cannot be simply assimilated into philosophy either. The ambiguity of the status of art in relation to philosophy is evident in Lacoue-Labarthe's description of the work of Hölderlin, one of the figures who exemplifies the critical element Lacoue-Labarthe sees in art. It is Hölderlin who, "through a movement of 'regression' if one wants (I will come back to this point: there is nothing pejorative about it), comes to touch something that dislocates the speculative *from within*."[4] Significantly, Hölderlin's work, whose central preoccupation, according to Lacoue-Labarthe's reading, is to address the question of the possibility and nature of a modern art, does not violently disrupt or overturn the speculative, nor does it originate in a space wholly alien to the speculative. Instead, it touches something within the speculative, and its effect is only to dislocate it.

The essays collected in *L'Imitation des modernes* should be read as a continuation of the line of questioning set forth in the critical reading Lacoue-Labarthe gives of Hegel's *Aesthetics* in "L'Imprésentable." In these later essays, he fully elaborates the historical-conceptual structure that gives rise to what in "L'Imprésentable" he calls "the nagging, paradoxical, and obscure suspicion that there is a possible literary *filiation* of philosophy" (54). As he puts it in "The Caesura of the Speculative":

> I would like to show—but this is hardly a thesis, given that the point, at bottom, ought to be evident—I would like to show that tragedy, or a certain interpretation of tragedy, explicitly a philosophical interpretation, and above all one wanting to be such, is the origin or the matrix of what in the wake of Kant is conventionally called speculative thought: that is to say, dialectical thought. ("Caesura," translation modified, 208)

The literary filiation of philosophy is evident in the "matricial" relationship between the interpretation of tragedy and speculative philosophy proper, but the ultimate implication of this thesis is not just that philosophy is rooted in its own interpretation of tragedy. Tragedy itself—that is, a discursive practice that is not explicitly philosophical and that philosophy itself has treated as other, as aesthetic, literary, or poetic—is implicitly part of this matrix in which the interpretation of tragedy also figures. This can be seen both in the way Lacoue-Labarthe juxtaposes them appositively in the above passage ("tragedy, or a certain interpretation of tragedy") and also in his conclusion that "the Oedipal scenario therefore implicitly contains the speculative solution. And everything has been prepared [by it] for that absolutization or paradoxical infinitization of the Subject [in which] philosophy will find its completion" (217).

Art and, more specifically, tragedy are thus the matrix of speculative philosophy, or, in other words, speculative philosophy is rooted in its aesthetic other. As a result, philosophy itself can be dislocated, though not overturned or dispensed with, its claim to truth contextualized in terms of its desire to provide the ultimate interpretation of tragedy. The critical power of tragedy (and more generally art) in relation to philosophy derives from the ambiguity of its status as matrix: both the other of philosophy and the same as philosophy. By implication, both aspects must be affirmed if tragedy is to retain its critical value. Much of Lacoue-Labarthe's work can be interpreted in terms of this double exigency.

And yet at certain points in his work, Lacoue-Labarthe appears to pull back from this position. Although he by and large maintains the tension between art and philosophy because that tension appears to be crucial in defining the critical role he assigns to art, he resolves it nonetheless at key moments in his analysis. In those moments, art emerges as absolutely other than philosophy, and, correspondingly, the speculative is in effect subjected to a dialectical operation governed not by philosophy but by art.

Lacoue-Labarthe's decision to subordinate the symmetry between philosophy and art to a conception of art which comprehends both itself and philosophy is evident in his essays on Diderot and Hölderlin, whose work taken together and interpreted in a certain critical light constitutes a substantial part, if not the essence, of the matrix from which, according to Lacoue-Labarthe, speculative philosophy (never completely) emerges. Put succinctly, the greater radicality of art corresponds to the contrast Lacoue-Labarthe establishes between the two writers and the privilege he assigns to one: that is, the greater critical power he attributes to Hölderlin in relation to the question of art. Hölderlin's greater radicality, of course, is almost imperceptible and does not prevent him from sharing much with Diderot. But the dissymmetry between Hölderlin and Diderot, *because* it is so slight, becomes immense in the terms of the logic that structures Lacoue-Labarthe's analysis of the relationship between philosophy and art.

And that dissymmetry corresponds, on the one hand, to the greater affinity between the work of Hölderlin and what Lacoue-Labarthe holds to be most destabilizing and disappropriating in art, and on the other, to the greater affinity of the work of Diderot with the speculative.

Diderot, Hölderlin, and Generalized Mimesis

In order to understand the distinction Lacoue-Labarthe ultimately draws between Hölderlin and Diderot—and between art and philosophy—it is important to grasp what from his perspective they share: a common position with respect to the crucial issue of representation or mimesis. Their common preoccupation with representation is what makes Diderot and Hölderlin the dominant figures in the tragic matrix of speculative philosophy. The basis of the special role Lacoue-Labarthe assigns their work in relation to speculative philosophy emerges in his interpretation of the notes where Hölderlin discusses ancient tragedy and the possibility of a modern tragedy. In Hölderlin's "rhythmic" conception of tragedy, there is a moment, a *caesura*, in Hölderlin's terms, in which, as Lacoue-Labarthe puts it, "the structure of tragedy itself becomes immobilized and paralyzed." It is at this moment that what appears is no longer " 'the alternation of representations but representation in itself' " (234). Representation itself, then, is for Hölderlin the subject of tragedy and not this or that content, this or that " 'consecution of representations.' " The importance given by Lacoue-Labarthe to this passage in particular and to any number of similar passages in Hölderlin's work indicates the central position mimesis holds in Lacoue-Labarthe's analysis of the relation between philosophy and tragedy.

In this passage, representation, or a certain concept of representation central to the speculative, is the something that Hölderlin touches that dislocates the speculative from within. In his essays on Hölderlin and Diderot taken as a whole, Lacoue-Labarthe more frequently uses the term *mimesis*, or imitation, rather than representation, to discuss the critical power of their work, as is suggested by the titles both of his essay on Diderot ("Diderot: Le paradoxe et la mimésis") and of the volume in which it and essays on Hölderlin are collected: *L'Imitation des modernes*. In *Heidegger, Art and Politics*, however, Lacoue-Labarthe brings forward a third term that not only is interchangeable with the other two but, he indicates, may even permit the critical dimension of the problem of imitation to be explored more fully and effectively. He introduces the term *identification* by saying that it is one he has "borrowed from Freud, because it is ultimately the only one we possess to designate what is at stake in the mimetic process. . . . Identification or appropriation—the self-becoming of the Self—will always have been thought of as the appropriation of a model" (*Heidegger*, 80–81). From Lacoue-Labarthe's perspective, the tradition that culminates in speculative philosophy has interpreted mimesis or representation as implying a reproduction that in each case is the mere copy of the original. From the standpoint of that tradition, identification could be interpreted only in similar terms.

The radicality of Lacoue-Labarthe's interpretation of the relationship between philosophy and art lies in his taking up the familiar—almost too familiar—term *mimesis/identification* and revealing its critical potential by redefining it in such a way that the relationship between original and copy appears in a problematic light. For Lacoue-Labarthe, the critical potential of the concept of mimesis is already implicit in Aristotle's *Poetics* and, more specifically, in his conception of art as the *perfection* of nature. In Lacoue-Labarthe's terms, this definition of art involves a paradox. It implies that art or, more specifically, tragedy, is *at once* imitation and original. For Aristotle, nature retains its originality insofar as art is an imitation of it, but art *also* has an originality inasmuch as the *perfected* nature it reproduces is not purely natural. Lacoue-Labarthe sees this paradox as evidence that Aristotle's *Poetics* already implies what he calls a *mimétologie*, that is, a theory of the "original" or poetic nature of representation—in other words, a notion of mimesis in which the re-production or copy is (also) "original."

Though the affinity between the work of Lacoue-Labarthe and that of Jacques Derrida is particularly evident in the former's discussion of mimesis, that same discussion also makes apparent an important difference between Lacoue-Labarthe's interpretation of Derrida and that of many of Derrida's other readers. From Lacoue-Labarthe's perspective, it would be false to convert immediately Derrida's notion of the "originary" character of writing or his own (Lacoue-Labarthe's) analysis of the "originary" character of mimesis into affirmations of the primacy of art or of the literary text in relation to philosophy. The original character of mimesis almost always implies quotation marks around the term *original* in his work. If this were not the case, Lacoue-Labarthe's position concerning the original character of mimesis would simply be an inversion of the philosophical interpretation of mimesis, and mimesis itself would simply be another form of origin. Lacoue-Labarthe's work involves a transformation, or at the very least an analysis of the ambiguity of the concept of mimesis, rather than a demystification of it, and this is why the term itself is neither simply positive nor simply negative for Lacoue-Labarthe.[5]

The ground for what Lacoue-Labarthe terms the deconstruction of the relation between philosophy and art is already being laid in the work of Aristotle. Nonetheless, while Aristotle's *Poetics* already implies a mimetology, Hölderlin and Diderot go much further, according to Lacoue-Labarthe. Unlike the *Poetics*, their work implies a generalization of his mimetic theory of art, "but one which can be such only in the abandonment of the terrain upon which Aristotle had constructed his own—that is, the terrain of the 'spectacular' relation" ("Caesura," 232). It is Hölderlin and Diderot who, at least in certain passages of their work, explicitly elaborate the major elements of a mimetology and also suggest the radically critical implications of such a mimetology in relation to speculative philosophy. Thus implicitly the work of Hölderlin and Diderot (and in certain respects that of Nietzsche and Heidegger) represents the interests of art with the greatest force, and this is true even though the mimetologies of Hölderlin and Diderot are elaborated in those texts where each writes not only as dramaturgist but also or even more as theoretician (41). Though he never says so explicitly, the underlying logic of Lacoue-Labarthe's decision to focus on these theoretical texts is formally consistent with the paradoxical logic that structures both the concept of mimesis as it is interpreted by Lacoue-Labarthe and his own texts. In appearance, Hölderlin and Diderot's theoretical and critical texts are the opposite of their literary (poetic and dramatic) texts. In fact, however, it is in their theoretical texts that Hölderlin and Diderot are perhaps closest to art.

Diderot and Hölderlin's work touches and dislocates the speculative in several closely related ways, but two are of particular importance. First, their work does not imply just a reversal but, rather, a total reformulation of the relationship between original and reproduction. Such a reformulation is explicit in Diderot's *Paradoxe sur le comédien*,[6] where the character identified only as "the First" states that, at least as far as the actor is concerned, identification comes first: the role played by the actor is pure creation, in the sense that it is not a reproduction or expression of his own, innate sensibility. While Lacoue-Labarthe uses the term *mimesis* rather than *identification* in "Diderot: Paradox and Mimesis," in the light of his subsequent remarks on mimesis and identification in *Heidegger, Art and Politics*, it seems entirely legitimate to read his text as though its theme were already mimesis *as* identification.

For Lacoue-Labarthe, the force of Diderot's text on acting lies in its assertion that the actor is without sensitivity, because, at least in terms of the art of the actor, this implies the primary nature of identification. The actor does not possess qualities which he then projects into his role; rather, in projecting himself into his role, he invents the qualities of that role out of nothing, that is, through his art alone. Identification is not a secondary process that establishes a link between the character of the actor and the character he or she is to portray but, rather, a primary process that coincides with the purely spontaneous artistic activity of the actor.

Hölderlin's work also transforms the significance of mimesis/identification, not so much in relation to art per se but, just as important, in terms of the relationship between the ancient and the modern. Modernity is a major—if not the major—theme of the essays collected in *L'Imitation des modernes*, because in Lacoue-Labarthe's terms it is one of the most important figures of mimesis. The concept of the modern implies a concept of mimesis, inasmuch as the ancient is traditionally conceived as the model or the original—whether positive or negative—for the modern. Because of its paradoxical nature, the essentially specular relation between the ancient and the modern constituted and in a sense still constitutes a gigantic double bind for modernity, according to Lacoue-Labarthe. It is as if the ancient were saying to the modern: " 'Be like me' / 'don't be like me' " ("Caesura," 223), and, as a consequence, as if the modern were condemned in advance to fail to equal—that is, condemned to be the *mere* imitation of—the ancient.

More than any other philosopher or poet since Kant, Lacoue-Labarthe argues, Hölderlin was able to dislocate the essentially specular relation between the ancient and the modern.[7] In the terms of the mimetology implicit in the work of Hölderlin, the modern no longer appears to be the mere repetition of an original model. This is what Hölderlin, in "his final thinking on the Greeks"–his "ultime pensée . . . sur les Grecs"–grasped, in a manner that upset the vision of the Greeks shared by Schiller and Winckelmann.[8] Hölderlin saw that what was "proper" to the ancient Greeks, that special quality as a people that made them inimitable, *"never took place"* ("Hölderlin," 246). In the terms of this insight there is no longer any place for the "'imitation of Antiquity'" (247) in the traditional sense. Hölderlin in effect recognized that the modern cannot take the place of the ancient precisely because the latter "never took place." But for that very same reason, the modern is no longer condemned to be the mere repetition of the ancient.

A common sense of the "originality" of mimesis/identification is not all Diderot and Hölderlin share. Equally important, a *generalized* theory of mimesis such as is indicated in the work of each–in Diderot's case by his theory of acting, in Hölderlin's by his conception of the relation between the ancient and the modern–necessitates the elaboration of a logical framework that is just as radically at odds with traditional philosophical thought. This logic (Lacoue-Labarthe, borrowing from Hölderlin, calls it a "hyperbologic") is the other major element linking their work from Lacoue-Labarthe's perspective. According to him, the hyperbologic, like Hölderlin's dislocation of the opposition between the ancient and the modern, is indicated in Hölderlin's texts on tragedy.

At first glance the hyperbologic appears to have much in common with dialectical logic, inasmuch as it is through a comparison of the two that one learns what each in essence is. The similarity between them is crucial because it reveals that, just as art is not merely the *opposite* of philosophy, so the hyperbologic is not merely the *opposite* of dialectical logic. The importance of this point is clear: if the hyperbologic *were* the opposite of dialectical logic, then the relationship between the two logics would itself be dialectical, and in this sense the hyperbologic would still be a subordinate form of logic. The dialectic could still legitimately speculate on the hyperbologic–that is, interpret its relationship to the hyperbologic in dialectical terms and see it as another version of dialectical logic.

From Lacoue-Labarthe's perspective, the affinity between the hyperbologic and the dialectic is thus the indication of the radical nature of the difference between them. Though he never makes the point explicit, it is not difficult to discern that the relationship between the two forms of logic is not itself dialectical but rather hyperbological: that is, the hyperbologic is so radically different from the dialectic because it resembles the dialectic so closely. The hyperbologic is nothing more than a generalization of the dialectical principle of the exchange of contraries, in which the process of exchange between the opposing terms is unlimited: in which no absolute term exists to close off and provide an ultimate reconciliation to the process of opposition and exchange. "In its greatest rigor, [the hyperbologic] cannot be reduced to any (philosophical) logic of identity and opposition, including dialectical logic, because it refuses to assure the *Aufhebung* of difference and because it unceasingly confirms what Hölderlin would have called the *Wechsel*, the infinite exchange or alternance of opposing terms."[9] A hyperbologic is an integral part of a mimetology because only such a logic can account for a conception of mimesis or identification in which the original is the copy and vice versa, and in which the possibility of exchange between these two opposites is unlimited—that is, in which neither the copy or the original can ever be determined to be original.

In Lacoue-Labarthe's view, it is not incidental by any means that Diderot formulated his theory of acting as a paradox. A mimetology of necessity implies paradox, not in the weak sense of an unorthodox opinion, but in the logical sense of the identity of opposites.[10] It is thus virtually inevitable that Diderot's theory of acting, simply because it takes identification to be "original," should also take the logical form of a paradox, or a hyperbologic: the more devoid the actor is of any intrinsic sensibility, the more adept he will be at rendering every form of sensibility or passion. Or, in other words, the actor (the original) is nothing and, in artistic terms, becomes something only through imitation or identification. For the actor at least, imitation/identification is "original."

Diderot's Betrayal of Generalized Mimesis

The critical force of art in relation to philosophy is thus evident in the paradoxical character of the relationship between mimesis and the speculative, that is, between Hölderlin and Diderot, on the one hand, and Hegel, on the other. The identity between mimesis and the speculative, between art and philosophy, is repeatedly indicated by Lacoue-Labarthe. It determines the emphasis he places on theoretical and critical texts rather than poetic or properly tragic texts in highlight- ing the critical force of art. More important, it is evident in his view that mimesis, even what he calls generalized mimesis, is *only* a dislo- cation or generalization of the speculative. But the difference between mimesis/identification and the speculative, between art and philoso- phy, is also being asserted in this description of the speculative, for, in terms of either a dialectical or a hyperbologic, these slight differ- ences are in fact immense and decisive.

Lacoue-Labarthe's essays on Diderot and Hölderlin thus exemplify the general critical strategy in terms of which he addresses the rela- tion between art and philosophy. But these same essays also reveal that at moments Lacoue-Labarthe in effect chooses between the exi- gencies imposed by the paradoxical relationship of philosophy and art. As a result of this choice, the paradoxical relationship progresses and appears in his work as one of *op*-position. In this respect, Lacoue- Labarthe *decides* (to use a term he himself has used) the question of art and in effect assigns an essence to it, an essence that corresponds to pure identification or mimesis. This is the case not because Lacoue- Labarthe is ultimately defending art against philosophy. In his terms there is a radicality of philosophy (exemplified by such figures as Nietzsche and Heidegger) that is a hyperbological consequence or complement of the radically critical value of art. It is the case, rather, because Lacoue-Labarthe, in the last instance, is defending a pure or generalized form of mimesis or identification against an impure or speculative version of it—because in order to save the value of art he must sacrifice the speculative.

As we have seen, Lacoue-Labarthe's interpretations of Diderot's work and of Hölderlin's illuminate each other. But his comparison of them also reveals what from his perspective is a serious limitation of Diderot's text on acting. The *Paradoxe sur le comédien* reveals the critical power of identification, but it also betrays an attempt to control it and neutralize its disruptive force—to "seek in mimesis [itself] the remedy for mimesis" (266). It is in this light, Lacoue-Labarthe argues, that we should interpret the First's insistence on the capacity of the great actor to repeat his role at will and always in the same directed man- ner. This view of the actor reveals Diderot's intention to impose a lim-

itation on identification, "to master it by definitively stopping the vertigo" it induces (263), by distinguishing two forms of identification. In
making this distinction, Diderot repeats a gesture that is

> absolutely classical. The active, virile, formative, properly artis-
> tic or poietic mimesis (deliberate and voluntary alienation, origi-
> nating from the gift of nature, and presupposing no preliminary
> subject . . .) *against* passive mimesis: the role that is taken on
> involuntarily, dispossession (or possession)—an alienation all
> the more alienating in that it occurs constantly from the basis of
> the subject as a material support. (265)

"With regard to Aristotle"—or, Lacoue-Labarthe might have added, to
Hegel—"one can see that there is still absolute fidelity" (265). The distinction between the two forms of mimesis represents an attempt to
think one form as the more original and is thus a repudiation of a generalized theory of mimesis.

Confronted with the vertigo induced by a generalized mimesis,
Diderot pulls back: "Diderot halts the paradox and closes, for himself, what for others (and for a long time) he opens up: fundamentally, the enigmatic possibility of thinking the identity without identity
of contraries" (263). In thus pulling back, Diderot defines his place in
a history that Lacoue-Labarthe qualifies as being "not solely empirical, but not ideal or pure either." It is the "history of the completion
of philosophy" ("Caesura," 212), the history in which Hölderlin,
Nietzsche, and Heidegger are ultimately the principal figures, the
others for whom Diderot opened up a possibility that in the end he
closed off for himself. In the ultimate analysis, Diderot's place,
though indeed within this history, is nonetheless relatively marginal
or at any rate prefatory. And the principle including/excluding Diderot from this history is that of generalized mimesis.

The radical and critical nature of generalized mimesis is thus exemplified more forcefully and more purely in the "tradition that Diderot
paradoxically inaugurated—in Germany" ("Diderot," 261, translation
modified), than in the work of Diderot himself. The distinction
Lacoue-Labarthe makes between Diderot and the tradition he inaugurated in Germany reflects and confirms the radical and critical function of art itself in relation to (speculative) philosophy, which is
characterized above all as an attempt to limit and control mimesis.
But clearly, this same distinction also marks the point in Lacoue-

Labarthe's argument where generalized mimesis and the sense of art that corresponds to it are being *opposed* to the speculative and to philosophy. Just as Lacoue-Labarthe argues that Diderot's decision concerning mimesis is indicated in the distinction he makes between an active and a passive mimesis, so Lacoue-Labarthe indicates his own decision concerning art in the distinction he makes between two mimetologies, one of which is general and the other of which is limited; one of which is Hölderlinian and the other of which is Diderotian; and finally, one of which is German, the other of which is by implication French or at any rate non-German.

Lacoue-Labarthe readily concedes the point that Hölderlin and the group of writers and theorists to whom his work is compared by Lacoue-Labarthe are not the only figures concerned with the problem of mimesis in the form in which they dealt with it: as the imitation of the ancient by the modern. Nonetheless, in *Heidegger, Art and Politics*, he argues that the Germany that was the context for Hölderlin's work had a special perspective on this problem:

> The agonistic (and consequently mimetic) rivalry with the ancient obviously does not apply to Germany alone. It is in general a foundation of modern politics. . . . What distinguishes Germany, however, is the fact that from the Revolution onwards, or rather from its imperialistic accomplishment, which coincides with the appearance of speculative idealism, . . . Germany rejected the neoclassical—and "Latin"—style of *imitatio* (which also implies the rejection of the political form ultimately taken by neoclassicism, i.e., the Republican form) and sought, not without difficulty, to find a style proper to it. . . . A mimetic *agōn* with France was thus added to that with Greece, such that it was not merely a question of wresting from France the monopoly over ancient models (and therefore over art, culture, and civilization), but it became necessary also to "invent" a Greece which up to that point had not been imitated, a sort of meta-Greece, if you will. (78–79, translation modified)

Lacoue-Labarthe's explicit theme in this passage is German politics, but what he says here unquestionably applies to philosophy as well—the whole argument of *Heidegger, Art and Politics* being that the two cannot be separated.

Lacoue-Labarthe's own perspective on the Germany (and the Greece) he is describing in this passage is clearly critical, and his interpretation of Hölderlin is that his perspective on Germany (Greece) is analogously critical. Nonetheless, the implication of Lacoue-Labarthe's argument is that if it does not suffice to be a German idealist in order to grasp the paradoxical character of the relation between the ancients and the moderns, only someone whose work can be situated at "the limit" ("Caesura," 212) of German idealism is in a position to do so.[11] This is why Diderot's concern for the ancient falls outside Lacoue-Labarthe's field of investigation—though there is a great deal to be said on the subject, even and perhaps especially with respect to the *Paradoxe*, which is Lacoue-Labarthe's particular focus—why Hölderlin, rather than Diderot, is in a better position to have grasped the radical implications of the mimetic dilemma posed for the modern by the ancient.

The distinction Lacoue-Labarthe makes between Diderot and Hölderlin in terms of the problem of the modern is thus complex, because Diderot is included in and excluded from the field defined by generalized mimesis. In this sense it recalls Hegel's (and Lessing's) sublation of Diderot in his (their) own dialectic of identification. For Lacoue-Labarthe, Diderot is almost German in much the same sense that he is for Lessing (and Goethe and Hegel). And for Lacoue-Labarthe too, Diderot's tacit Germanness is a function of his position with respect to identification—and thus with respect to the Greeks. Of course, Lacoue-Labarthe's Greeks (and his Germans) are different from the Greeks of Lessing, Winckelmann, Schiller, and Hegel. That is to say, the privilege of the Greeks (and ultimately of the Germans) in Lacoue-Labarthe's (and, according to him in Hölderlin's) eyes is to be a "non-people" occupying a "non-place," or, in Lacoue-Labarthe's own terms, "a people, a culture constantly showing itself as inaccessible to itself" ("Hölderlin," 247). But for that very reason, Lacoue-Labarthe's Greeks could be argued to be the *same* as those of Hegel—the same because they are the opposite. That is to say, Hölderlin's Greeks are the same because their impropriety is Greek (and German) rather than French (or any other national entity one might name). Their impropriety is thus proper to Greece/Germany; it is at bottom what, Lacoue-Labarthe holds, "distinguishes" Greece/Germany (*Heidegger*, 78).[12]

The special character of Hölderlin's relation to the people whose relationship to the Greeks is itself special parallels the special position of Hölderlin's work in relation to a generalized theory of mime-

sis. The privilege—and it *is* a privilege—Lacoue-Labarthe attaches to
the German is indicative of an implicit attempt to break out of the
double bind of the copy and the original, of the ancient and the modern, and of art and philosophy. It is indicative, that is, of an underlying privilege given to art. This privilege is of course complex and
problematic, inasmuch as the implication of Lacoue-Labarthe's text is
that art, like Greece and ultimately like Germany, never took and
never takes place, that it has no place that would belong purely to it
and nothing that is proper to it. As Lacoue-Labarthe puts it, what is
in question with respect to the actor as he is presented in Diderot's
Paradoxe is "the absence of any *proper* quality in one who intends to
take up (or proves suited for) representation and production" ("Diderot," 257). Still, also like Greece (Germany), the privilege of art consists in occupying this non-place. Thus, the non-place of art is in the
end being indicated as absolutely other than the place of the speculative, despite all the precautions Lacoue-Labarthe takes to respect the
exigency of the hyperbologic and avoid progressing toward a dialectic.

At stake, then, in Lacoue-Labarthe's reading of Diderot is nothing
other than art itself as the other of philosophy, more particularly, of
speculative philosophy. It is in terms of this alternative that he can
view Diderot's *Paradoxe* both as an opening toward and as a betrayal
of the most radical possibilities of identification and art, that he can
sublate the *Paradoxe* in his own dialectic of identification, in his theory
of a generalized—and Greek/German—form of mimesis.

Reading the *Paradoxe* with/against Lacoue-Labarthe

As we have seen, Lacoue-Labarthe attributes greater critical value to
the work of Hölderlin than to that of Diderot because Hölderlin is
closer to a concept of art as pure *poiesis*, as the absence of any proper
quality, and thus closer to a corresponding generalization of the
mimetic. But as we have also seen, Diderot's work holds an important
place in this critical scheme, even if it is not the primary or dominant
one. Despite Lacoue-Labarthe's reservations about the *Paradoxe sur le
comédien*, in certain respects its significance for him seems to be very
nearly as great as the significance of *Le Neveu de Rameau* for Hegel in
the *Phenomenology*. Just as Hegel sees the Nephew as a particularly
radical figure of philosophical consciousness, so Lacoue-Labarthe

sees the discourse of the First, one of the two characters whose dialogue is presented in the *Paradoxe*, as one of a very few instances in which an explicit attempt to generalize the mimetic principle can be discerned. And while Lacoue-Labarthe's interest in an art that would have a particularly critical value in relation to philosophy leads him to both Diderot and Hölderlin, it is in Diderot's essay on acting that identification/mimesis emerges as the central element of theater and of art generally speaking. In the overall organization of *L'Imitation des modernes*, Hölderlin is ultimately given a more important place than Diderot, but Lacoue-Labarthe's essay on Diderot comes first nonetheless: it introduces the theme of imitation, whose analysis he pursues in the essays on Hölderlin, Nietzsche, Heidegger, Derrida, and Lyotard, which appear along with "Diderot: Paradox and Mimesis" in the original French collection.

Grasping what Lacoue-Labarthe finds most significant and critical in Diderot's *Paradoxe* is thus crucial in order to understand fully what is most critical and forceful in Lacoue-Labarthe's own analysis of the problem of art. In identifying his own interpretation of mimesis so closely with a text (or at any rate with certain elements of a text) by Diderot, Lacoue-Labarthe gives his position force, clarity, and concreteness. But while much or all of what makes that analysis especially powerful is evident in his reading of Diderot, it also serves to raise questions concerning the ultimate implications of his critical reassessment of the relation between philosophy and art. Just as Hegel's philosophy is opened to challenge in terms of its reading of *Le Neveu*, so Lacoue-Labarthe's more critical position is opened to challenge in terms of his interpretation of the *Paradoxe*.

The character of the Nephew occupies the stage in an almost exclusive manner in Hegel's interpretation of *Le Neveu de Rameau*, and, in a similar manner, Lacoue-Labarthe's reading of Diderot is focused not only on one text, the *Paradoxe sur le comédien* but, more particularly, on one figure in that text. In Lacoue-Labarthe's case, of course, that figure is rhetorically complex, inasmuch as it is split between two textual functions:

> The author—Diderot—thus occupies two places simultaneously (that is, in the same text). And, moreover, two incompatible places. He is the First, one of the two interlocutors. Or at least he presents himself as such. But he is also the one who, putting himself overtly in the position of author or general narrator, sets

himself apart from the First or is able, even if only in play, to set himself apart from him and to constitute him as a character. ("Diderot," 250, translation modified)

Lacoue-Labarthe's object in this passage is to underscore the complexity of the subject who authors the *Paradoxe*. The Diderot who writes here is both the narrator and a character (the First), and thus in a sense he is neither. These remarks on the character of the narrator/character relationship prefigure Lacoue-Labarthe's discussion of the paradox on acting in the body of his analysis of Diderot's text. Only in that discussion are their implications fully developed, and thus any objection to them that does not take that discussion into account is premature. Nonetheless, certain issues central to Lacoue-Labarthe's interpretation of Diderot are already being decided in these preliminary remarks because, however complex the figure of Diderot may be in Lacoue-Labarthe's reading of the *Paradoxe*, the narrator and the First still form a single figure. That is to say, they are implicitly opposed to the Second, who is thrust into the background in Lacoue-Labarthe's comments on the subject of the *Paradoxe*, even though he notes in passing that the Second "has constantly, from the beginning [of the dialogue] forced the other to speak" (248, translation modified.)

Lacoue-Labarthe's decision to focus on the First/the narrator corresponds to a second decision—to define the paradox of acting in terms of the thesis of the First—that the great actor is devoid of sensitivity ("sensibilité"). Lacoue-Labarthe thus diverges from many commentators of the text, for whom the paradox of the *Paradoxe* lies in the contradiction between what is said about acting in this text and what is said about it in the *Entretiens sur le Fils naturel*, where the character Dorval argues that the actor, like other artists, "feels intensely, and reflects little."[13] Instead, Lacoue-Labarthe emphasizes that the thesis of the First in and of itself implies a paradox; the less the actor feels, the greater his capacity for representing feeling or passion.

Lacoue-Labarthe is certainly justified in writing that the commentators who have defined the paradox in terms of the contradiction between the respective theses of the *Entretiens* and the *Paradoxe* have sought to resolve this contradiction in order to reconstitute an "aesthetic without paradox." Yvon Belaval's study *L'Esthétique sans paradoxe de Diderot* (Paris: Gallimard, 1950) illustrates Lacoue-Labarthe's contention very well. Belaval more than once acknowledges that Diderot appears to overtun himself when he argues, in the *Entretiens*, that the actor is an enthusiast, and yet, in the *Paradoxe*, portrays him as totally lacking in sensitivity. Nonetheless, Belaval concludes his study with the statement that "it is clear the *Paradoxe* does not contradict in the least [Diderot's] aesthetic" (304), without ever effectively explaining why the contradiction between the *Paradoxe* and Diderot's other texts is not real but only apparent.

Belaval's claim notwithstanding, there *is* indeed a contradiction between the two works. But if Belaval never addresses it, neither does Lacoue-Labarthe. Such an omission is not in and of itself significant, in the sense that Lacoue-Labarthe's reading of the *Paradoxe* must be judged on its own terms, for what it does, not for what it does not do. Nonetheless, within the frame of the *Paradoxe*, the Second is the representative of the *Entretiens*, that is, of the thesis that sensitivity and feeling are the signal faculties of the actor. Lacoue-Labarthe's reading of the *Paradoxe*, and more specifically his privileging of the narrator/the First, is thus directly connected to his decision not to treat the contradiction between the two works. Thrusting the Second into the background permits Lacoue-Labarthe to frame the paradox essentially in the terms of the First, that is, to proceed as though the contradiction *between* the *Entretiens* and the *Paradoxe* were not also a contradiction within the *Paradoxe*, not a part of the paradox of the *Paradoxe*.

What exactly is the paradox of the *Paradoxe*? Lacoue-Labarthe insists it does not lie in the idea that reflection, rather than sensitivity, is the quality distinguishing the exceptional from the mediocre actor. As we have seen, the paradox is that "one must oneself be *nothing*, have *nothing* proper," in order to do everything, that is, in order to play all sorts of roles, characters, et cetera ("Diderot," 258). Thus the quality distinguishing the exceptional actor is not so much reflection understood as an intellectual as opposed to an emotional capacity but, rather, reflection understood as the "absence of any *proper* quality" (257). This is why the gift accorded to the actor must be understood as "*the gift of nothing*" (259). The paradox is thus that the great actor is, in his essence as actor, nothing.

Reflection, understood as the absence of any proper quality, thus becomes the dominant theme in Lacoue-Labarthe's analysis because it is in terms of the emphasis placed in the *Paradoxe* on reflection that this text can be argued to effect a generalization of mimesis, that is, can be interpreted as indicating the "original" nature of imitation or identification. The passions of the character are not reproductions of passions felt by the actor but, rather, a spontaneous creation of the actor/artist, which, because of its very spontaneity, cannot be considered proper to the actor or artist. Passion, however, is consistently deemphasized by Lacoue-Labarthe, inasmuch as it is implicitly associated with a limited mimetic theory: that is, with a theory that sees the work of art as the imitation of a preexisting passion, as the expression of a pre-given subject.

In this interpretation, the paradox of the *Paradoxe* is not resolved, but it is nonetheless truncated. By insisting so strongly on the idea that the actor is nothing in himself (that is, that he is without sensibility or passion), Lacoue-Labarthe understates the importance of the other aspect of the paradox—that he is *everything* (that is, capable of representing all sorts of passions) because he is nothing:

> The Second: To listen to you, the great actor is everything and nothing.
> The First: And perhaps it's because he is nothing that he *is* par excellence everything. (Diderot, *Paradoxe*, 341, my emphasis.)

The terms in which the paradox is formulated here are significant. They differ from the more prudent versions of the paradox offered elsewhere in the text: for example, in the passage where the First argues that the talent of the actor consists in "so scrupulously rendering the exterior signs of passion that you are taken in" (312). In these other formulations of the paradox, imitation is still active *rather than* passive, and the active nature of acting maintains a distance between the actor and his role. The actor, as author of his role, can still, at least logically, be distinguished from it, his creation.

But the logic of the paradox leads inexorably beyond such a prudent formulation of it. The sign that the great actor is nothing in himself is that he can represent passion perfectly and truly—that he can identify totally with his role. Were there certain elements of passion he could not render, were his portrayal of the passions of a given character limited in any way—that is, were there any possibility of distinguishing between the actor and his role—it would indicate that a natural sensibility or passion enters into and determines his art. That is why the actor who plays his role perfectly, *is* his character: "is par excellence everything" (341).

In this fuller and less prudent version of the paradox, identification is as much passive as it is active—it is still as much a mimesis in the narrow sense as a "pure and ungraspable poiesis (in withdrawal, and always withdrawn in its presence): a productive or formative force, energy in the strict sense, the perpetual movement of presentation" (259). The activity by which the actor creates his role is also a passivity through which the qualities of his character take possession of him, and he becomes the character. The full version of the paradox, in other words, can be viewed as consistent *both* with Diderot's insistence on the importance of the role of observation in art *and* with the (opposite) view that the activity of the artist is spontaneous and creative.

Equally important, in the fuller version of the paradox, the actor is still described as being without sensitivity or passion, but, paradoxically, these same qualities are not subtracted from him. Instead, sensibility or passion itself now has been revealed as conforming to the logic of paradox: passion is always concealed when it is revealed, and vice versa. Where passion is present, the spectators will not see passion on the stage. Where passion is absent, the spectators will see it on the stage. In short, where passion is concerned, not only is more less. All is none and none is all. The actor whose natural sensitivity is more passionate is less able to represent passion and the actor who is without natural sensitivity is better able to represent passion. That is to say, the actor who *is* more passionate *is* less passionate, and vice versa. The First, then, in defending his thesis on acting, never succeeds in convincing the Second not because his arguments are not strong enough but because the position of each presupposes the other—because identification presupposes (indifferently) both activity and passivity, passion and reflection.

It is thus impossible for the argument of either the First or the Second to prevail in purely theoretical terms. But it is just as impossible to demonstrate the validity of either argument on the basis of practice, because the theater can only provide evidence that supports both equally well. The spectator of a given play cannot determine whether the actor who gives an exceptional performance is dominated by passion or reflection, as the First concedes in talking to himself while the Second accompanies him, absorbed in his own thoughts:

> Supposing a consummate actor ceases playing with his head, that he forgets himself, that his heart gets involved, that sensibility overcomes him, that he gives in to it. He will make us drunk with pleasure. —Perhaps. —He will transport us with admiration. —It's

not impossible; but it's on the condition that he will not abandon
his system of declamation and that the unity [of declamation] will
not disappear, otherwise you will swear he has gone mad. . . .
Yes, in that case you would have a fine moment, I agree. (376)

In this hypothetical instance when the great actor forgets himself and
is overcome by feeling, it would still be impossible to tell if reflection
were not playing an important role, if the habits of his craft were not
continuing to dominate him to some extent. But precisely for that reason, it is impossible to determine that an actor, in an especially fine
moment, is *not* ruled by passion. Both the First and the Second can thus
with an equal appearance of justice appeal to the play to lend support
to their positions and undercut the arguments of the other (370). "What
difference does it make, indeed, if they [the actors] feel or if they don't
feel, as long as we don't know?" (358), the First exclaims at one point.
The paradox lies in the fact that it makes no difference.

That the paradox points to the interchangeability of passion and
reflection explains why so many of the arguments in the *Paradoxe* are
similar to those found in the *Entretiens*. Whereas Belaval takes such similarity to be the sign that there is, at bottom, no paradox in Diderot's aesthetic theory, it is rather the indication that the paradox lies in the
double-edged nature of the argument being made in each text rather
than in a simple contradiction between them. In the *Entretiens*, for
example, Dorval defends the thesis that the excellence of the actor consists in his sensitivity by arguing that only such sensitivity can enable
him to feel the emotions felt by his character and guide him unerringly
in finding the gestures and accent appropriate to those emotions. The
gestures and accents employed by the great actor are thus the natural
signs of passion, and the ability to reproduce them is taken by Dorval
to be an indication of the actor's proximity to passion and nature rather
than the degree to which he has mastered the technique of acting and
the conventions of a specific, national theater.

Dorval's argument in the *Entretiens* is evoked with particular force in
a passage from the *Paradoxe* in which the First argues:

But the case of violent pleasures is like that of profound
sufferings—both are mute. A sensitive, tender friend sees a friend
long lost to absence. The latter reappears unexpectedly. At once,
the heart of the first is moved. He runs, he embraces, he wants to
speak. He cannot. He stammers half words, he doesn't know what
he's saying. . . . Judge by the truth of this picture the falseness of

> these theatrical dialogues where two friends have so much pres-
> ence of mind and control themselves so well. (334)

A critique of traditional acting techniques and conventions is still being
made in the *Paradoxe* as it was in the *Entretiens*, and the spontaneous gestures and stammering language of passion still provide the model
against which acting is to be judged. If in the case of the great actor
reflection dominates passion, there are nonetheless at least two forms
of reflection, one totally at odds with passion (or perhaps one could say,
dialectically related to it), another having the greatest possible affinity
with (or perhaps one could say, hyperbologically related to) it. It is quite
true that, as Lacoue-Labarthe remarks in passing, Diderot never makes
a *"serious* apology for frenzy or confuses genius with manic delirium"
("Diderot," 262). But it is equally true that he never seriously writes an
apology for this other type of reflection—or for an acting that would be
stilted, conventional, or stylized. "Nothing," writes Lacoue-Labarthe,
"is being rejected in relation to inspiration, except frenzied possession"
(262, translation modified). And, correspondingly, reflection is not
being defended en bloc, but rather only insofar as it has an affinity with
a passion whose transmission or representation it makes possible.

Lacoue-Labarthe's decision to treat the paradox in terms of the theme
of reflection, understood as the indication of the absence of any quality
that would be proper to the artist, is thus clearly at the antipodes of the
organicist logic in terms of which other commentators of Diderot have
treated—and sought to resolve—the paradox of his aesthetic. But however dramatically Lacoue-Labarthe's interpretation differs from an
organicist one, it too amounts to an attempt if not to resolve then at least
to subject the paradox of the *Paradoxe* to a limitation, one that makes
apparent what in Lacoue-Labarthe's terms is the radical, critical power
of Diderot's conception of acting. For Lacoue-Labarthe, the subordination of passion to reflection in this text is tantamount to a revelation that
what is proper to art is nothing, that is, that art is totally lacking in anything that would be proper to it. By treating the theme of reflection as
totally dominant, Lacoue-Labarthe can assimilate Diderot's text on acting with a conception of art that sees it as radically other than speculative philosophy, thanks to its lack of any "properness," thanks to the
absence of any qualities that would make it possible to identify the
artist, and hence art itself, as a subject.

Given this interpretation of the *Paradoxe* and of the problem of identification, Lacoue-Labarthe's ultimate conclusion that Diderot betrays the most radical possibilities of mimesis when he pits "active, virile, formative, properly artistic or poietic mimesis," which "presupposes no preliminary subject," against "passive mimesis" (265) comes as something of a surprise. As I have argued, this conclusion can be contested on the basis of the many elements of the *Paradoxe* which indicate that the two versions of mimesis are indistinguishable or identical. But what makes it surprising is that Lacoue-Labarthe himself explicitly attaches critical value to the thesis of the First—that is, to a conception of mimesis as pure poiesis—and has himself separated it from passive mimesis in his reading of the *Paradoxe* in order to highlight its significance. The very form of mimesis with which Lacoue-Labarthe identifies its critical potential (a mimesis of reflection rather than passion) thus becomes the form he identifies with the mimesis of Aristotle, a specular form of mimesis in which the *absence* of subjectivity can be converted into a *form* of subjectivity, thanks to the active nature of the mimetic process.

This apparent reversal in Lacoue-Labarthe's interpretation could be argued to be necessary in view of his argument that Diderot's own strategy in regard to mimesis is contradictory: in Lacoue-Labarthe's words, it reveals an attempt to "seek in mimesis a remedy for mimesis" (266). But given the complexity of the Diderot who authors the *Paradoxe*, a complexity perhaps even greater than that suggested by Lacoue-Labarthe, it is extremely difficult to argue that there is *a* strategy with respect to identification in this text. If the text does unquestionably place an emphasis on the theme of reflection and on an active form of mimesis, it does so against a background in which the indeterminacy and the indifference of reflection and passion, active and passive mimesis, are consistently being indicated as well. The point is not that Diderot has already said what Lacoue-Labarthe tells us about mimesis in his reading of Diderot. It is, rather, that by adopting what is ultimately a critical stance in relation to Diderot, Lacoue-Labarthe reveals, despite himself, not just the limitation of *Diderot's* version of mimesis, but the limitation of what for him is the most critical version of it—if you will, of his own version of mimesis. Even a generalized form of identification or mimesis must of necessity be linked to a subject and in this sense be dialectical; this is the underlying logic that compels Lacoue-Labarthe to separate active from passive mimesis in order to reveal the critical potential of Diderot's the *Paradoxe* and also to criticize this same text as an attempt to reappropriate imitation for a subject.

Can there be an art that is pure identification, that is the absolute other of philosophy, that is, of philosophy understood as the speculative? In the light of Lacoue-Labarthe's analyses of Diderot and Hölderlin, one would have to say no, both because of and despite what he says. It is not just that Hölderlin's theoretical texts are "speculative through and through." It is—this would be the ultimate implication of Lacoue-Labarthe's analysis, the one from which he pulls back when he distinguishes between Diderot and Hölderlin—because the hyperbologic is none other than the speculative itself, in its strange relationship of nonidentity with itself. The critique of the speculative thus involves underscoring not only its affinity with paradox but also its own nonidentity, its own radically critical potential.

Identification belongs exclusively to neither philosophy *nor* art, and it would be false to attach any privilege to art based on its purportedly greater affinity with the essence of identification, or with a generalized rather than a limited form of it. The philosopher or artist can (legitimately) limit identification, that is, find in identification resources that can be turned against identification. But the significance of such a discovery is always ambiguous. Identification triumphs over the effort to control it—and also manifests itself in the effort to control it. In other words, there is no art without identification, but there is no pure art and no pure identification: that is, there is no art that is not philosophical and speculative. The critique of speculative philosophy is thus an "infinite task" because it is one that necessitates a continual critical questioning of the "other" of philosophy—of art—as well.

CHAPTER 8

Sexual Identification and the Social:

 Freud and Beaumarchais

> *The whole evening I had been in high spirits and in a combative mood. . . . And now all kinds of insolent and revolutionary ideas were going through my head, in keeping with Figaro's words and with my recollections of Beaumarchais' comedy which I had seen acted by the* Comédie française. *I thought of the phrase about the great gentlemen who had taken the trouble to be born, and of the* droit du Seigneur *which Count Almaviva tried to exercise over Susanna.*
>
> —Freud

Freud's "Politics" of Identification

In Freud's essays on society, including *Totem and Taboo, The Future of an Illusion, Group Psychology and the Analysis of the Ego,* and *Civilization and Its Discontents,* the theme of identification consistently emerges as central for understanding the nature and existence of social formations from a psychoanalytic standpoint. Freud's concept of identification provides him with a perspective from which to criticize existing social formations and existing social theories, and it is also fundamentally intertwined with the various elements of his own, complex view of society. And yet, despite Freud's attempts to define it and despite the way it is illuminated by his interpretation of society, his concept of identification is problematical, encompassing (at least) two tendencies or alternatives. In the words of Philippe Lacoue-Labarthe and Jean-Luc Nancy, the first involves a "massive identification with the Father," that is, a privileging of the identification between father and son as the model in terms of which identification in general must be defined, while the second is "another problematic of identification" in which not only the father-son model of identification but identity itself is in question.[1]

In *Group Psychology and the Analysis of the Ego,* Freud turns to the psychoanalytic concept of identification in order to take the first step in the elaboration of the contribution of psychoanalysis to the theory of groups. In the chapter "Identification," he states that identification is "known to psycho-analysis as the earliest expression of an emotional tie with another person."[2] Before the ego has taken on a definite form and hence before the other can become an object for the ego, the individual is already capable of forming a tie with the other through identification (18:106). Since Freud's principal object in *Group Psychology* is to understand how groups are formed, how they preserve themselves, and how they resist disintegration, his discussion of identification here focuses on its role in the establishment and maintenance of social ties or bonds and on the way it roots them in the deepest and earliest phases of psychological development.

Nonetheless, in the same chapter of *Group Psychology*, Freud also shows that identification can be a disruptive force in relation to the individual and therefore by implication in relation to the group as well. In a form of identification that he asserts is characteristic of melancholia, the ego has identified itself with an object upon which it now seeks to take revenge. In a case such as this, we see that identification can alienate as well as create a bond, though in this case it alienates one portion of the ego from another:

> These melancholias . . . show us the ego divided, fallen into two pieces, one of which rages against the second. This second piece is the one which has been altered by introjection and which contains the lost object. But the piece which behaves so cruelly is not unknown to us either. It comprises the conscience, a critical agency within the ego, which even in normal times takes up a critical attitude towards the ego. (18:109)

Melancholia shows us a more spectacular version of the ambiguous functioning of identification "even in normal times." It reveals that the process of identification can be a disruptive one in which one portion of the ego rages against another.

The reasons for this disruptive aspect of identification, even in normal times, are clear by the time Freud writes *Civilization and Its Discontents*, if not earlier: that portion of the ego which has split itself off and become the superego is in the service of the aggressive instincts, and the rage it directs against the first part of the ego derives its force and persistence from them.

What happens to [the individual] to render his desire for aggression innocuous? Something very remarkable, which we should
never have guessed and which is nevertheless quite obvious.
His aggressiveness is introjected, internalized; it is, in point of
fact, sent back to where it came from—that is, it is directed
towards his own ego. There it is taken over by a portion of the
ego, which sets itself over against the rest of the ego as superego, and which now, in the form of "conscience," is ready to put
into action against the ego the same harsh aggressiveness that
the ego would have liked to satisfy upon other, extraneous individuals. (*Civilization*, 21:123)

The introjection described here, like that described in the case of the
melancholic in *Group Psychology*, is a form or variant of identification.
"By means of identification, [the child] takes the unattackable authority into himself. The authority now turns into his super-ego" (*Civilization*, 21:129). When identification is understood in terms of the model
provided by the introjection of the authority-figure, it appears significantly more complex than when Freud defines it as "the earliest
expression of an emotional tie with another person." It now appears
not only as a form of unification but also of dissociation (Lacoue-
Labarthe and Nancy, "Le Peuple juif ne rêve pas," 65) in which the
ego can become divided from itself and therefore, by implication,
from the other with which it identifies. Because of the dissociative
nature of identification, it is never completely clear whether, as
Lacoue-Labarthe and Nancy put it, the superego "is a SuperEgo," (as
we might say a Superman) or instead a "beyond-the-ego [un au-delà
du Moi]" (62).

The more complex description of identification has become necessary in great part because aggression has entered the picture and is
now seen to play a role in identification as important as love. This is
a significant point not because aggression is being designated as the
dominant instinct but, rather, because love and aggression now disso-
ciate the instinctual itself, thus problematizing in advance any attempt
to define or redefine the subject in terms of affect or instinct. The split
between the superego and the ego reveals itself to be a repetition of
an "original" dissociation at the level of the instinctual itself. And just
as the subject of identification becomes radically problematic in the
light of the conflict between the ego and the superego, so "there is no
subject of ambivalence" (64).

The implications of the more complex view of identification in relation to the social are clear. The bonds between individuals are, or at any rate can be, undermined in the very process of their formation. At the same time, the process of identification can no longer be said to be governed by the individual—it is the process of identification that defines the individual as dissociation/association. The individual is constitutively open not just to an other or to others as a group but also to an alterity that belongs neither to the other, nor to the group, nor to the individual himself or herself.

Freud's sense of the problematic nature of the relationship between psychoanalysis and politics corresponds in large part to the more complex view of identification that emerges in these two major essays. In *Civilization and Its Discontents*, Freud formulates what for him is one of the most powerful objections to the political relevance of psychoanalysis in the following terms:

> I would not say that an attempt . . . to carry psychoanalysis over to the cultural community was absurd or doomed to be fruitless. But we should have to be very cautious and not forget that, after all, we are only dealing with analogies [between the individual and civilization] and it is dangerous, not only with men but also with concepts, to tear them from the sphere in which they have originated and been evolved. . . . As regards the therapeutic application of our knowledge, what would be the use of the most correct analysis of social neuroses, since no one possesses authority to impose such a therapy upon the group? (21:144)

Psychoanalysis has no clear practical relevance to politics, since no political or social agency exists that could serve as the psychoanalyst of society or use its authority to impose the analysis and therapy of a properly psychoanalytical authority such as Freud.

This state of affairs is no accident in terms of the picture of society that emerges from *Civilization and Its Discontents* in particular. Quite the contrary: according to that essay, it is the necessary consequence of the process through which societies are formed. Because the "inclination to aggression constitutes the greatest impediment to civilization" (21:122), the aggressive instincts must of necessity be most severely restricted by society. As a result, the process of identification linking the members of a group to any figure of authority will always be ambivalent. There can be no form of social authority whose legitimacy is not (unconsciously) contested, who is not an object of (unconscious) aggression. The same is true, of course, in the case of psychoanalysis. But the psychoanalyst works with his patient in an "environment, which is assumed to be 'normal'" (21:144), whereas the social or political authority-figure has no such context within which to place his analysis of society. As a result, there is no way for him to convert negative identification, which comprises an aspect of every relationship to authority, into something positive.

The character of identification itself thus limits the practical relevance of psychoanalysis to politics. But the ambiguous social significance of identification also implicitly constitutes a crucial political insight, one in terms of which the weaknesses of a broad range of political theories and regimes can be understood. From Freud's perspective, the critical implications of the ambivalence of identification are perhaps most obvious with respect, if not to the communist system, then at any rate to communist political theory:

> I have no concern with any economic criticisms of the communist system; I cannot enquire into whether the abolition of private property is expedient or advantageous. But I am able to recognize that the psychological premises on which the system is based are an untenable illusion. . . . Aggressiveness was not created by property. It reigned almost without limit in primitive times, when property was still very scanty, and it already shows itself in the nursery almost before property has given up its primal, anal form. (21:113)

From the standpoint of Freud, the fatal flaw in the psychological premises of communist political theory is that it does not recognize the "instinctual" nature of aggression. But the communist system does not escape from or eradicate aggression by refusing to recognize its primary nature, according to Freud. On the contrary, that system subsists only insofar as it too provides an outlet or means of expression for aggression, which in the case of communist societies is directed against the bourgeoisie (21:115). Freud concludes his remarks on the communist system by wondering, "with concern," what will become of the aggression directed at the bourgeois once the bourgeoisie has ceased to exist.

Liberal, democratic regimes and liberalism itself, however, are based on an equally defective theory of identification and equally

faulty "psychological premises." Such regimes actively promote identification in order to maintain themselves, but the form of identification they foster is a reductive one that impoverishes them:

> Perhaps we may also familiarize ourselves with the idea that
> there are difficulties attaching to the nature of civilization which
> will not yield to any attempt at reform. Over and above the tasks
> of restricting the instincts, which we are prepared for, there
> forces itself on our notice the danger of a state of things which
> might be termed "the psychological poverty of groups." This
> danger is most threatening where the bonds of a society are
> chiefly constituted by the identification of its members with one
> another, while individuals of the leader type do not acquire the
> importance that should fall to them in the formation of a group.
> The present cultural state of America would give us a good
> opportunity for studying the damage to civilization which is
> thus to be feared. (21:116)

Identification provides the psychological basis for the formation of
groups, but it is a concept and process that includes variants, of
which the identification of the members of a given group with one
another constitutes only one. The other, ultimately more important
form of identification is that between the members of the group and
those Freud considers to be of the leader type. The psychological poverty of groups is the result of the emphasis placed on identification
between the members of the group at the expense of identification
with a leader or leaders.

If one analyzes this condemnation of liberalism in the light of the
model of identification provided by the creation, through introjection,
of the superego, its meaning becomes clearer. The aggressiveness of
the superego does indeed represent a danger from the social standpoint, an "impediment to civilization." But the superego is not just a
more aggressive form of the ego; it is also a higher form of it, one that
lies beyond the ego and its narrow, narcissistic claims. In grounding
itself in the identification between the sons, liberal regimes protect
themselves to some extent from the aggressiveness of the social
instances that correspond to the superego. But they also rob themselves of the opening to alterity symbolized by the superego. As a
result, liberal society is reduced to an association of egos, who, even
when they are supposedly concerned with others (the other brothers),
are in fact concerned only with other versions of themselves. In short,

choanalysis directly and art indirectly both indicate the importance and fundamental character of the unconscious hostility of the sons toward the father, and thus both point to the social forces that make any political authority, even their own, uneasy at best. But this is precisely why, in Freud's terms, any truly legitimate political authority is founded in the authority of the father: because such an authority best exemplifies and provides an outlet for the ambivalent character of identification.

As we have seen, Freud's politics of identification is critical of all political interpretations of identification that would reduce or ignore its ambivalent character, as well as of political regimes that exploit its destructive force to consolidate their own authority. And yet Freud's own concept of identification, however complex, is itself in the end reductive of the very ambivalence whose importance he underscores in his political reflections. By identifying the father-son relationship as the one that best exemplifies the ambivalent character of identification, Freud indirectly indicates that for him there are other relationships in which identification is not as ambivalent, or in which, if it is still ambivalent, identification does not play the fundamental role. In this sense, the privilege he attaches to the father-son relationship itself could be argued to be founded on a reductive concept of identification, which would provide the background against which ambivalent father-son identification could emerge.

The exact sense in which Freud's own discussion of relations to others involves a reductive form or concept of identification becomes apparent when one compares passages from his essays on society. Note the contrast between the passages in which the ambivalence of the father-son relationship is designated as the most central for understanding the nature of society and other passages in which Freud stresses the ambivalent nature of virtually *all* forms or instances of identification: "The evidence of psycho-analysis shows that almost every intimate emotional relation between two people which lasts for some time — marriage, friendship, the relations between parents and children — contains a sediment of feelings of aversion and hostility, which only escapes perception as a result of repression" (18:101). If all intimate emotional relations that last for some time are ambivalent, then the emphasis placed in Freud's essays on society on the identification between the father and son seems arbitrary. The father-son relationship would provide just one example among others of the ambivalence of identification, and not necessarily the supreme or original example.

It is obvious that from Freud's perspective the identification among the sons and the political values associated with it are secondary and derivative with respect to those he associates with the identification between father and son. Perhaps the most important of the son's values, in his view, is "the demand for equality," which he holds to be "the root of social conscience and the sense of duty" (18:121). Important though this demand may be, Freud argues that, because it is linked to the identification among the sons or members of the group, it is still of secondary importance: "The demand for equality in a group applies only to its members and not to the leader. All the members want to be equal to one another, but they all want to be ruled by one person" (18:121). The demand for equality is not fundamental when viewed from the standpoint of the psychological development of the individual, or of the human species. It is always subordinate in theoretical terms to identification between father and son, not because the son identifies positively with the father and therefore elevates him above all other individuals, but because the positive and negative elements of identification are *both* realized to the maximum in this relationship.

Though Freud attaches less importance to identification among the sons (members of a group) than to that existing between the leader (or father) and the group (or sons), it is nonetheless more important than another form of identification, that between mother and son. This is mentioned only in a note in *Group Psychology* and in a parenthetical aside in *Civilization and Its Discontents*. Given the manner in which psychoanalysis centers on the development of the male rather than the female child, it comes as no surprise that Freud's essays on society have nothing to say about the identification between daughter and father, daughter and mother, or sister and brother, or among sisters. But even on the face of it, his view of the importance of the identification between father and son would seem to require some discussion of the reasons why this, rather than the identification between mother and son, should be viewed as the more significant form of identification.

The reason Freud holds the identification between mother and son to be not only of lesser importance but ultimately so insignificant that its lesser importance need not even be justified is evident in his assessment of it, brief though it may be. To the statement that "almost every intimate emotional relation between two people which lasts for some time . . . contains a sediment of feelings of aversion and hostility," he appends the following note: "Perhaps with the solitary exception of the relation of a mother to her son, which is based on narcissism, is not disturbed by subsequent rivalry, and is reinforced by a rudimentary attempt at sexual object-choice" (*Group Psychology*, 18:101). An equally brief remark in *Civilization and Its Discontents* makes essentially the same point: "Aggressiveness . . . forms the basis of every relation of affection and love among people (with the single exception, perhaps, of the mother's relation to her male child)" (21:113). Though identification is the "earliest expression of an emotional tie with another person," it is in effect preempted here by a relationship to an object—to the mother as member of the opposite sex and, therefore, as sexual object. By contradicting his own law that identification predates all other forms of relation to the other, Freud is able to make an exception to the universal rule of ambivalent identification. The implications of this exception are clear. Despite the tremendous significance of the mother-son relationship in terms of the development of the individual, because of its lack of ambivalence, it is totally without significance from the standpoint of *social* psychology.[3]

The privilege Freud attaches to the ambivalent identification between the father and the son thus depends on the theoretical subordination of identification among the sons and also on the presupposition that the mother-son relationship in its essence is free of any fundamental hostility.[4] This presupposition contradicts Freud's own pronouncement concerning the universality of ambivalence and is also implicitly reductive of the more complex sense of identification that leads him to criticize liberal regimes, in particular. It indicates that, despite the importance he attaches to ambivalence, there is nonetheless a *subject* of identification, according to Freud, more specifically a male subject, whose masculinity preempts identification and thus makes it possible to select a model form of identification from among the myriad instances of identification. The paternal authority whose interiorization results in the emergence of the superego is indeed other for the son, but it is nevertheless still recognizably the same because of the masculinity (and authority) they share as males.

While Freud opposes his own view of the ambivalent nature of identification to the psychological premises of liberalism and communism and uses it to criticize the sinister practices of fascism, that view can itself be opposed to another view, in terms of which the lack of ambivalence of the mother-son relation would no longer be considered self-evident and identification among the sons and daughters—and the corresponding demand for equality—would no longer appear derivative with respect to the relationship of the group to its leaders. In this other view, identification itself would be more fundamental than any instance or model of identification, whether based on paternal authority or maternal narcissism. As a result, there would be no subject of identification, properly speaking; the subject would be dissociated in principle and from the very beginning; it would be split by an alterity that is the property of no single subject, even a symbolic one. It would thus be a social subject in a radical sense, but neither a patriarchal nor matriarchal model of society would be able to account for what Kant would have called its unsocial sociability.

Like the authority of psychoanalysis itself, such a view of the psychological bases of the political would be problematical: it would not clearly designate any political authority that might implement it. But just as psychoanalysis provides certain insights into the importance and function of the individuals of the leader type in the life of groups, so such a view, provided its psychological bases and implications were spelled out, would be a potential source of insight into the demand for equality. It would illuminate that demand from a perspective that, while it may no longer be strictly psychoanalytical, would, nonetheless, like psychoanalysis, take account of the ambivalent character of identification—of *all* instances of identification.

Beaumarchais's *Le Mariage de Figaro*: Sexual Identification and the Demand for Equality

The term *identification* is not explicitly found in the work of Beaumarchais any more than it is in the work of Lessing or Diderot. However, a process of identification is the implicit central principle of both his critical texts—in which he justifies and explains his own work and also, to a greater or lesser extent, the value of the *genre sérieux*—and of his plays (with the possible exception of his early "parades"), from his first melodramas to *Le Barbier de Seville* and *Le Mariage de Figaro*, and even to his last melodrama, *La Mère coupable*. Beaumarchais's concept of identification, like Lessing's, is implicit in his interpretation of the distinctive form of pity that both tragedy and drama (and even, eventually, a comedy such as *Figaro*) are capable of inspiring. What makes pity central to drama, he argues, in a manner that recalls Lessing, is the self-reflexive quality it takes on in the theatrical context. The interest we feel for the characters of a given play is "the involuntary sentiment through which we apply this event [by which they are affected] to ourselves, the sentiment which puts us in the place of the one who suffers, in the midst of his situation."[5] Pity, in other words, becomes dramatically significant when it is transformed by the art of the dramatist into identification, when it "puts us in the place of the one who suffers."

Beaumarchais's admiration for Diderot relates directly to his conviction that the *genre sérieux* described in the *Entretiens sur le Fils naturel* and exemplified in Diderot's plays represents the most serious modern attempt to strengthen and deepen theatrical identification. Beaumarchais's concern with the central role played by identification also links his own early (and late) attempts at melodrama with his best-known work, *Le Mariage de Figaro*, even though, at first glance, this celebrated comedy seems far removed from the tone, language, characters, and ethico-aesthetic values of the *genre sérieux*.[6] In the eyes of Diderot and Lessing, a central—if not the central—innovation of the *genre serieux* serving to strengthen the identification of the spectators with the principal characters is the substitution of middle-class for aristocratic or royal heroes and heroines. Beaumarchais echoes them both in the essay that serves as a preface to his *Eugénie* (an essay in which he explicitly pays homage to Diderot and identifies himself as his disciple): "The more the man who suffers is of an estate close to mine, the greater the hold his misfortune has on my soul" ("Essai," 39).

Several years later, Beaumarchais was to write of his abandonment of drama in the "Lettre sur la critique," which serves as a preface to *Le Barbier de Seville*; but he describes this abandonment in terms that make it clear he has not given up the aims of the *genre sérieux*, even if he is no longer a practitioner of it:

> Previously, out of weakness, I presented you, at different times, with two sorry dramas; monstrous productions, as we know! For between tragedy and comedy, no one any longer doubts that

> nothing exists. The point has been decided, the master has said it, the school reverberates with it. . . . Present men of average condition crushed and unhappy! Tsk, tsk! They must never be shown unless they are scoffed at. Comic citizens and unhappy kings, there you have the whole of existing and possible theater; and I hold myself to have been told as much; it's done, and I don't want to quarrel anymore with anyone. (*Théâtre*, 22–23)

In this passage, Beaumarchais's attachment to what for him is the central principle of the *genre sérieux* is as obvious as his sarcasm. According to the criterion Beaumarchais himself provides here, *Le Mariage de Figaro*, if not *Le Barbier* itself, still conforms in the most crucial respect to the basic model of drama, inasmuch as its central figures are still a man and a woman of average condition, that is, "of an estate close to mine."

If *Figaro* is viewed from the perspective of Beaumarchais's critical texts on the theater, it becomes apparent that it represents more a culmination of and continuing commitment to his reflections on and experiments with the *genre sérieux* than a radical break with them. When contrasted with the clever valets of the comedies in the decades preceding *Figaro*, the figure of Figaro appears as an obvious attempt to create a comic hero with whom the spectator can nonetheless identify because he is a man like ourselves. A fuller interpretation of the play only serves to deepen and strengthen this initial impression. In the central conflict between Figaro and the count, as well as in the myriad conflicts among all the different characters, identification emerges as the decisive issue in terms of which both the aesthetic and the political aims of the play can be formulated and elucidated.

In his preface to *Figaro*, Beaumarchais indicates the central role played by identification in the play as a whole in a passage in which he discusses the "profound morality that makes itself felt in the entire work" (151). He quotes an incident from his play by way of illustration: the count, thinking he has caught his unfaithful wife, shows a door to his gardener and demands that he enter it and bring out his wife, whom he supposes to have dishonored herself and thereby him. To this the gardener replies that there surely is a Providence, since it is only fair that the count, who has himself been responsible for there being so many dishonored women in the region, should now in turn be dishonored ("Preface," 151). In this instance, as throughout the play, a character is ridiculed not because he has departed from or transgressed norms of propriety, reason, or morality that prevail in the society at large but, rather, because he is caught in a conflict with *his own* proclaimed norms and values, which he consistently holds up for others but fails to apply to his own conduct.[7] As Figaro puts it in addressing the count in the final act: "You rule everything here, except yourself" (act 5, scene 12, p. 323). In order better to take advantage of others, the character—in these two cases the count—has deliberately refused to refer the situation he sees before him back to himself. He has refused, in other words, to put himself in the place of the other.

The conflict described in *Figaro* does not simply pit those of average condition against the members of the aristocracy, even if the class distinctions among the characters are highly significant. It is a conflict that plays itself out in terms of a general process of identification that encompasses identification along class lines but is not limited to it. At first glance, this conflict based in and on identification seems to oppose those who identify with others to those who are unwilling or unable to do so. It appears that the count is the character most unwilling or least able to identify with the other characters, whereas they are united against him by their ability to identify with him and with each other. Despite specific conflicts between Bartholo and Figaro, Bazile and Figaro, and Figaro and Antonio, all the male characters in *Figaro* are ultimately united against the count because of his superior social position and his political and legal authority over them.[8] In this sense they identify with each other and are capable of joining forces against him, as is evident in the final act when they go with Figaro to the garden in order to catch the count in the act of seducing Suzanne. But, equally important, in doing this they are all working in essential harmony not only with Suzanne, but even with the countess. In this sense, then, the basis of their common identification extends beyond class alone.

The identification among the women characters is even more self-evident, so much so that it seems Beaumarchais, like Rousseau before him and Freud after him, is indicating that the woman better exemplifies (positive, unambivalent) identification than the man, and that the mother exemplifies it best of all. Though the count's interest in Suzanne would seem to represent a potential source of serious conflict between the countess and her servant, in fact harmony prevails, and, with perhaps one very slight exception, the two women work in concert throughout the play. Marceline is the only female character to express jealously and bitterness for more than a moment, and she is also, if only briefly, the count's only feminine ally. But, significantly, she is both of these only prior to the scene in which she learns that Figaro is her son. Then she abruptly ceases to be the spiteful old duenna and becomes someone radically different, not only the tender mother of Figaro but also the staunch supporter of Suzanne.[9] It is relatively easy, then, to interpret Marceline's sudden transformation as the most striking confirmation of the spontaneous, natural character of a feminine form of identification, which would be best exemplified in the relation between the mother and the child. Identification or natural pity would cause the mother to put herself in the place of the other—that is of her (male) child—and identify unhesitatingly both with his interests and with those of all other women—that is to say, with all other mothers or potential mothers.

The last scene of act 1 provides one example of the way the positive identification of the characters with one another opposes them to the count: when Figaro is joined by virtually all the other characters in the play (with the exception of Marceline and Antonio) in asking the count to reiterate publicly his renunciation of the *droit de seigneur* and bless Figaro's marriage to Suzanne. Similarly, in the final act, the count is obliged to acknowledge that he has lost a battle of wits that pitted him against the other characters as a group: "I wanted to outsmart *them*; *they* have treated me like a child" (*Figaro*, act 5, scene 19, p. 328, my emphasis). The countess is the one who indicates that the count's isolation from the others stems from a lack of (self-reflexive) pity. At the end of the play, she says that, were he in her place, he would say, "No, no" to his own request for forgiveness, precisely because he cannot put himself in the place of the other. But she, who implicitly has done just that, pardons him once again.[10]

When *Le Mariage de Figaro* is read as an articulation of the fundamental nature of a positive, feminine form of identification, it appears to express a liberal ideology, and its revolutionary implications seem to be restricted to the overthrow of monarchy and the establishment of a liberal regime of the type Freud describes critically when he speaks of "the psychological poverty of groups." The psychological premise of this liberalism would be a reductive concept of identification that ignores its ambivalent character and thus denies aggression,

while nonetheless providing it with an outlet in the form of the humil-
iation of the count. It would be a concept of identification based on
the model of the relationship between the mother and the child, and
the supposed absence of ambivalence in this relationship would be
taken as indicative of the true nature of identification. Identification
would be subject to perversion in certain (feudal) forms of society,
but there would always exist a possibility of restructuring society,
through either reform or revolution, thanks to and in accordance
with the underlying, natural form of (positive) identification—thanks,
in Freud's terms, to the way maternal love protects the son from paternal jealousy. But we should not forget that such positive identification
is, in Freud's terms, profoundly narcissistic.

What appears, at least on the surface, to be the feminine form of
identification is not the only model for identification offered in the
play, however. An equally important and perhaps even more archaic
or primary form of it provides the key to the character of Chérubin.
Of course, Chérubin has a great deal in common with the women
characters. Nonetheless, adjectives such as *spontaneous* and *natural*,
which could be used to describe the form of identification the women
seem to exemplify when they act in concert, do not seem altogether
adequate to describe the case of Chérubin. Because it is totally undis-
ciplined, uncontrolled, and perhaps uncontrollable, the form of identification represented by Chérubin is a force disruptive not only of the
hierarchical society represented in *Figaro* but potentially of any imaginable political order.

As depicted in the figure of Chérubin, identification appears to be
the "earliest expression of an emotional tie with another person," so
early, that it predates the emergence of the ego or sense of self: "My
need to say 'I love you' to someone is so bad, that I say it all by myself,
running across the park, to your mistress, to you, to the trees, to the
wind which takes them away with my lost words. Yesterday, I ran into
Marceline" (*Figaro*, act 1, scene 7, p. 186). Chérubin's love is the expression of a form of identification so primary that it does not distinguish
between the self and its object. Thus Chérubin says, "I love you" all
by himself. Because it cannot distinguish between itself and its
object, it is equally unable or unconcerned to distinguish between
different objects: Franchettte, Suzanne, the countess, the trees, or
Marceline all suit Chérubin equally well.

The barely adolescent Chérubin is, as Beaumarchais claims in his presentation of the characters of the play, "without project, without knowledge, and entirely caught up in each event" (168). Because of his youth he lacks definition in either social or psychological terms. Correspondingly, he is without jealousy or vanity. From either standpoint, he is a character without a character, a subject without a self. Indeed, the profound sense of his lack of maturity also lies in the idea that his narcissistic identification with the objects of his love is more primitive than the ego, rather than an expression of it, as seems to be the case with the adult characters. In identifying with the women characters and in effect viewing them as part of himself, he does not make them into his property but, rather, takes on—or rather partakes of—their feminine character.

The radical character of the form of identification exemplified by Chérubin is evident not only in the way he confuses himself with the object(s) of his love. The action of the play similarly confuses him with the other characters. It is because of his protean nature that Chérubin is less a distinct individual than a kind of cipher that can be substituted for or play the role of any other character. He can be dressed up like Suzanne and sent in her place to a rendezvous with the count. But he can also be substituted for the countess, as in the general confusion of the last act, when he (among others) is led from the pavilion by the count in the conviction that "she" is Rosine. Or, in another instance, in the first scenes in which he appears (act 1, scenes 7, 8, and 9), Chérubin is a double for the count, who unwittingly takes what had, seconds before, been Chérubin's place behind the chair when Bazile pays a surprise visit to Suzanne. By the end of the play, Chérubin's value as a substitute for the other characters is so well established that, in the crescendo of mistaken identities that makes up the concluding scenes, one has the sense that all the characters have been "Chérubinized," that is, transformed into similarly protean entities any one of which can be put in the place of—that is, identified with—any other.

We have seen how, in excepting the relationship between the (male) child and the mother from the universal law of ambivalence, Freud makes "rudimentary object choice" a factor in their relationship and thus indicates that the identification between mother and child is sexually determined even in its most fundamental and archaic form. In contrast, the character of Chérubin points to a different interpretation of the mother-son relationship and ultimately of identification in general. Chérubin's significance in this regard is highlighted in a remark Beaumarchais makes in connection with his character in his directions to the actors of Le Mariage de Figaro, "Caractères et Habille-ments de la Pièce." Chérubin is "what every mother, at the bottom of her heart, would perhaps like her son to be, even if she suffered greatly as a result" (168). This "universal son" thus offers the key to interpreting the mother-son relationship from the perspective of Le Mariage de Figaro.

Significantly, the role of this universal son, according to a second remark from Beaumarchais's directions, "can be played, as it was played, only by a young and very pretty woman" (168). The universal son is (also) a daughter. The text of the play frequently exploits the sexual ambiguity that this casting of the role imparts to Chérubin, especially in the second act, when he is dressed up in one of Suzanne's dresses by Suzanne herself and the countess, but else-where as well. "Ah how white his arm is," exclaims Suzanne to the countess in the course of the scene in question; it's "like a woman's! It's whiter than mine!" (act 2, scene 6, p. 213). The feminine aspect that the character of Chérubin takes on thanks to the casting and the situations in which he finds himself constitutes an important link between him and the women characters. But it also has the paradox-ical effect of separating him from them. For, because of his femininity, Chérubin is *neither* completely masculine *nor* completely feminine. The result is that the form of identification linking this "son" to the "mothers" (the women characters) cannot be said to represent simply an attempt at an object-choice, however rudimentary. Or, what amounts to the same thing, it represents a radically problematic object-choice, one that is indifferently masculine and/or feminine. Inasmuch as it presupposes no natural sexual determination whatso-ever—that is, neither a subject nor an object—the form of identifica-tion exemplified by Chérubin's anarchic love would be even more primary than the identification Freud supposes to be the basis of the mother-son relation.

Of course, it could be argued that in introducing the character of Chérubin into the play, Beaumarchais has done nothing to undercut seriously the view that *Figaro* is an expression of liberal ideology. The affinities between Chérubin and the women characters can be inter-preted as just one more factor isolating the count from those charac-ters who exemplify the force of identification. In support of such a view, it could be argued that the count and Chérubin can be opposed by the different nature of their desire. In Chérubin's case, it appears to be spontaneous and unmediated, but in the count's case, it appears to be calculated and expressive of his own (desire for) mastery over others. Whereas Chérubin's love is "self-less," the count appears to love out of vanity and a sense of self, which express themselves as a consciousness of his rank and a willingness to use his social advantage to prevail in any conflict, large or small. The count, of course, pretends he wants to be loved for himself, for his intrinsic or natural merit. But he repeatedly shows that what he counts on at bottom are his money and position. The jealous nature of his love is an expression of his vanity, the infallible sign that his is a selfish, as opposed to selfless love. The count's desire transforms women into mere objects, mere pieces of property to be jealously guarded, as the countess puts it, "for honor but not for love," or, in the case of Suzanne, exploited or simply bought. That is, Chérubin appears to be one more example of a character whose capacity for identification, excessive though it may be, has no purpose other than to highlight his own differences with the count in much the way that the more adult forms of identification oppose the other characters to the count.

Despite these differences, however, the affinity between the count and Chérubin is in fact undeniable. Perhaps the clearest sign of the link between them lies in the count's constantly finding himself in Chérubin's place. As the count unwittingly follows Chérubin from the house of Franchette to the room of Suzanne, to the chambers of the countess, it becomes clear that only adulthood separates them. Furthermore, the resemblance between the two characters is implicitly part of what excuses the countess's feelings for Chérubin. They are the logical consequence of the similarity between this younger version of her husband and her husband himself. The count's inability to remain faithful to the countess is a sign of the extent to which he has remained a child, and he himself is obliged to acknowledge that he has been treated like a child (and deservedly so) when he is confronted by the other characters at the end of the play (act 5, scene 19, p. 328). In the terms of the play, it would be more exact to say he has behaved like Chérubin.

If *Figaro* focused only on the contrast between the count, on the one hand, and the women characters and Chérubin, on the other, it could be seen as a play about the perversion of natural identification by a feudal or monarchic form of government. But because of the affinities between Chérubin and the count, and because of the way those affinities indirectly link the count to the women characters, Beaumarchais's psychological premises appear quite different from those Freud attributes to liberalism and communism. Despite all that separates him from Chérubin, when the two characters are compared, the count can be seen to exemplify not an absence of or incapacity for identification but, rather, *another form* of identification, perverted though it may seem.

In treating others as the mere extension of himself, as property, the count too identifies himself with them: he reveals that the boundaries of his ego, like those of Chérubin's, are not fixed, but rather continually fluctuating. The violence he directs against others (not just Figaro, but Suzanne and the countess as well) is the sign not of a failure to identify but, rather (to borrow the language of Freud), of an aggressiveness inherent in identification or (in a language closer to that of Beaumarchais) of a jealousy inherent in all forms of love.

This aggressive component is foregrounded in the character of the count, particularly in the scene in which his jealousy puts him on the verge of breaking down the door to the countess's dressing room in order to learn the identity of the person inside. But it is present in the less spectacular instances of jealousy experienced by almost all the other characters, as we see in the concluding scenes of the play. The ambivalent character of all love relationships finds a comic expression as slaps intended for one character land on the cheek of another, money intended to buy the favors of a mistress ends up as a contribution to her marriage dowry, and attempts to identify the guilty party produce a host of suspects. Suzanne and Figaro in particular, who have withstood jealousy relatively well in the previous acts, succumb to it here. The generalization of jealousy in the final scenes of the play is highly significant. If the count, in the words of the preface, is "always humiliated, without ever being debased" (151), it is at least in part because, in the terms of the play, there is something legitimate about his jealousy and vanity. In Freud's terms, one could say it is because there is something instinctual about aggression. It must be recognized as a power equal to—and invariably fused with—love.

Beaumarchais's handling of the theme of jealousy indicates that for him, as for Freud, identification is by nature ambivalent. But it is when Beaumarchais is compared to Freud that one instance of jealousy emerges as perhaps the most significant of all—the jealousy of Marceline. The reason why her jealousy is significant is obvious: because it indicates that, Rousseau and Freud notwithstanding, even the mother-son relationship is characterized by jealousy and ambivalence. As Beaumarchais himself indicates in his directions, the recognition scene in which Marceline learns she is Figaro's mother is critical not only in terms of her character but in relation to the play as a whole as well. It involves an about-face for the character and a correspondingly difficult challenge for the actress. It is as if the actress were required to represent two completely different characters in a single play: the jealous, scheming, and vindictive Marceline who is willing to do anything to force Figaro into marrying her, and the generous, loving Marceline who will do anything to help bring about his marriage with Suzanne.

It is obvious that the dual nature of Marceline is the most important element in her character, and yet the significance of the duality is ambiguous. It could be interpreted in strict Freudian terms as an indication that the instincts of the mother are so strong that they overcome the woman's natural disposition to jealousy. But it can also be interpreted as the indication that the two sides of Marceline are in fact one, that maternal love can overcome jealous love only because it is a form of (jealous) love—and thus never fully overcomes jealousy. Marceline claims that her designs upon Figaro were only the sign of a maternal love that had been temporarily thrown off course and out of character by her ignorance of their true relationship: "My heart was drawn to him, but it was fooled as to why—it was our blood-relation that was calling me" (act 3, scene 18, p. 275). But Figaro himself laughingly points out that it is not so easy to separate the two when he tells her at the end of their recognition scene, "And you, my mother, kiss me . . . as maternally as you can" (act 3, scene 16, p. 273).

The play as a whole confirms the view underlying Figaro's ironic remark: unambivalent mother love and aggressive, jealous sexual love are not radically different but, rather, poles or aspects of a single emotion, love.[11] The countess's relationship to her godson Chérubin offers another instance in which a female character's maternal feelings for a younger man vie but also fuse with a form of love more appropriate in the countess's case to her relations with the count. In affectionately addressing Figaro more than once as "my son," (Figaro, act 1, scene 1, p. 171; act 1, scene 10, p. 199), Suzanne indicates that their love too is fused with love of a mother-son type. But if all this seems to confirm that the dominant tone of the relationships between Suzanne and Figaro, Marceline and Figaro, and the countess and Chérubin is the result of a lack of ambivalence, a lack normally associated with maternal love, it also indicates that in each case maternal love is tinged with a sexual and aggressive element. In the "Lettre sur la critique," Beaumarchais claims that, given Figaro's ignorance concerning the identity of his father and mother, he, Beaumarchais, could easily have made a tragic sequel to *Le Barbier de Seville* or turned *Le Barbier* itself into a tragedy in which Figaro would have become a modern Oedipus (145). It could be argued that the shadow of *Phèdre* also hangs over *Le Barbier de Seville* and especially *Figaro* because of the ambiguous character of the relations between Marceline and Figaro—that is, because of the ambivalence of maternal love.[12]

Figaro is thus both an interrupted *Oedipus and* an interrupted *Phèdre*, a tragedy made comic because of the way it plays with love and aggression and shows them to be constantly fused; that is, it shows that each is constantly being transformed into the other. Significantly, Figaro's anguish over whether Suzanne loves him or not ends when she pommels him in the last act for having deceived her and for having been suspicious of her own fidelity: "Is *this* love?" she asks, as she slaps him. "*Santa Barbara!* yes, it's love" he answers in delight (*Figaro*, act 5, Scene 8, p. 318). The ambivalence of the mother-son relationship puts the (aggressive) mother in the position of the (aggressive) father and at the same time reveals the tie between aggression and love—it reveals, in other words, that the father is also a "mother." This universalization of ambivalence is indicative of what all the characters in the play share with Chérubin: a formlessness, a lack of self that is the condition/the result of this perpetual transformation of aggression into love and the identification of each character with all the others. From the perspective of *Figaro*, it can be said that the other with whom I identify is not a paternal other, but (and) neither is it merely another version of "myself," precisely because ambivalent identification radically puts the self itself into question.

The character of Figaro should also be understood in relation to the primary form of identification exemplified by Chérubin. Figaro's equivocal social status is an important indication of what these two characters share. Even before he learns who his parents are, Figaro is of course less a servant than a member of the middle class, and, in the terms of the *genre sérieux*, this makes him the character with whom the spectator can most readily identify. Nonetheless, class alone is not what determines Figaro's status, as is clear if one contrasts him with his father, the doctor Bartholo. Unlike his father and the heroes of, for example, Beaumarchais's drama *Les Deux Amis*, Figaro is defined less by a stable social and economic position than by a checkered itinerary that does not necessarily appear to have reached its end point even after he learns the identity of his father. As he describes himself in the soliloquy of the final act, he is barber, playwright, essayist, journalist, gambler, and servant to the count (act 6, scene 3, pp. 305–6). His illegitimate birth also makes his social status indeterminate.

In short, what makes Figaro a strong example of the constitutive, primary nature of identification is what could be called, borrowing from Diderot, Figaro's "equal aptitude for all sorts of characters and roles,"[13] an aptitude that corresponds to his social indeterminacy. Unlike the count, whose outlook and essence are wholly determined by his aristocratic birth, Figaro remains socially undetermined in much the same way Chérubin remains sexually undetermined. This is why he can be barber, playwright, essayist, journalist, gambler, and servant to the count with equal success. Figaro's lack of a fixed social status corresponds to a sense of self that is equally unfixed or indeterminate. As he puts it at the end of the same soliloquy in which he narrates his chaotic history: "Forced to travel the route upon which I have embarked without knowing it, just as I will leave it without wanting to, I have strewn it with as many flowers as my gaiety permitted me to. Again, I say my gaiety without knowing if it's mine any more than the rest, nor what is this *I* with which I am concerned: a formless assemblage of unknown parts" (*Figaro*, act 6, scene 3, pp. 306–7). Figaro is, in effect, "all and nothing," to borrow once again from Diderot's *Paradoxe*. He is all, because he takes so many different forms, and nothing, because this multiplicity of forms is the indication of a certain formlessness that frustrates his own attempts to know himself. In terms of Diderot's *Paradoxe*, it is no accident that literary occupations predominate among the roles Figaro has played. His affinity for writing and the theater is consistent with the indeterminacy of his social and moral nature.

In Figaro's long, dramatic soliloquy, *Figaro* (once again) verges on tragedy. Figaro appears as another version of Hamlet, whose very being is in question along with his marriage to Suzanne. This is indicated not only in what he says about himself but perhaps even more forcefully in the rhetorical confusion of his speech, a confusion that culminates in the line, "There is an argument: its you, its him, its me, its thee, no, it isn't us. Ah—then who is it?," (act 6, scene 3, p. 306). In a moment in which Figaro appears to have lost control over his own language, what is being indicated is not only the radical indeterminacy of his nature but a correspondingly radical confusion between himself and others. The radical loss of self depicted in this scene and in Figaro's language is in addition a strong affirmation of the social. This interpretation is confirmed inasmuch as it is not through sheer introspection that this "crisis" (act 6, scene3, p. 307) has been precipitated but, rather, because of his identification with another—because of his feelings for Suzanne. It is in terms of a sense of the primary nature of the social that the comedy is interrupted by this tragic moment, and then resumes once again.

One could of course argue that from a standpoint such as Freud's, Figaro's artistic nature does not make him radically indeterminate but, on the contrary, is perhaps the clearest expression of what makes him an "individual of the leader type." He could be seen as an embodiment of the epic poet, whose identity and authority are based on art. A similar argument could be made in terms of the perspective of Lacoue-Labarthe in his reading of Diderot's *Paradoxe sur le comédien*, though in Lacoue-Labarthe's terms, it would place Figaro in a negative, rather than positive light. According to such an argument, Figaro's lack of qualities, his impropriety, would in fact be the source and the sign of his mastery as an artist, of a (superior) form of subjectivity. In support of such a view, one might stress that Figaro's advantage in relation to the count is not simply that of an industrious member of the middle class but also that of the artist, who understands the ambivalent nature of aggressiveness and knows how to arouse and deflect it in order to achieve his political ends. This would be why Figaro defines politics using terms equally appropriate to acting: because politics is quite literally an art, and because the natural leader is a consummate actor-artist. Political intrigue, Figaro does indeed argue, is not much. It involves only:

> feigning to ignore what one knows, to know what one ignores;
> to understand what one doesn't understand, to not understand

what one does understand; above all, doing things beyond one's forces; making a big secret out of the fact that there isn't one; hiding behind closed doors to sharpen pens, and appearing profound when one is, as they say, only empty and hollow; playing a role well or badly. (act 3, scene 5, p. 251)

Though in this speech Figaro speaks disdainfully of politics or intrigue, it is, as Suzanne affirms, his proper sphere (act 1, scene 1, p. 174). It is a sphere in which role playing, defined in the same paradoxical terms as in Diderot's *Paradoxe,* is everything. The political artist, like the actor, can feign everything because he is nothing; he too is, in effect, his own antithesis.

Politics and art thus merge in the figure of Figaro in much the same way as in Freud's description of the epic poet, the first individual of the leader-type to distinguish himself from the group of sons who participated in killing the primal father. And, just as the art of the epic poet is a means to realize specific political ends, so Figaro can be seen as using his art to bring about his marriage to Suzanne and cement his own position in society.

In Figaro's case, the specific work of the artist is the festival planned for the evening of the *folle journée,* the twenty-four hours in which the action of *Figaro* is supposed to take place. But given the art he must deploy to make the festival come to pass, his work comes to stand not only for the projected festival but also for the events leading up to it. At one point the count, in an expression of frustration and confusion, exclaims, "Are we performing a comedy?" (act 4, scene 6, p. 289). The implication is that he and the other characters are indeed performing a comedy, and that Figaro, thanks to his talent as actor and man of intrigue, has pretensions of being its director. As he tells Chérubin and Bazile: "We must rehearse boldly: let's not be like those actors who give their worst performance the day the critics are the most alert. We won't have another chance to do it better. Let's know our roles well today" (act 1, scene 10, p. 200). These instructions could be interpreted narrowly in terms of the need to rehearse for the festival Figaro plans for the evening of the same day. But they also clearly relate to the events of the play as a whole. The alert critics are none other than the count and those who are in his pay; and Figaro and the other actors will not get another chance to improve their performance, because life cannot be done over again. The epic poem must work its political effects the first time it is presented. If it does not, there will be no chance for a repeat performance.

Though there are important formal parallels between Beaumarchais's Figaro and Freud's epic poet, the fate of art and the artist is not the same in Beaumarchais's play as in Freud's essay *Group Psychology,* or in Diderot's *Paradoxe* as interpreted by Lacoue-Labarthe.

In the simplest terms, this is because, though the play ends happily from Figaro's perspective, it is not thanks to his art alone. The count himself proves to be no mean artist, and he succeeds if not in wholly determining the outcome, then at least in delaying it. But Figaro's most obvious rivals for political and artistic power are the women, in particular the countess and Suzanne. The count testifies to their comic and thus political talents in act 2, scene 19, when Suzanne emerges from the Countess's dressing room: "Madame . . . you know how to act very well. . . . We think we know something about politics, and we are only children. It is you, it is you, Madame, that the King ought to make his ambassador to London! Your sex must have carefully studied the art of feigning in order to do it so successfully!" (p. 229). In the context in which they are uttered, these lines of course have an ironic significance: The countess was in reality not feigning at all but rather appeared guilty and frightened because she was under the impression that Chérubin was trapped in her dressing room, not Suzanne. But the final act of the play confirms the count's observations nonetheless. It shows that the countess is capable of turning in an excellent performance as Suzanne, and Suzanne plays her role as countess equally well. Just as important, this last act has been "written" by the countess in that she has persuaded Suzanne to tell the count she will meet him in the garden despite Figaro's orders and has also decided that she herself will go to the garden disguised as Suzanne. Suzanne puts it thus: "Madame, your project is charming! I have just been thinking about it. It reconciles everything, ends everything, embraces everything" (act 2, scene 26, pp. 243–44).

Of course everything in the play does not come about in exactly the terms projected by the countess and Suzanne either. Figaro injects an element of his own when he sees through Suzanne's disguise and then proceeds to arouse her indignation and jealousy by proclaiming his love for "the Countess." The countess too learns a lesson from her husband when he confides to "Suzanne" that the countess has not "sufficiently studied the art of sustaining [his] inclination" for her (act 5, scene 7, p. 313). The last act of the play thus identifies the characters with one another by showing that each is an actor-artist, and therefore each is by implication without a fixed identity. What underlies this generalization of art—and hence this democratization of political authority—is the revelation that the alternative itself of either paternal authority or maternal/narcissistic love is inadequate.

Uneasy though the relationship between psychoanalysis and politics may be according to Freud, it is in principle possible to reconcile them if there is one relationship free of ambivalence and if there is an individual of the leader type, whether artist or psychoanalyst, who understands and knows how to exploit ambivalence. But by formulating its demand for equality in terms of a concept of identification that is as original as any form of object-choice, Beaumarchais's *Figaro* presents an even greater challenge to political authority, even to one that takes the form of art. It shows that there is no political or aesthetic authority that is not rooted in a concept of identification, and thus there is no form of authority that can underestimate the complexity of identification—a complexity that is ultimately exemplified in each of the ambiguous characters in the play—without itself paying a severe price. It reveals that all authority is in some sense without authority, given the ambivalent role of identification on which it is based. The political problem is not that of finding a (substitute for) paternal or maternal authority but, rather, of conceiving of a form of equality based on the identification of the individuals of a group not with one another but rather with *the other*.

Because it indicates the universality and primary nature of identification, *Figaro* also points out the limitations of the model of tragedy that underlies Freud's social psychology and psychoanalysis as a whole. If the identification between the father and the son is no longer privileged, then *Oedipus* (or *Hamlet*) is no longer the supreme tragedy. This does not mean that *Figaro* denies the existence of conflict between the father(s) and the son(s); quite the contrary. It means only that it is one form of conflict among others and that its claim to be the ultimate form of conflict is arbitrary. That *Figaro* has a serious aim—that is, that it is a comedy and not a tragedy, but also a comedy interrupted by tragedy—can be seen as a consequence of the way it places the conflict between the father and the son in a context that exceeds the explanatory power of *Oedipus*, understood as the model tragedy, and of psychoanalysis, understood as the theory modeled after this model.

Figaro can thus be seen as a modern tragedy, which achieves its effects through a generalization of the tragic principle of ambivalent identification, and which in an analogous manner implies the generalization of equality outside the realm of the mutual identification of the sons both with each other and with any form of natural paternal authority, no matter how ambivalent. The politics of psychoanalysis reaches its limit in such a context, not just because, as Freud would have it, psychoanalysis has no authority to impose its analyses and cures on society, but also because in the end it conceives of equality only in terms of a highly restrictive form of identification, because it cannot conceive of a non-Oedipal—that is, not necessarily masculine (or feminine)—form of authority, which would be rooted in the "other" rather than in the self.

Conclusion:

♦ Tragedy and the Problem of Culture

In *The Birth of Tragedy,* Nietzsche denounces the thinkers who see tragedy as little more than the occasion for the discharge of emotions or
for the vindication of a moral vision of the universe, and he accuses
them of having had "no experience of tragedy as a supreme *art.*"[1] The
criticism expressed here reflects an essential aim of Nietzsche's essay:
to free his own interpretation of tragedy from extra-aesthetic problems and frameworks, which in his view have traditionally prevented
a genuine understanding of tragedy. And yet this same work also
shows Nietzsche himself to be as concerned with extra-aesthetic
issues as with aesthetics per se. What Nietzsche offers his reader is a
philosophical interpretation not only of the tragic art of the Greeks
but of Greek culture as well, as is evident in the manner in which he
consistently defines the tragic and the Greek each in terms of the
other. And when, in the "Attempt at Self-Criticism," Nietzsche later
rejects the "artists' metaphysics" lurking in the background of *The
Birth of Tragedy,* he shows the importance that the cultural dimension
of the problem of tragedy still has for him by expressing his regret
that, because of its shortcomings, *The Birth of Tragedy* failed to do justice to what he calls the Greek problem (24).

In terms of the works of the figures discussed in the preceding
pages, Nietzsche's views on the relation between culture and tragedy
appear in no way exceptional. Only a reading itself narrowly committed to a restrictively aesthetic interpretation of tragedy could overlook
the cultural dimension and implications of the interpretations and versions of tragedy offered in the works of these various theorists and
playwrights.

Hegel's reading of *Antigone* is an important and revealing case in
point. We have seen that from his perspective *Antigone* is not only an
aesthetic object in the usual sense but also, just as fundamentally, a
cultural object. This does not mean that Hegel sees the play as a mere
representation of Greek life: for him it *is* that life, that is, *Antigone* is

the concrete embodiment of the Greek ethical community, the very substance and essence of Greek existence. When Hegel embraces tragedy, and more specifically, *Antigone* as models for philosophy itself, he thus simultaneously embraces (Greek) culture and history. They too cannot be mere objects for philosophy; philosophy must find itself in rather than merely opposing itself to them.

But as we have also seen, in defining the Greek ethical community in terms of an opposition between abstract, Kantian morality and the real existence of an ethical-cultural community, Hegel sets up a dialectic between reason and culture whose culmination lies in reason—or in philosophy. Given the interdependence of culture and tragedy in Hegel's reading of *Antigone,* his famous dictum that "art is for us a thing of the past" tells us as much about the relation of speculative philosophy to Greek culture as to (Greek) art. In neither case should it be read as the expression of crude nostalgia. The pastness of Greece, like the pastness of art, is as necessary from the philosophical standpoint as the organic wholeness that makes Greece a golden age of philosophy, art, and ethical life. The historical-conceptual movement through which Greek culture becomes a thing of the past is synonymous with the speculative dialectic itself, and thus without this movement there would be no modernity and no philosophy in Hegel's sense. The dialectic leads us to both art and culture, but it also leads beyond culture just as it leads beyond art.

The project of embracing culture in order to transcend it is also evident in Hegel's reading of *Le Neveu de Rameau,* where Rameau's Nephew exemplifies the absolute alienation of cultural consciousness, an alienation that is produced by a culture that has attained the highest stage of properly cultural development. As we have seen, however, such absolute alienation not only is the consequence and expression of cultural development; in Hegel's terms, it also leads immediately to the transcendence of culture. From this perspective, the dialectic between speculative reason and "the French" is identical to the dialectic between speculative reason and "the Greeks." In each case it is a question of coming to terms with or producing the rational principle of a particular culture and, thereby, transcending it. But in each case the given culture can be transcended not because reason has taken form in another culture but only because, in its ultimate form, reason transcends any specific culture, or—what amounts to the same thing—because reason institutes a universal culture.

By finding in Greek culture an embodiment of the synthesis of reason, art, and ethics to which philosophy itself aspires, Hegel, one could argue, roots philosophy itself, if only momentarily, ..1 a specific culture and thus despite himself imposes a cultural limitation on philosophy. It is true that the place and importance he gives to Greek culture in his philosophycal system make the universality of speculative reason problematic. But the role played by the Greeks in Hegel's philosophy does not in and of itself necessarily indicate the total imprisonment of philosophy in an ethnocentric perspective. Hegel embraces Greek culture because for him it exhibits the traits of a universal, ideal culture. In its organic wholeness, in the manner in which everything in the culture is determined by the culture (that is, in the dynamic harmony it institutes between nature and culture, art and life, reason and practical activity), Hegel's version of classical Greece echoes prior attempts to imagine or find in history a golden age and a historical or mythical culture that could serve as a model for the understanding of culture generally.

If Hegel is not the first thinker to conceive of the problem of culture in such terms, he is certainly not the last either. Claude Lévi-Strauss's *Tristes Tropiques* provides a more recent example, even though, at first glance, it would be easy to see Lévi-Strauss as an anti-Hegelian theorist of culture.[2] Lévi-Strauss's anthropology explicitly grows out of a critique of historical theories of culture, which in his view are derived from dialectical philosophy. In his celebrated polemic with Jean-Paul Sartre, Lévi-Strauss rejects these theories and the work of those who accept them without question, on the grounds that by equating culture with history, they are in fact privileging a particular form of culture — the European — as the only true one.[3] *Tristes tropiques* recounts Lévi-Strauss's search for an ethnographic method that would make it possible to meet non-European cultures on their own terrain and describe them in terms that do not simply reflect the cultural presuppositions of the ethnographer. For him culture is not just an object among others for the theorist. It includes the theorist within its compass, and in this sense only a highly self-reflexive and self-critical anthropology is capable of describing and analyzing other cultures.

Important though his differences with Hegel are, *Tristes tropiques* nonetheless reveals what Lévi-Strauss shares with him as well. Their affinity is particularly clear in Lévi-Strauss's analysis of the culture of the Nambikwara tribe of Brazil. From Lévi-Strauss's perspective,

Nambikwara society includes the fundamental elements in terms of which all cultures can be interpreted. Its stability, homogeneity, and humanity provide the foundation of not only Nambikwara culture and others with which its resemblance is obvious but implicitly even those cultures in which this foundation is overlaid with and obscured by technological innovation and historical transformation. And the same qualities that make Nambikwara culture the purest example of culture also make it a New World equivalent of the Golden Age of Greece, a Brazilian ethical community in which Lévi-Strauss senses "an immense kindness, a profoundly carefree attitude, a naive and charming animal satisfaction and—binding these various feelings together—something which might be called the most truthful and moving expression of human love" (293).

The tone and character of his description of Nambikwara society are not all that recall Hegel's interpretation of the "immaculate world"[4] of Greek culture, however. By showing that reason can reconcile itself with practical life while at the same time elevating it to the level of reason itself, Hegel's interpretation of Greek culture also serves as a justification of the absolute character of both reason and philosophy, which can now be seen to encompass culture and practical life within themselves. In a similar manner, by showing that the essential elements of all human life are found in Nambikwara culture, Lévi-Strauss's interpretation of Nambikwara society legitimates the concept of culture itself, which is now seen as encompassing all other spheres and modes of existence. It also legitimates anthropology, as opposed to history or philosophy, as the form of theory that encompasses all others. Lévi-Strauss's ethnography is radically different from—even opposed to—Hegel's theory of culture in that it reverses the hierarchy between reason and culture and makes culture the dominant term. But the concept of culture and the corresponding science of anthropology that replace speculative philosophy are nonetheless fundamentally similar to it. The encompassing of the ethnographer by culture is now no longer a limitation of anthropology itself but the confirmation of the absolutely determining character of culture generally. Lévi-Strauss is far from being a proponent of absolute reason, but he does implicitly bestow an absolute status on culture and in the process makes anthropology the only discipline that could legitimately claim to provide absolute knowledge.

Any number of other descriptions of culture that see it as all-encompassing, as the fundamental phenomenon in terms of which other phenomena must be situated and analyzed, depend on similar models of culture — or, one could say, similar myths of culture. In privileging a model (of) culture in terms of which all specific forms of culture can be understood and accounted for, such descriptions attempt to place themselves within but also, implicitly, beyond culture. Hegel's ethnocentrism, if it can be called that, is not radically different from an ethnocentrism underlying certain forms of cultural criticism — even those that are decidedly anti-Eurocentric in their strategies and goals — which do not involve a questioning of the idea that there can be a single concept of culture, which conceive of culture as a totality or assume that there can be *a* model for culture or *a* model culture.

What makes the relationship between speculative philosophy and Greek culture particularly problematic, then, is not only that the central place Hegel gives to the interpretation of *Antigone* permits us to situate speculative philosophy in terms of its interpretation of classical Greece. As long as the wholeness and oneness of (a) culture is sustained, it is always possible to embrace culture and transcend it, to acknowledge one's roots in a specific cultural context and to claim simultaneously to have attained universality. What poses a much graver problem from a Hegelian standpoint is that Greek culture should be radically and originally disrupted by tragic conflict, that its harmony should be revealed as mythical. When Hegel's interpretation of *Antigone* is read in a critical light, Greek culture appears at odds with itself, radically split by tensions that give it a dramatic complexity and dynamic and rob it of any unifying theme or structure that might serve to define its nature. The sublime or tragic dimension that Hegel imparts despite himself to his description of Greek culture undercuts *both* the attempt to situate theory within culture *and* the opposite (but in the terms of the dialectic, the essentially identical) attempt to place theory beyond culture.[5]

There is no way to convert culture into an absolute ground without obscuring or reducing the tensions lurking within any given culture. The conflict between "the law of the man" and "the law of the woman" uncovered by Hegel in his reading of *Antigone* is significant for exactly this reason. In cultural terms, it is an absolute conflict insofar as Antigone and Creon are both embodiments of the same culture or ethical community but also radically opposed. Hegel's concept of culture and ultimately perhaps all concepts of culture are problematic, at least in part because of the way conflict between "the law of the woman" and "the law of the man" undercuts not just cultural harmony but even the very attempt to define a given society or group of individuals in exclusively cultural terms. In reading *Antigone* with and against Hegel, what emerges is a sense of the mythical character not only of Hegel's Greece but of any culture—or any sex—that is viewed as being self-authentifying or self-defining.

In the terms of my analysis, Hegel's Greece is not the only culture originally disrupted by tragic conflict. Neither France nor Germany emerges intact from their conflict over the tragic, which both divides and unites them. Each is engaged in the construction of a mythical antiquity that would permit it to define, by contrast, its modernity, and in this sense each is involved in a struggle to create and shape its own identity. This struggle in and of itself indicates the problematic nature of that identity, the way in which neither French nor German culture can be seen as the true heir of Greek culture, but only as sites of recurrence for certain of the conflicts that make the concept of Greece and the concept of (Greek) culture themselves problematic. Equally important, each is engaged in a struggle with other modern European cultures for an aesthetic/cultural supremacy, and in this sense the Europe to which the France of Corneille, Racine, and Diderot and the Germany of Hegel and Freud belong also appears as a problematic entity, where similarity does not necessarily produce harmony but, rather, conflict. What France and Germany have in common with Greece is not a community of values that would be founded in tragedy, in philosophy, or in anything else but, rather, a disharmony and antagonism that excludes each from, as much as it makes each a part of, some larger or more original political-cultural entity.

In my readings of modern French tragedies as in my readings of Hegelian and Freudian theory, society (or what I have also called, borrowing from Hegel, the ethical community) is continually disrupted by the problematic nature of sexual identity and identification. The texts of Freud are especially significant from this perspective. In terms of the interpretation I have presented of Freud's work, it can be said that the imperatives of civilization and culture are constitutive of rather than external to individual psychology: this is one sense, and not the least important, of Freud's discovery that the unconscious is structured like a tragic drama. Moreover, as we have seen, it is not only Oedipus whom Freud discovers in the unconscious, but Hamlet as well—not only sexual desire but also the repression or punishment of sexual desire by culture and civilization. Similarly, the individual is produced not by nature or biology but, rather, by a complex process of identification that links him or her both to others and to him- or her self, and the fundamental status that Freud gives to identification is another sign that for him the individual is defined by culture. There is no identity or sexuality outside culture, that is, outside the complex process of identification that creates, rather than stems from, individual identity.

But an equally important implication of my reading of Freud is that our relationship to culture is no less uncomfortable or even painful as a result of its being rooted in the deepest layers of the psyche, in the instincts, if you will. The superego, which is harsh "even in normal times," is no less demanding because it draws its force from the instincts rather than from external authorities alone. The conflict between the individual and culture is no less real or dramatic for being internal to the individual. The existence of this conflict is just what indicates the limitations of culture, the element or elements that, without being distinct from culture, cannot be contained by it or understood wholly in cultural terms.

From Freud's perspective, the relationship between culture and what he calls the instincts is highly complex. But what limits its complexity and makes it possible to produce a theory of that relationship is what Freud takes to be the fact of the relatively more marginal relation of women to culture. When he writes that women have no sense or only a weak sense of justice, that their relationship to authority is erotically tinged and masochistic, he effectively removes the feminine from the sphere of conflict between culture and instincts. Women, for Freud, participate in cultural life more spontaneously than men because their relatively weaker aggressive instinct is not as difficult to overcome. But for the very same reason, they are also less well integrated into cultural life, whose condition is precisely the overcoming of aggressiveness.

Of course, Freud stresses that recognizing the deep-seated nature of the conflict between aggressiveness and civilization, between instincts and culture, will not provide mankind with any moral comfort. But he can nonetheless be seen to take comfort of a different sort from his analysis of this conflict. He is perhaps a moral pessimist, but he remains in many ways a theoretical optimist, confident that both culture and the instincts can be simultaneously theorized. In order to do this what is needed is that their dialectic be clarified in and through a description of the masculine path to civilization, and that the feminine, because of the way it blurs the distinction between instinct and culture, be marginalized in or excluded from the theory of culture. There is unquestionably a dialectic of culture and instinct in the work of Freud, and the ends of that dialectic, the idea that it has an end and a discernible direction, however negative, depend on the way his theory of culture excludes the feminine from the cultural.

In terms of Freud's own theory, then, as well as in terms of the tradition within which he situates it when he claims to have at last discovered the source of the fascination *Oedipus* holds for us, "the feminine" represents a particularly sensitive term, the site where the dialectic of culture and what culture cannot contain within it stalls or is interrupted. The cultural significance of feminine masochism and, more broadly, of femininity, is just this: that there is no origin (and hence no end) for the dialectic of instinct and culture. That dialectic "begins" in and through a primary and ambivalent identification with others, a process that Freud himself identifies with femininity, but which he reveals, despite himself, is the very foundation of masculinity and culture as well. As I have shown in my analyses of Antigone, Camille, Eriphile, Manon, and Beaumarchais's women characters, the question of the feminine is critically significant insofar as these various feminine figures cannot be simply opposed to but, instead, *mirror* the society and the masculine figures with which they find themselves in conflict. They are neither the other of (their) culture nor the same.

It is important to keep in mind that no individual or group could legitimately claim to speak in a univocal manner as or for feminine figures such as these and certainly not for something like the feminine in general, just as it would be impossible to speak as or for the masculine, the European, the Greek, the French, the German or, for that matter, the non-Western. To assume that one can speak for or as such cultural totalities is to fail to recognize the complexity of identification, that is, the ambivalence of all instances of it as well as the conflict between culture and instinct that any instance of identification inevitably brings into play. Equally important, to privilege these or other figures of the same type, to make of them the *absolute* other of a defined culture or philosophy, is to make them into another version of the same culture. Their critical significance lies instead in their place being as much within the particular culture or philosophy they can be used to contest and undermine as outside it. But for just that reason, no one culture or concept of culture, no one philosophy alone can define them or determine their destiny.

◆ Notes

Introduction: The Birth of Philosophy and Psychoanalysis

1. G. E. Lessing, *Hamburg Dramaturgy*, trans. Helen Zimmern (New York: Dover Publications, 1962), 179.

2. Sigmund Freud, *The Interpretation of Dreams*, *The Standard Edition of the Complete Psychological Works of Sigmund Freud* (London: Hogarth Press, 1953), 3:149.

3. Immanuel Kant, *The Critique of Judgement*, trans. James Creed Meredith (Oxford: Oxford University Press, 1952), 151.

4. In the essays on Hölderlin and Diderot which are the principal texts I analyze here, as well as in several of his other essays, Lacoue-Labarthe's main theme is mimesis rather than identification. But in *Heidegger: Art and Politics: The Fiction of the Political*, trans. Chris Turner (Cambridge, Mass.: Basil Blackwell, 1990), Lacoue-Labarthe writes of the term *identification* that "it is ultimately the only one we possess to designate what is at stake in the mimetic process" (80). In Lacoue-Labarthe's terms, then, *mimesis* and *identification* are interchangeable, inasmuch as identification can be considered a form of mimesis; but, even more, *identification* is the term for the mimetic process which best indicates its nature and the critical problems that arise when one attempts to understand it.

Chapter 1   The Identities of Tragedy: Nietzsche, Benjamin, Freud

1. What is new in the new historicism—for example, what distinguishes it from traditional historicisms—is its emphasis on the discursive, that is, on a historical object that comprehends language as part of itself rather than being the referent of language, but which, as a result, loses what, from the perspective of a traditional historicism, is its objective character.

2. Friedrich Nietzsche, *The Birth of Tragedy and the Case of Wagner*, trans. Walter Kaufmann (New York: Random House, 1967), 95.

3. Walter Benjamin, *The Origin of German Tragic Drama*, trans. John Osborne (London: NLB, 1977).

4. Thus Nietzsche characterizes the Apollinian as not just illusion but *delusion* when he writes that "it can even create the illusion that the Dionysian is really in the service of the Apollinian and capable of enhancing its effects—as if music were essentially the art of presenting an Apollinian content" (*Birth of Tragedy*, 128).

5. Thus, according to Nietzsche, what Euripides destroyed was not just the

Dionysian element of tragedy but the Apollinian as well, inasmuch as in destroying the one, he could not fail to destroy the other: "The intricate relation of the Apollinian and the Dionysian in tragedy may really be symbolized by a fraternal union of the two deities: Dionysus speaks the language of Apollo; and Apollo, finally the language of Dionysus; and so the highest goal of tragedy and of all art is attained" (130).

6. See Paul de Man's reading of *The Birth of Tragedy* in "Genesis and Genealogy (Nietzsche)," *Allegories of Reading* (New Haven, Conn.: Yale University Press, 1979), in which he undermines the distinctions between the terms of Nietzsche's principal oppositions and thus the absolute privilege given to the Dionysian. De Man argues that the "diachronic, successive structure of *The Birth of Tragedy* is in fact an illusion," because "whenever an art form is being discussed, the three modes represented by Dionysos, Apollo, and Socrates are always simultaneously present and that it is impossible to mention one of them without at least implying the others" (85).

7. This is the argument of Gilles Deleuze, *Nietzsche et la Philosophie* (Paris: Presses Universitaires de France, 1967). Deleuze stresses the incommensurability between Nietzsche's concept of Dionysian tragedy and traditional philosophical concepts, especially the dialectic: "In general the dialectic is not a tragic vision of the world but, on the contrary, the death of tragedy, the replacement of the tragic vision with a theoretical conception (with Socrates), or better still with a Christian conception (with Hegel)" (21). In a subsequent passage he makes this same point even more forcefully and succinctly: "No compromise is possible between Hegel and Nietzsche" (223).

8. G. W. F. Hegel, *Aesthetics: Lectures on Fine Art*, trans. T. M. Knox (Oxford: Oxford University Press, 1974–75), 1196.

9. A similar perspective on Shakespeare can, of course, be found in the work of German critics beginning at least with G. E. Lessing's *Hamburg Dramaturgy*, trans. Helen Zimmern (New York: Dover Publications, 1962). Perhaps even more significant, it is still to be found in the work of Nietzsche, at least in the period of *The Birth of Tragedy*. In a note from 1870–71, he writes that "only the primal German spirit in Shakespeare, Bach, etc., has emancipated itself from" the influence of the Romans on modern art (quoted by John Sallis, *Crossings: Nietzsche and the Space of Tragedy* [Chicago: University of Chicago Press, 1991], 139). This passage is important in terms not only of the way it casually assimilates Shakespeare and the German but also of the way it opposes the Greek and German to the Latin (and hence also to the French). Sallis's book on Nietzsche and tragedy articulates a very interesting and at times persuasive interpretation of the place of *The Birth of Tragedy* in relation to Nietzsche's work as a whole and more generally in relation to Western metaphysics. What is most questionable about it is the lack of weight given to Nietzsche's own subsequent criticisms of his early work as expressing an artists' metaphysics. The passage quoted above and others of a similar type are interpeted by Sallis only in terms of the degree to which Nietzsche's concept of tragedy breaks with traditional philosophy (which Sallis defines in a fairly narrow sense). He thus reads them without attempting to offer a discussion of their cultural or political significance.

10. Nietzsche writes that Kant and Schopenhauer lay the ground for a "tragic culture" because their work triumphs "over the optimism concealed in the essence of logic" (*Birth of Tragedy*, 112). And in "the noblest intellectual efforts of Goethe, Schiller, and Wincklemann," we see how "the German spirit has so far striven most resolutely to learn from the Greeks" (121).

11. Sigmund Freud, *Civilization and Its Discontents, The Standard Edition of the Complete Psychological Works of Sigmund Freud* (London: Hogarth Press, 1953), 21:115. All further citations of works by Freud refer to this edition.

12. Friedrich Nietzsche, *On the Genealogy of Morals, Ecce Homo*, trans. Walter Kaufmann and R. J. Hollingdale (New York: Random House, 1969), 243. Walter Kaufmann points out that Nietzsche similarly distances himself from the use of such terms as *Aryan* and *Semitic* and the concern with racial and cultural purity they connote when he later writes in a note: "Contra Aryan and Semitic. Where races are mixed, there is the source of great cultures" (quoted in *The Birth of Tragedy*, 70–71, n. 5).

13. For example, in a fairly typical passage from his "Lettres sur Oedipe," Voltaire writes condescendingly of the Greeks that "with all their intelligence and all their culture, [they] could not have a correct idea of the perfection of a [tragic] art that was only in its infancy" (*Oeuvres complètes de Voltaire* [Paris: Garnier Frères, 1877], 1:26). Had the Greek playwrights been born in modern France, Voltaire goes on, "they would have perfected the art that they practically invented" (27). In Voltaire's "Discours sur la Tragédie" (which he addresses to an Englishman, Lord Bolingbroke), he writes in a similar vein of Shakespeare's *Julius Ceasar*: "I do not pretend to approve of all the barbarous irregularities of which it is full; it is nonetheless amazing that there are not more in a work composed in a century of ignorance, by a man who did not even know Latin and who had no other master than himself" (1:316–17). Nonetheless, Voltaire himself, it is worth recalling, was no vulgar chauvinist, either in his work as a whole or even in his prefaces to his tragedies. As he writes in the "Discours historique et critique" published with *Don Pèdre*: "Those who lie . . . to humanity are often still animated by the stupidity of national rivalry. . . . Today, when Europe is divided among so many powers that balance each other; when so many peoples have their great men in every genre, whoever wants to flatter his country too much runs the risk of displeasing the others, if by chance he is read by them, and ought not to expect appreciation [even] from his own countrymen" (6:252).

14. The philosophers and theorists who fall within this general category and who will be treated in the course of this study are Hegel, Lessing, and, in a somewhat different sense Freud, Auerbach, and even Philippe Lacoue-Labarthe, who has taken up once again, but this time critically, the "German" investigation of the problem of art.

15. Sigmund Freud, *Group Psychology and the Analysis of the Ego*, 18:105.

16. Jean Starobinski, "Hamlet et Oedipe," *La Relation critique* (Paris: Gallimard, 1970). This point is more fully developed in chapter 4.

Chapter 2   Philosophical Identification, Tragedy, and the Sublime:
Hegel, Kant, and *Antigone*

1. G. W. F. Hegel, *Aesthetics: Lectures on Fine Art*, trans. T. M. Knox (Oxford: Oxford University Press, 1974-75), 13.

2. Martin Heidegger, "The Origin of the Work of Art," *Poetry, Language, Thought*, trans. Albert Hofstadter (New York: Harper & Row, 1971), 79.

3. Jacques Derrida, *Glas* (Paris: Galilée, 1974), 171.

4. Friedrich Nietzsche, *The Birth of Tragedy and the Case of Wagner*, trans. Walter Kaufmann (New York: Random House, 1967), 120-21.

5. A. W. Schlegel, *Course of Lectures on Dramatic Art and Literature*, trans. John Black (New York: AMS Press, 1965).

6. Jean-Luc Nancy, *Le Discours de la syncope: 1. Logodaedalus* (Paris: Aubier-Flammarion, 1976), 36.

7. Immanuel Kant, *The Critique of Judgement*, trans. James Creed Meredith (Oxford: Oxford University Press, 1952), 151.

8. Sigmund Freud, *The Interpretation of Dreams*, *The Standard Edition of the Complete Psychological Works of Sigmund Freud* (London: Hogarth Press, 1953), 4:149.

9. See especially Hannah Arendt, *Lectures on Kant's Political Philosophy*, ed. Ronald Beiner (Chicago: University of Chicago Press, 1982); Jean-François Lyotard, *L'Enthousiasme: La Critique kantienne de l'histoire* (Paris: Galilée, 1986).

10. Jean Hyppolite, *Genèse et structure de la Phénoménologie de l'esprit de Hegel* (Paris: Aubier, 1946), 313.

11. Immanuel Kant, *Critique of Pure Reason* (Garden City, N. Y.: Doubleday, 1966), 89.

12. Gilles Deleuze, *Kant's Critical Philosophy: The Doctrine of the Faculties*, trans. Hugh Tomlinson and Barbara Habberjam (Minneapolis: University of Minnesota Press, 1984), viii.

13. Martin Heidegger, *Kant and the Problem of Metaphysics*, trans. James S. Churchill (Bloomington: Indiana University Press, 1962), 167.

14. As Heidegger puts it, in the first edition, Kant brought the possibility of metaphysics before an abyss, but, in the second edition, he drew back from it (*Kant*, 173).

15. "Only the concept of freedom," Kant asserts in the Second Critique, "allows us to find the unconditioned for the conditioned and the intelligible for the sensuous without going outside ourselves" (*Critique of Practical Reason*, trans. Lewis Beck White [Indianapolis: Bobbs-Merrill, 1956], 109). In this passage, Kant makes it clear that the unconditioned necessity is indeed located not only outside reason but within it as well.

16. The relation between Hegel's interpretation of tragedy and his philosophy as a whole has been treated by several of his most distinguished modern commentators. Already in 1940, P. Bertrand argued, in "Le Sens du tragique et du destin dans la dialectique hégélienne," *Revue de métaphysique et de morale* 47 (1940), that "it is therefore no exaggeration to affirm that, from 1799 on, Hegel's meditation on the Tragic and Destiny and the dialectical movement that results

from them assured his possession of his method" (176). Jean Hyppolite's *Genèse et structure de la Phénoménologie de l'esprit de Hegel* and, more particularly, his *Introduction à la philosophie de l'histoire de Hegel* (Paris: Seuil, 1983) also devote much attention to Hegel's conceptions of destiny and tragedy and argue that the reconciliation that is to be effected by the movement of history is effected first in Hegel's work through his interpretation of the tragic. Jacques Derrida's *Glas*, though not centrally concerned with the problem of tragedy, presents a highly detailed and complex assessment of the place of Hegel's interpretation of *Antigone* in his philosophy as a whole. Finally, there is Peter Szondi's essay "The Notion of the Tragic in Schelling, Hölderlin, and Hegel," *On Textual Understanding and Other Essays*, trans. Harvey Mendelsohn (Minneapolis: University of Minnesota Press, 1986), which I shall discuss later in the chapter.

17. Hegel, *Article de Iena sur le droit naturel*, quoted in Hyppolite, *Genèse et structure de la Phénoménologie de l'esprit de Hegel*, 2:330.

18. G. W. F. Hegel, *Phenomenology of Spirit*, trans. A. V. Miller (Oxford: Oxford University Press, 1977), 280.

19. H. R. Jauss, "Dialogique et dialectique," *Revue de métaphysique et de morale* 89, no. 2 (April–June 1984): 172.

20. G. W. F. Hegel, *Philosophy of Right*, trans. T. M. Knox (Oxford: Oxford University Press, 1967), 115.

21. In *The Tragic Vision* (Chicago: University of Chicago Press, 1960), Murray Krieger introduces his analyses of several masters of modern prose fiction (Gide, Malraux, Camus, Dostoevsky, Mann, Kafka, Conrad, and Melville) with a discussion of Hegel's conception of tragedy as embodied in the *Aesthetics*. Krieger's general strategy stems from a critique of Hegel's concept of the tragic in terms of what he calls its "attempt to create a metaphysical equivalent for the unity of the Greek world," an attempt that in Krieger's view accounts for Hegel's stress on "the conclusive power of tragedy" and "his insistence on the absoluteness, the wholeness, the indivisibility" of the ethical substance (5). Krieger responds to this Hegelian tragic vision with one that takes the "subversive tragic hero" as its focus and sees him as "fulfilling a proper human function and even a proper human obligation in standing with his integrity as an individual outside the universal" (6–7).

22. In *Speculum de l'autre femme* (Paris: Minuit, 1974), Luce Irigaray says of this same passage that the relationship between the brother and the sister is "an ideal settlement [*départagement*], in which the (ethical) substance of matriarchy and patriarchy would coexist, in an untroubled peace and a relationship without desire. The war between the sexes would not take place. But this moment, of course, is mythical and *this Hegelian dream* is already the effect of a dialectic produced by patriarchy" (269). For Irigaray, a war between the sexes is inevitable. Moreover, she goes on to imply that that war stems from the absolute nature of the difference beween the sexes, when she writes of bisexuality that it works only *with* the patriarchical dialectic to assure "the connection and the passage one into the other of each sex" (269). In contrast, I argue that conflict between the sexes has its basis in (a certain) bisexuality, but also that that bisexuality prevents the war of which Irigaray writes from

being total—since the conflict in question is as much within each sex as between them.

Chapter 3   The Interrupted Dialectic of Modern Tragedy: Hegel, Corneille, and the Feminine Challenge to *Aufhebung*

1. G. W. F. Hegel, *Aesthetics: Lectures on Fine Art*, trans. T. M. Knox (Oxford: Oxford University Press, 1974–75), 605.

2. Certainly, Hegel himself does not acknowledge his departure from Aristotle but instead takes pains to portray his philosophy of fine art as consistent with the *Poetics*. His "official" posture is identical to that of Lessing. Hegel too sees himself as part of and perhaps even as the preeminent figure in a return to Aristotle, from whose true principles the French, in particular, have strayed. And yet the instance mentioned above is not the only one in which he appears to chose a rather different path from that taken in the *Poetics*. In particular, one could argue that Hegel never successfully brings his criticism of theories of art which are based on the affect associated with the work of art into line with his professed posture of fidelity to Aristotle's fundamental principles. (Among such theories one would have to classify the *Poetics*, given the central nature of the notion of catharsis in Aristotle's analysis of tragedy, and, to be sure, Kant's *Critique of Judgment*.) Instead, Hegel argues unconvincingly that Aristotle was not really talking about "mere feelings of pity and fear" but instead about "the nature of the subject-matter by which its artistic appearance is to purify these feelings" (*Aesthetics*, 1197).

3. In Martin Heidegger, *Poetry, Language, Thought*, trans. Albert Hofstadter (New York: Harper & Row, 1971), 80.

4. In Hegel's lexicon this term does not refer to pity or self-pity and does not have the negative connotation it commonly has in contemporary usage. It means, rather, the tragic passion that animates a given character or characters.

5. G. W. F. Hegel, *Phenomenology of Spirit*, trans. A. V. Miller (Oxford: Oxford University Press, 1977), 406–7.

6. Pierre Corneille, *Le Cid, Théâtre complet* (Paris: Garnier, 1971), 1:725.

7. Pierre Corneille, "Discours de la tragédie," *Théâtre complet*, 1:36.

8. This is a paraphrase of Hegel's characterization of the heroes and heroines of Greek tragedy: "the Greek, with his plasiticty of consciousness, takes responsibility for what he has done as an individual and does not cut his purely subjective self-consciousness apart from what is objectively the case" (*Aesthetics*, 1224).

9. Pierre Corneille, *Oedipe, Oeuvres complètes* (Paris: Seuil, 1963), ll. 1149–58, p. 580.

10. F. W. J. Schelling, *The Philosophy of Art*, trans. Douglas W. Stott (Minneapolis: University of Minnesota Press, 1989), 254.

11. Pierre Corneille, *Horace, Théâtre complet*, 1:830.

12. See Serge Doubrovsky, *Corneille ou la dialectique du héros* (Paris: Gallimard, 1963), 107–19.

13. "As soon as Rodrigue provides Chimène with the opportunity to 'punish' him [for the murder of her father], her aim of punishing him changes immediately into a desire for legal justice, which postpones its execution. . . . All the arguments of Chimène can be brought back, in fact, to one: she wants to obtain *through the mediation of others* . . . what the Master [that is, the authentic Corneillean hero] must take on himself alone. We are brought back to a behaviour typical of bad faith" (Doubrovsky, *Corneille*, 111).

14. Doubrovsky's other major theoretical reference in *Corneille* is, of course, Hegel, in particular his "dialectic of master and slave." That Corneille's texts lend themselves so well to a Hegelian reading is accepted by Doubrovsky as a natural consequence of their analogous philosophical positions. As a result, he never discusses the possibility that the convergence between Hegel and Corneille is historical in nature and therefore as much a consequence of what Hegel owes to tragedy as of what Corneille achieved as a thinker of subjectivity.

15. Thus Doubrovsky writes that in the case of Rodrigue, we see that "the conversion of the animal 'I' into the heroic 'I' consecrates the advent of the aristocratic ethic, which at last overcomes nature" (*Corneille*, 113).

Chapter 4   The Uneasy Identification of Psychoanalysis and Tragedy: Freud and Racine

1. F. W. J. Schelling, *The Philosophy of Art*, trans. Douglas W. Stott (Minneapolis: University of Minnesota Press, 1989), 253.

2. In the *Aesthetics: Lectures on Fine Art*, trans. T. M. Knox (Oxford: Oxford University Press, 1974–75), G. W. F. Hegel devotes little attention to the problem of tragic guilt, which he treats almost exclusively in terms of the plasticity of the heroes of (ancient) tragedy, who do not distinguish between their responsibility in relation to unconsciously and consciously performed deeds (see especially p. 1214). But while it is doubtless of some significance that Hegel has recourse to the term *unconscious* in order to describe the guilt of the tragic Greek heroes, his explicit position — at least in an early text in which he addresses the question of tragic guilt and its irrational nature more squarely — appears to be much closer to that of Schelling: "*Tragedy* resides in the fact that the moral nature, in order not to become entangled with its inorganic nature, separates the latter from itself as a fate, and places it over against itself; and through the recognition of this fate in the course of the battle, it is reconciled with the divine being, which is the unity of both" (Hegel, "Über die wissenschaftlichen Behandlungen des Naturrechts, seine Stelle in der praktischen Philosophie, und sein Verhältnis zu den positiven Rechtswissenschaften," quoted in Peter Szondi, "The Notion of the Tragic," *On Textual Understanding and Other Essays*, trans. Harvey Mendelsohn [Minneapolis: University of Minnesota Press], 49). For Hegel too, tragic guilt exemplifies the tension between freedom and necessity and represents a dialectical reconciliation of that tension in which necessity is respected, but not at the expense of freedom.

3. Sigmund Freud, *The Interpretation of Dreams*, *The Standard Edition of the*

Complete Psychological Works of Sigmund Freud (London: Hogarth Press, 1953), 4:262. All further citations of works by Freud refer to this edition.

4. "Oedipus and Hamlet are the mediating images between Freud's past and his patient: they are the guarantees of a common language. This series of recognitions thus imposes itself as constitutive of the path of analytic thought itself and not as an example of its appplication to an exterior domain" (Jean Starobinski, "Hamlet et Oedipe," *La Relation critique* [Paris: Gallimard, 1970], 315).

5. This question is addressed by Jean-François Lyotard in his essay "Oedipe Juif": "What is there in *Hamlet* that is not in *Oedipus*? There is *non-fulfillment* [*inaccomplissement*]. One can see it as the psychological dimension of neurosis or the tragic dimension of thought. But it has an altogether different dimension. Oedipus fulfills the destiny of his desire; the destiny of Hamlet is the non-fulfillment of desire: this chiasmus is the one implied between what is Greek and what is Jewish, between the tragic and the ethical" (Lyotard, "Oedipe Juif," *Dérive à partir de Marx et Freud* [Paris: Union Générale d'Editions, 1973], 175). Lyotard's extremely complex interpretation of Freud's relation to Oedipus and Hamlet deserves to be considered both in its own right and in terms of its links to Lyotard's work as a whole. But with regard to the more immediate concerns of my own reading of Freud, what interests me is not so much the alternative Lyotard proposes between *Oedipus*, the Greek, and the tragic, on the one hand, and *Hamlet*, the ethical, and the Jewish on the other, but rather the "still (or already) Jewish" and "still (or already) ethical" qualities of the Greek and the tragic—in other words, the way in which Freud's work indirectly suggests that from the standpoint of psycholanalysis, *Hamlet* exemplifies the nature of the unconscious *and therefore of the tragic* as well as and perhaps even better than *Oedipus*.

6. This article is the focus of Philippe Lacoue-Labarthe's analysis of Freud and his relation to tragedy in "La Scène est primitive," *Le Sujet de la philosophie* (Paris: Aubier-Flammarion, 1979), an essay to which my own analysis is particularly indebted.

7. Of course, Freud's interpretation of *Oedipus Rex* in *The Interpretation of Dreams* already raises the issue of repression. He writes that "we shrink back from [the figure of Oedipus] with the whole force of the repression by which those [incestuous] wishes have since [childhood] been held down within us" (*Interpretation of Dreams*, 4:263). But this repression is external to the spectator's experience of the play and is not related by Freud to the "profound and universal power to move" of the Oedipus legend, both of which are presented as being rooted in the pleasure afforded by the positive expression the play and legend give to unconscious wishes.

8. According to his associate Max Graf, Freud wrote "Psychopathic Characters" in 1904; but he himself never published it. It was first published by Graf in 1942 in the *Psychoanalytic Quarterly*. Reflecting on the historical circumstances of the (non)publication of this brief text, Philippe Lacoue-Labarthe remarks that it "represents an enigma, among all [Freud's] posthumous texts, not only because Freud did not publish it (or did not want to publish it, or did

not write it with a view to publication), but because he probably 'forgot' its very existence, and because he, in any case, *divested* himself of it. This circumstance is sufficiently unusual, if it is not unique, to attract attention, even to intrigue" (Lacoue-Labarthe, "La Scène est primitive," 187).

9. "Here the precondition of enjoyment is that the spectator should himself be a neurotic, for it is only such people who can derive pleasure instead of aversion from the revelation and the more or less conscious recognition of a repressed impulse" (Freud, "Psychopathic Characters," 7:308–9).

10. Thus it comes as something of a surprise when Jacques Lacan, in his own interpretation of *Hamlet*, "Desire and the Interpretation of Desire in *Hamlet*" (*Yale French Studies* nos. 55–56 [1977]), remarks that he knows of no commentator who has noted the importance of the theme of mourning in *Hamlet* (39).

11. In his *Aesthetic Theory*, trans. C. Lehnhardt (New York: Routledge & Kegan Paul, 1984), Theodor W. Adorno contrasts Freud's and Kant's aesthetics. He stresses that Freud's is focused on wish fulfillment and is therefore "interested," in Kant's terms, whereas Kantian aesthetics, based on the concept of the "disinterestedness" of aesthetic pleasure, appears from a Freudian perspective as a "castrated hedonism" (18). Adorno also notes, however, that the two thinkers have something important in common—an "underlying subjective orientation" (15–16). Unlike Adorno, I would lay greater stress on the affinity between Kant and Freud, but, like him, I see that affinity in terms of the "subjective orientation" of each—if by that one means their common concern with the ambivalent and in part painful process of identification which each indicates is constitutive of the subject.

12. In *Pouvoirs de l'horreur* (Paris: Seuil, 1980), Julia Kristeva devotes a portion of her analysis to a concept of primary repression that is for her an essential component of what she calls the abject, which she defines as "the 'object' of primary repression" (20). In Kristeva's terms, the primary form of repression that has the abject as its "object" presupposes no subject or object in the usual sense. She thus describes it as "the capacity of the speaking being, always already inhabited by the Other, to divide, reject, repeat. Without there being *a* division, *a* separation, *a* subject/object already constituted" (20). But though Kristeva argues that primary repression presupposes no subject or object, it does, in her view, have a single *cause*, which she asserts lies in "maternal anxiety, which is incapable of satisfying itself in the ambiant symbolic" (20). Thus, the primary form of repression finds its purest expression in the relation of the mother to her child: "it is necessary to recognize that this narcissistic topology is supported by nothing other, in psychosomatic reality, than by the mother-child dyad" (77).

13. Jacques Lacan, "Introduction au commentaire de Jean Hyppolite sur la 'Verneinung' de Freud," and Jean Hyppolite, "Commentaire parlé sur la 'Verneinung' de Freud," both in Jacques Lacan, *Ecrits* (Paris: Seuil, 1966).

14. The *Standard Edition* translation of the same passage is as follows: "Negation is a way of taking cognizance of what is repressed, indeed, it is already a lifting of the repression, though not, of course, an acceptance of what is repressed" ("Negation," 19:235–36).

15. This explicit admiration of and even fascination with art as well as the more complex theoretical ambiguities underlying it are the subject of Sarah Kofman, *The Childhood of Art*, trans. Winifred Woodhull (New York: Columbia University Press, 1988).

16. Roland Barthes, *Sur Racine* (Paris: Seuil, 1963), 9–10.

17. André Green, *Un Oeil en trop: Le Complexe d'Oedipe dans la tragédie* (Paris: Minuit, 1969), 195.

18. Charles Mauron, *L'Inconscient dans l'oeuvre et la vie de Racine* (Gap: Publication des Annales de la Faculté des lettres d'Aix-en-Provence, 1957), 21.

19. Jean Racine, *Iphigénie, Oeuvres complètes de Racine* (Paris: Gallimard, 1950), 671. All further citations of works by Racine refer to this edition.

20. A practice that, as we have seen, contrasts markedly with that of Corneille, who, while also claiming to remain faithful to the ancients, nonetheless diverges openly from Aristotle on this point ("Discours de la tragédie," *Théâtre complet* [Paris: Garnier, 1971], 1:36–38).

21. Hegel criticizes Phèdre on the same grounds he criticized Rodrigue: because of a lack of firmness of character, which in her case manifests itself in the fact that the responsibility for her actions is not hers alone but is shared with Oenone: "It is equally contrary to individual decision if a chief character in whom the power of a 'pathos' stirs and works is himself determined and talked over by a subordinate figure, and now can shift the blame from himself on to another—as e.g., Phèdre in Racine's [play] is talked over by Oenone" (*Aesthetics*, 241). In the case of Racine, as in the case of Corneille, Hegel shows himself to be unsympathetic to what is most modern in his portrayal of character.

22. There is an obvious convergence here between two conceptions of guilt. One would be derived from the Greeks and their tragedies. The other would be derived if not from Jansenism per se, then from a "radical" Jansenism, which would stress not so much the wholesale refusal of the world by the tragic hero/Christian, as Lucien Goldmann would have it (*Le Dieu caché* [Paris: Gallimard, 1955]). Rather, it would stress the guilt of *even* the elected few, who, like those who are condemned, have done nothing themselves to merit their election but owe it to God alone and, in this sense, are no more innocent than those who are condemned. Clearly these two Racines—the one pagan and the other Christian—are not contradictory but, rather, complementary. Though one appears to belong to a historical period of longer duration, stretching from Greek antiquity to the seventeenth century, and the other appears to belong to a more limited historical period, beginning with the emergence of Jansenist theology in France, it would be an oversimplification to separate them too radically. Hegel, for example, consistently treats Christianity as the *Aufhebung* of Greek culture, and in this sense it is already immanent in Greek culture as the solution to its antinomies. But one could argue, borrowing Hegel's terms while reversing his conclusions, that in terms of its conception of the ineluctability of guilt, a certain form of Jansenism is the sign of the persistence of the tragic and the Greek within Christianity.

23. In "The Economic Problem of Masochism," Freud writes that "a sense of guilt, too, finds expression in the manifest content of masochistic phanta-

sies; the subject assumes that he has committed some crime (the nature of which is left indefinite) which is to be expiated by all these painful and tormenting procedures. This looks like a superficial rationalization of the masochistic subject-matter, but behind it there lies a connection with infantile masturbation" (14:162). In "The Dissolution of the Oedipus Complex," this sense of guilt related to infantile masturbation becomes the castration complex whose dissolution results in the institution of the superego (14:176).

24. Here again, however, though the logic of his own description of the superego appears to lead toward a notion of primary guilt, Freudian theory can be seen resisting such a notion as well as calling for it. The resistance is evident in the conviction, expressed with greatest clarity in *Totem and Taboo* and reiterated in *Civilization and Its Discontents*, that every individual carries with him, as part of the biological substratum upon which his psyche is grafted, a kind of genetic memory of the original sin of humanity—the murder of the primal father by his sons.

25. In terms of Racine's plays, the primary nature of guilt would thus illuminate—or be illuminated by—the manner in which guilt and the erotic are continually intertwined, to the extent that punishment and erotic fulfillment become virtually indistinguishable. One of the most spectacular instances of such contamination of the erotic and the ethical occurs when Phèdre's declaration of love is rejected by Hippolyte, and she responds by attempting to take her own life, and hence punish herself, with *his* sword. But Eriphile's death is equally relevant to this question. It too has both an (auto)erotic and ethical dimension, inasmuch as it can be seen both as (self-)punishment for her crimes against Iphigénie and as the satsifaction of the masochism that makes her love her abductor, Achille.

26. This does not mean, of course, that the psyche as a whole is fundamentally unconcerned with reality according to psychoanalysis. As Jean Laplanche and J.-B. Pontalis argue in their *Vocabulaire de la psychanalyse* (Paris: Presses Universitaires de France, 1967), 138–42, the concept of "reality testing," though not fully determined in Freud's psychoanalytic theory, nonetheless cleary indicates his intent to give an account of the realism of the psyche, albeit one that does not negate the complexity and specificity of its structure. In "The Ego and the Id," Freud calls reality testing one of the important functions with which the ego is entrusted. The psyche has reality inscribed within it, in the figure of the ego, which then enlists reality on its side in its conflicts with the id and superego. But because the ego is only one character among others on the psychic stage, reality appears as a contested value rather than something that is self-evident and pre-given. The situation of the psychoanalyst or theorist would implicitly be analogous to that of the ego. As Sam Weber has put it, psycholanalysis is not a science of observation, or, rather, psychoanalysis is the "science" that reveals that observation is "a function of conflictual desires" (*The Legend of Freud* [Minneapolis: University of Minnesota Press, 1982], 25).

27. Once the superego has been instituted, Freud writes, "the distinction . . . between doing something bad and wishing to do it disappears en-

tirely, since nothing can be hidden from the super-ego, not even thoughts" (*Civilization and Its Discontents*, 21:125).

28. As G. E. Lessing puts it in his *Hamburg Dramaturgy*, trans. Helen Zimmern (New York: Dover Publications, 1962): "It is true it is [the French] who boast of most obedience to rules, but it is they also who give to these rules such extension that it scarce repays the labour to bring them forward as rules; or else regard them in such a left-handed and forced manner, that it generally offends more to see them observed thus instead of not at all" (134).

29. "The unalterability of an exclusive locality for a specific action is one of those rigid rules which the French especially have drawn from Greek tragedy and the remarks of Aristotle. But Aristotle only says of tragedy that the duration of the action should not normally exceed one day, and he does not touch at all on the unity of place which even the Greek poets did not abide by in the strict French sense" (Hegel, *Aesthetics*, 1164).

30. Barthes describes the Oedipal situation, albeit without naming it, in the terms Freud uses to characterize it in *Totem and Taboo*: "Incest, rivalry between brothers, the murder of the father, the rebellion of the sons, these are the fundamental themes of Racinian theater" (Barthes, *Sur Racine*, 21).

31. Goldmann notes this same characteristic of Racine's plays but interprets it from the standpoint of the predominance in them of the theme of passion: "If, with the exception of Titus, the tragic characters of his plays are women, it is because passion is an important element of their humanity, and because the seventeenth century would have accepted this only with difficulty in a masculine character" (*Le Dieu caché*, 352).

32. A typical example from the early eighteenth century can be found in l'abbé Prévost's *Mémoires et avantures d'un homme de qualité*, *Oeuvres complètes* (Paris: Leblanc, 1810–16), 1:394. Prévost puts the criticism of Racine in the mouth of a Spaniard, who calls Racine a "pleureux" and who quite naturally admires Corneille.

33. "Whereas in boys the Oedipus complex is destroyed by the castration complex, in girls it is made possible and led up to by the castration complex. . . . The difference between the sexual development of males and females at the stage we have been considering is an intelligible consequence of the anatomical distinction between their genitals and of the psychical situation involved in it; it corresponds to the difference between a castration that has been carried out and one that has merely been threatened" (Freud, "Some Psychical Consequences of the Anatomical Distinction between the Sexes," 19:256–57).

Chapter 5 The Sexual Interruption of the Real: Auerbach and *Manon Lescaut*

1. Erich Auerbach, *Mimesis: The Representation of Reality in Western Literature* (Garden City, N.Y.: Doubleday, 1957), 391.

2. See David Carroll, "Mimesis Reconsidered: Literature/History/Ideology," *Diacritics* 5, no. 2 (Summer 1975). Carroll argues that Auerbach's theory of

realism retains even today an "active, critical side" that can be used "to under-mine the dominant ideologies and philosophical systems of the various histor-ical periods treated [in *Mimesis*], to show the historical roots of all philosophical and esthetic systems, and to argue for historical diversity." Car-roll also argues, however, that the critical side of *Mimesis* is quickly replaced "with another system." This other system reveals an Auerbach "intent on reducing the complexity of the real to the fullness of the present" and deny-ing the fundamental complexity of history, a complexity that Carroll argues can be seen in historicism's own "repeated attempts to reconstruct after the fact a present which necessarily escapes it" (12).

3. G. W. F. Hegel, *Aesthetics: Lectures on Fine Art*, trans. T. M. Knox (Oxford: Oxford University Press, 1974), 44–46.

4. Auerbach writes in the epilogue that the character of *Mimesis* was deter-mined to an important extent by the (arbitrary) limitations of the libraries of wartime Istanbul (492). He also stresses that "a systematic and complete his-tory of realism would not only have been impossible, it would not have served my purpose." *Mimesis*, he continues, is not based on a preconceived system, but rather, its purpose assumed form "only as I went along" and was "guided only by the texts themselves," the great majority of which "were cho-sen at random on the basis of accidental acquaintance and personal prefer-ence" (491).

5. Martin Heidegger, "The Origin of the Work of Art," *Poetry, Language, Thought*, trans. Albert Hofstadter (New York: Harper & Row, 1971), 27.

6. Thus "Voltaire falsifies reality by an extreme simplification of the causes of events," so that his works are at bottom "propaganda pieces for the Enlight-enment" (Auerbach, *Mimesis*, 360). In Schiller's *Miller the Musician* "it is pre-cisely the strong and bold coloration of the revolutionary tendency which impairs the genuine character of the realism" (388). In the case of Goethe, his attitudes and political "utterances interest us in the present connection not so much immediately in that they illustrate Goethe's conservative, aristocratic, and anti-revolutionary views, but rather mediately because they explain how Goethe's views prevented him from grasping revolutionary occurrences with the genetico-realistic-sensory method peculiar to him on other occasions" (395).

7. This is true not just of *Manon Lescaut* and eighteenth-century French lit-erature but of the age of Goethe as well, an age in which "the combination of a forceful realism with a tragic conception of the problems of the age simply does not occur. This is the more striking and, if you will, the more paradox-ical since it was precisely the German intellectual development during the sec-ond half of the eighteenth century which laid the aesthetic foundation of modern realism. I refer to what is currently known as Historism" (Auerbach, *Mimesis*, 391).

8. Hegel, of course, never refers to *Manon Lescaut* in his *Aesthetics*. Nonethe-less, certain of the broad lines of his assessment of the "intermediate genres" are strikingly similar to Auerbach's. For Hegel, as for Auerbach, the intermed-iate genres represent an attempt to reconcile comedy and tragedy. Thus, just

as they are very close in their aim to that of modern tragic realism for Auerbach, so for Hegel they are very close to the aim of the philosophy of fine art, in that they share in its dialectical character. But Hegel is also like Auerbach in considering that the intermediate genres, and especially the drama, represent something of a literary dead end: "In the center between tragedy and comedy there is a third chief *genre* of dramatic poetry which yet is of less striking importance, despite the fact that it attempts to reconcile the difference between tragedy and comedy: or at least, instead of being isolated in sheer opposition to one another, these two sides meet in it and form a concrete whole. . . . But on the whole the boundary lines of this intermediate kind of dramatic poetry are less firm than those of tragedy and comedy. Moreover this kind almost runs the risk of departing from the genuine type of drama altogether or of lapsing into prose" (Hegel, *Aesthetics*, 1202–4).

9. Thus it comes as no surpise, given his relatively strong commitment to modernity, that Corneille should himself have transgressed the rules governing the separation of styles with the creation of the heroic comedy and entertained the project of creating an additional genre that would give everyday subjects the same serious treatment afforded by tragedy to kings and princes (see Corneille, letter to De Zuylichem, which serves as a preface to his *Don Sanche d'Aragon*, *Oeuvres complètes* [Paris: Seuil, 1963], 495–97). In defending the need for such a new genre, he argues that modern playwrights could produce a form of drama even more faithful to the imperative that tragedy move us by the arousal of pity and fear, because characters who are like us are more likely to produce the required tragic emotions in us. Thus, while Lessing was to see Corneille as the evil genius of modern drama, Lessing's central idea concerning the drama is formulated by Corneille in precisely the same terms Lessing will use.

10. Antoine-François Prévost d'Exiles, *Manon Lescaut* (Paris: Garnier-Flammarion, 1967), 130.

11. Antoine-François Prévost d'Exiles, *Mémoires et avantures d'un homme de qualité, Oeuvres complètes* (Paris: Leblanc, 1810–16), 1:105.

12. In *Reading the Romantic Heroine* (Ann Arbor: University of Michigan Press, 1985), Leslie Rabine argues that Prévost's novel should not be read in terms of the conventions of literary realism, an important component of which is the presupposition that the reader can discover the individuality of each character. This is true in the case of des Grieux since, according to Rabine, "in a completely realist text des Grieux's behavior would not remain so inexplicable as it does to Renoncourt in *Manon Lescaut*" (60). But Rabine goes on to argue that it is even more crucial to set aside the "realist" conception of character when analyzing the figure of Manon: "However much Manon's discourse is contained in des Grieux's discourse like quotations in another writer's text, her own subtext is not totally repressed by his supertext. Bringing it out needs an interpretation not based on a realist reading that asks: Who is the *real* Manon behind the paper? It needs instead a symptomatic reading which seeks to find the 'not said' in what is both repressed and indirectly implied by the language of the text" (72).

13. Voltaire, "Discours sur la tragédie," *Oeuvres complètes de Voltaire* (Paris: Garnier Frères, 1877), 2:323.

14. "Never in [Racine's] plays is love an episodic passion: it is the foundation of all his plays. It is their principal interest. It is the most theatrical of passions, the most fertile in sentiments, the most varied. It must be the soul of a theatrical work or be banished entirely. If love is not tragic, it is insipid; and if it is tragic, it must reign alone. It is not made for second place. It is Rotrou, it is even the great Corneille, it must be confessed, who, in creating our theater, almost always disfigured it by these made-to-order love affairs, by these amorous intrigues that, not involving true passions, are not worthy of the theater." Voltaire, "Lettre à M. Scipion Maffei," *Oeuvres complètes*, 4:182.

15. Voltaire, "Lettre à Mademoiselle Clairon," *Oeuvres complètes*, 4:9.

16. A. W. Schlegel, "Comparaison entre la Phèdre de Racine et celle d'Euripide," *Sämmtliche Werke* (Hildesheim: Georg Olms Verlag, 1972), vol. 14.

17. Jean Racine, *Bérénice*, *Oeuvres complètes de Racine* (Paris: Gallimard, 1950), act 2, scene 2, p. 485.

18. This sociology of the feminine condition, which is implict in *Manon Lescaut*, is explicitly spelled out in Prévost's *Mémoires d'un honnête homme*, *Oeuvres complètes*, vol. 33.

19. Antoine-François Prévost d'Exiles, *Campagnes philosophiques ou Mémoires de M. de Montcal*, *Oeuvres complètes*, vol. 12.

Chapter 6   The Dialectic and Its Aesthetic Other: The Problem of Identification in Diderot and Hegel

1. G. W. F. Hegel, *Aesthetics: Lectures on Fine Art*, trans. T. M. Knox (Oxford: Oxford University Press, 1974–75), 1171.

2. "Whoever wishes to laugh with his reason," Lessing writes toward the end of the *Hamburg Dramaturgy*, trans. Helen Zimmern (New York: Dover Publications, 1962), "he goes to the theater once and never goes again" (253). Lessing's view, of course, is that it is imperative to transform this situation, to create a theater in which reason has a place.

3. When A. W. Schlegel, in his *Course of Lectures on Dramatic Art and Literature*, trans. John Black (New York: AMS Press, 1965), criticizes Lessing's "lingering faith in Aristotle," he explicitly rejects Lessing's attempt both to bring art into the purview of philosophy and to make criticism indispensable to the artist (511).

4. Hegel's criticism of the *Poetics* in this respect is veiled, but nonetheless unambiguous. In the introduction to the *Aesthetics*, he states that the investigation of fine art has become for many thinkers "an investigation of the feelings, and the question has been raised, 'what feelings should be aroused by art, fear, for example, and pity? But how can these be agreeable, how can the treatment of misfortune afford satisfaction?' Reflection on these lines dates especially from Moses Mendelssohn's times and many such discussions can be found in his writings. Yet such discussions did not get far, because feeling

is the indefinite dull region of the spirit" (*Aesthetics*, 32). Though Mendelssohn's work is the explicit object of Hegel's criticism, the view that art should arouse feelings of "fear, for example, and pity" certainly does not, even for Hegel, "date especially from Moses Mehdelssohn's times" but rather from ancient Greece and the *Poetics*.

5. Roger Laufer, "Structure et signification du *Neveu de Rameau*," *Revue des sciences humaines* no. 100 (1960): 399–423.

6. Roland Desné, Introduction to Denis Diderot, *Le Neveu de Rameau, Le Rêve de d'Alembert* (Paris: Editions Sociales, 1984).

7. G. W. F. Hegel, *Phenomenology of Spirit*, trans. A. V. Miller (Oxford: Oxford University Press, 1977), 318.

8. H. R. Jauss, "Dialogique et dialectique," *Revue de métaphysique et de morale* 89, no. 2 (April–June 1984): 172.

9. Denis Diderot, *Le Neveu de Rameau* (Paris: Garnier-Flammarion, 1967), 138–39.

10. As Jean Starobinski has put it, "to ridicule is an *aesthetic* disparagement [of the other], a caricature of the image of the individual" ("Sur l'emploi du chiasme dans *Le Neveu de Rameau*," *Revue de métaphysique et de morale* 89, no. 2 [April–June 1984]: 184).

11. Jean-François Lyotard, *Le Différend*, (Paris: Editions de Minuit, 1983), 142.

12. Philippe Lacoue-Labarthe, "L'Imprésentable," *Poétique* no. 21 (1975): 54.

13. In this particular respect as in others, Lyotard's interpretation of Kant strongly recalls that of Theodor Adorno. In his *Aesthetic Theory*, trans. C. Lehnhardt (New York: Routledge & Kegan Paul, 1984), Adorno writes: "The ascendance of the sublime is identical with the need for art to avoid 'playing down' its fundamental contradictions but to bring them out instead. No longer is reconciliation the result of conflict. The only aesthetic purpose is to articulate this conflict" (282). Adorno, however, though he has many positive things to say about Kant's aesthetics, is at the same time unquestionably more critical of Kant's work (and more open to the work of Hegel) than is Lyotard. Thus he also writes: "It might be better to stop talking about the sublime completely. As it is, the term has been corrupted beyond recognition by the mumbo-jumbo of the high priests of art religion" (283).

14. Jean-François Lyotard, "The Sublime and the Avant-Garde," *Artforum* (April 1984): 40.

15. "My soul agitated by two opposed movements, I didn't know if I would abandon myself to my desire to laugh or to a transport of indignation. I was suffering. . . . He noticed the conflict taking place within me" (*Le Neveu*, 60). "As for me, I didn't know if I should stay or flee, laugh or become indignant. I stayed, with the intention of turning the conversation toward a subject that would banish from my soul the horror with which it was filled" (138). "If he left the singing part, it was in order to take up the instrumental; . . . taking hold of our souls and holding them suspended in the most singular state I have ever experienced" (149).

16. As, for example, when Diderot bases his negative assessment of Challe's *Hector Reproaching Paris for His Cowardice* on a comparison between a

dramatic passage from the *Illiad* and Challe's pictorial rendition of it: "In order to judge whether or not Challe's Hector is Homer's Hector, let us see if the discourse the old poet put in the mouth of his character would be by chance appropriate to the character depicted by the painter" (Denis Diderot, *Salon de 1765* [Paris: Editions Hermann, 1984], 112). In a similar spirit, Diderot criticizes Badouin for not having chosen the appropriate moment in the dramatic action that forms the basis for his *Retiring of the Bride*, as "our friend Greuze" would have done (*Les Salons*, *Oeuvres esthétiques* [Paris: Editions Garnier, 1968], 472).

17. "The different passions succeeded one another on his face. One could identify tenderness, anger, pleasure, pain" (*Le Neveu*, 65).

18. In *Histoire de la folie à l'âge classique* (Paris: Editions Gallimard, 1972), Michel Foucault devotes several pages to a reading of *Le Neveu de Rameau* in which he argues that it represents a whole complex of subterranean historical forces that were changing the way the classical age both conceived of and experienced madness. *Le Neveu de Rameau* is thus included by Foucault in a select group of texts with those of Nietzsche, Artaud, and Roussel because it also does what they purportedly do: it directly manifests the disruptive force of madness in history. For Foucault, the Nephew represents "the immediate pressure of being in unreason, the impossibility of mediation" (367). In making the Nephew into a particularly radical figure of madness, Foucault neglects, in my view, the complex interaction of reflection and passion in Diderot's portrait of him.

19. Denis Diderot, *Entretiens sur le Fils naturel*, *Oeuvres esthétiques*, 103–4.

Chapter 7 The Tragic Matrix of Speculative Philosophy: Generalized Mimesis and the *Paradoxe sur le comédien*

1. The most important modern German philosopher Lacoue-Labarthe subtracts from this Hegelian tradition is thus Heidegger. In *Heidegger, Art and Politics: The Fiction of the Political*, trans. Chris Turner (Cambridge, Mass.: Basil Blackwell, 1990), Lacoue-Labarthe takes a stance more critical of Heidegger than in any of his earlier essays. Nonetheless, even in this work, he continues to insist on what separates Heidegger from Hegel and consequently what separates Heideggerean philosophy from what he calls the speculative. He speaks of the "incommensurability that exists, by definition, between a thesis on being and the question of being" and attacks the "dishonesty—but such a dishonesty is banal nowadays—of reducing the theses of Heidegger to the theses of the philosophical tradition" (11, translation modified).

2. Philippe Lacoue-Labarthe and Jean-Luc Nancy, *The Literary Absolute*, trans. Philip Barnard and Cheryl Lester (Albany: State University of New York Press, 1988), 17.

3. Philippe Lacoue-Labarthe, "L'Imprésentable," *Poétique* no. 21 (1975): 54.

4. Philippe Lacoue-Labarthe, "The Caesura of the Speculative," *Typography: Mimesis, Philosophy, Politics*, ed. Christopher Fynsk (Cambridge, Mass.:

Harvard University Press, 1989), 227, translation modified. This volume groups together selected essays from both *Le Sujet de la philosophie: Typographies I* (Paris: Aubier-Flammarion, 1979); and *L'Imitation des modernes: Typographies II* (Paris: Galilée, 1986).

5. In *Readings in Interpretation: Hölderlin, Hegel, Heidegger* (Minneapolis: University of Minnesota Press, 1987), Andrzej Warminski misses or ignores this ambiguity, particularly as concerns the positive, critical side of Lacoue-Labarthe's concept of mimesis. He praises Lacoue-Labarthe's readings of Hölderlin, saying that they do not "flinch from formulating Hölderlin's insights in all their radicality" (37). But he goes on to criticize those same readings, arguing that they "attribute to Hölderlin a mimetic model of tragedy" (39). Lacoue-Labarthe's "mimetic" terminology has "outlived its use" and "cannot account for textual processes" to which "mimetic categories . . . are no longer pertinent" (139–40). With these statements, Warminski in effect refuses to engage in a discussion of whether or not Lacoue-Labarthe's concept of mimesis might indeed have a positive critical significance in relation both to tragedy and to what Warminski calls signification or figuration. He refuses, in other words, to entertain the possibility that textual processes can themselves function as an origin when they are seen as totally autonomous, and thus that mimetic terminology may not have "outlived its use," especially in a context where the "originality" of the text is a given.

6. Denis Diderot, *Paradoxe sur le comédien, Oeuvres esthétiques* (Paris: Editions Garnier, 1968), 306.

7. "If by 'completion of philosophy' is meant the exhaustion of a program, the realization or effectuation, the *thinking* of a bimillennial questioning of the Same out of which philosophy in its entirety has unfolded; if the completion of philosophy is the thinking of difference in the sense of that 'One differing in itself' (*En diapheron heauto*–Heraclitus) which Hölderlin made the most constant, most explicit motif in his questioning of the essence of the Beautiful and of Art, ever since he cited it in *Hyperion*; if, moreover, for reasons that cannot be developed here but that may be presumed familiar enough, the completion of philosophy is the passage over the gap or the closing of the wound (re-)opened, in extremis by Kant in the thinking of the Same; if, in short, it is this covering over of the Kantian crisis (the 'leap over Kant,' as Heidegger puts it) and of the loss of everything this crisis swept with it beyond any power of legislating, deciding, and criticizing–then Hölderlin (this is his singular position, his 'case,' if you like) will have represented, in this completion which he *too* brings about and to which he 'contributes' more than a negligible share, the impossibility of covering over this crisis, this wound still open in the tissue of philosophy, a wound that does not heal and that reopens constantly under the hand that would close it" (Lacoue-Labarthe, "Caesura," 212–13, translation modified).

8. Lacoue-Labarthe describes the decisive character of Hölderlin's insight in terms of a "teetering [on the brink]"–the word in French is *basculer*, which Fynsk translates with the weaker "shift" ("where things begin to [teeter]"–of the then dominant concept of the Greeks. Lacoue-Labarthe also stresses that

Hölderlin's view of the Greeks constitutes "an original intuition" and "an entirely different historical thought" ("Hölderlin and the Greeks," *Typography*, 242).

9. Philippe Lacoue-Labarthe, "A Jacques Derrida: Au Nom de *," *L'Imitation des modernes*, 238–39.

10. Philippe Lacoue-Labarthe, "Diderot: Paradox and Mimesis," *Typography*, 251–52.

11. In "The Nazi Myth," trans. Brian Holmes, *Critical Inquiry* (Winter 1990), Lacoue-Labarthe is equally if not more insistent on the unique status of Germany with respect to the problematic relation of the ancient (the Greek) and the modern and hence with respect to mimesis/identification: "Since the close of the eighteenth century, it is in the German tradition *and nowhere else*, that the most rigorous reflection on the relationship of myth to the question of identification is elaborated. The reason for this is, primarily, that the Germans . . . read Greek particularly well, and that this problem or this investigation of myth is a very old problem inherited from Greek philosophy and, above all, from Plato" (296–97, my emphasis).

12. As Andrzej Warminski argues, Lacoue-Labarthe's interpretation of Hölderlin "reinvents the Greeks—*la Grèce comme telle*" (*Readings in Interpretation*, 39).

13. Denis Diderot, *Entretiens sur le Fils naturel, Oeuvres esthétiques* (Paris: Editions Garnier, 1968), 104.

Chapter 8 Sexual Identification and the Social: Freud and Beaumarchais

1. Philippe Lacoue-Labarthe and Jean-Luc Nancy, "Le Peuple Juif ne rêve pas," *La Psychanalyse est-elle une histoire juive?* (Paris: Seuil, 1981), 58.

2. Sigmund Freud, *Group Psychology and the Analysis of the Ego, The Standard Edition of the Complete Psychological Works of Sigmund Freud* (London: Hogarth Press, 1953), 18:105. All further citations of works by Freud refer to this edition.

3. As we have seen, the mother-son relationship does play an important role with regard to the creation of the first modern political regime—that founded by the epic poet. But significantly, that role is entirely in keeping with the wholly positive nature of the identification between herself and her son, since it involves only the protection by the mother of her favorite, youngest son from paternal jealousy (*Group Psychology*, 18:136).

4. Though the mother-son relationship is the only one Freud exempts from the universal law of ambivalence in *Group Psychology* and *Civilization and Its Discontents*, in the *Introductory Lectures on Psychoanalysis* he also includes the father-daughter relationship in this exemption. Significantly, however, he nonetheless goes on to emphasize that the mother-son relationship better exemplifies love unadulterated by hostility: "There appears to be less danger [from unconscious hostility] to the relation between father and daughter or mother and son. This last provides the purest examples of an unchangeable

affection, unimpaired by any egoistic considerations" (*Introductory Lectures,* 15:206).

5. P.-A. Caron de Beaumarchais, "Essai sur le genre dramatique sérieux," *Théâtre complet de Beaumarchais* (Paris: Mignard, 1952), 39–40.

6. See P.-A. Caron de Beaumarchais, Introduction, *Théâtre* (Paris: Editions Garnier, 1980), iv. All citations of *Le Mariage de Figaro* refer to this edition.

7. Alternatively, the count is ready to punish others for actions that he himself has obliged them to commit, for example, as when he says to Chérubin in act 5, scene 15, "What were you doing in that salon?" To which Chérubin replies, "I was hiding, as you ordered me to" (*Figaro,* 325). This passage comes immediately before the one referred to by Beaumarchais in his preface.

8. A case in point is Bartholo, whose attitude toward Figaro is anything but fatherly. But in act 5, scene 2 when Bartholo begins to understand why he and several others have been called by Figaro to wait in the garden, he nonetheless expresses his solidarity with Figaro by offering the following piece of fatherly advice: "Remember that a wise main doesn't make trouble for himself with his superiors [*les grands*]" (*Figaro,* 303).

9. She says to herself when she learns of Figaro's plan to spy on Suzanne's rendezvous with the count: "I'll go watch out for Suzanne, or rather, warn her; she is such a pretty creature! Ah! when personal interest does not arm us against each other, we are all ready to support our oppressed sex against this proud, this terrible . . . (*laughing*) and nonetheless slightly boobish masculine sex" (*Figaro,* act 5, scene 1, p. 301).

10. When he learns that the woman he was trying to seduce was not Suzanne but the countess disguised as Suzanne, he cries out to the countess: "What! It was you, Countess? (*In a supplicating tone.*) Only a generous pardon . . ." To which she replies: "You would say 'no, no,' *in my place* [in fact he just has in the immediately preceding lines]. But as for myself, for the third time today, I grant you an unconditional pardon" (*Figaro,* act 5, scene 19, p. 327, my emphasis).

11. The view of the mother presented in *Figaro* can be contrasted not only with the one expressed by Freud in *Group Psychology* and *Civilization and Its Discontents* but also with that found in the work of three contemporary French feminist theorists and critics, Julia Kristeva, Luce Irigaray, and Hélène Cixous. In "Difference on Trial: A Critique of the Maternal Metaphor in Cixous, Irigaray, and Kristeva," in *The Poetics of Gender,* ed. Nancy K. Miller (New York: Columbia University Press, 1986), Domna Stanton argues that the critiques of phallocentrism made by each of these three writer-theorists depends on a "hidden ontology of the maternal metaphor" (161). The privileging of the pre-Oedipal, the equation of femininity with the maternal, and the lyricism with which the maternal is consistently evoked in their work, in Stanton's view, points to an "onto-theologizing" of the maternal. While the work of Irigaray, Cixous, and Kristeva is Stanton's principal focus in "Difference on Trial," the conclusion to her essay extends her critique to include the socio-historically oriented work of prominent American feminists: "These multi-disciplinary studies repeatedly extol pre-oedipal unboundedness, re-

latedness, plurality, fluidity, tenderness, and nurturance in the name of the difference of female identity" (176).

12. The titles of the two tragedies *Oedipe* and *Phèdre* appear side by side in Beaumarchais's preface to *Figaro*, where he cites them as the two foremost examples of tragic dramas in which incest is the principal subject (145).

13. Denis Diderot, *Paradoxe sur le comédien, Oeuvres esthétiques* (Paris: Editions Garnier, 1968), 306.

Conclusion: Tragedy and the Problem of Culture

1. Friedrich Nietzsche, *The Birth of Tragedy and the Case of Wagner*, trans. Walter Kaufmann (New York: Random House, 1967), 132.

2. Claude Lévi-Strauss, *Tristes tropiques*, trans. John and Doreen Weightman (New York: Antheneum, 1981) begins by evoking the diffuse Hegelianism that dominated the French university when Lévi-Strauss began his university training, and he himself attributes his decision to become an anthropologist to his sense of frustration at the shallowness of what he calls the mental gymnastics of dialectical reasoning (51).

3. Claude Lévi-Strauss, "History and Dialectic," *The Savage Mind* (Chicago: University of Chicago Press, 1966).

4. G. W. F. Hegel, *Phenomenology of Spirit*, trans. A. V. Miller (Oxford: Oxford University Press, 1977), 278.

5. In *The Birth of Tragedy*, Nietzsche, of course, sees that, in order to develop what he considers to be a more profound and more serious concept of tragedy than that bequeathed by Hegel and Romanticism, he needs to discover, or invent, not only a new conception of tragedy but also a new Greek culture. This other, deeper, and more serious Greek culture, which he contrasts with the more traditional image of "Greek cheerfulness," is Dionysian, just as the other, deeper and more serious form of tragedy is. In terms of his theory of Greek culture, as in terms of his concept of tragedy, the dominant tendency in *The Birth of Tragedy* is to replace the cheerful, Apollinian model of Greece with another, tragic and Dionysian model rather than to analyze Greek culture in terms of the irresolvable conflict between the two models.

Index

Designed by Joanna Hill

Composed by A. W. Bennett, Inc.
in Palatino text and display.

Printed on 50-lb. Glatfelter Natural,
and bound in Joanna Arrestox A cloth
by Edwards Brothers, Inc.